COGNITION
AND
ENVIRONMENT

COGNITION AND ENVIRONMENT

FUNCTIONING IN AN UNCERTAIN WORLD

Stephen Kaplan
and
Rachel Kaplan

Library of Congress Cataloging in Publication Data

Kaplan, Stephen, 1936–
    Cognition and environment.

    Bibliography: p.
    Includes indexes.
    1. Cognition. 2. Environmental psychology.
I. Kaplan, Rachel. II. Title.
BF311.K27   1983   153   82-13124

ISBN 0-914004-50-6 (pbk.)

Illustration for cover copyright © Diane and Joel Schatz, 1981

Ulrich's Bookstore
549 East University Avenue, Ann Arbor, Michigan 48104-2586

ISBN 0-914004-50-6
Printed in the United States of America

We have been guided and inspired
by the wisdom of William James and
D. O. Hebb. This book is dedicated
to that inspiration.

ABOUT THE AUTHORS

Stephen Kaplan is Professor of Psychology and of Computer and Communication Sciences at the University of Michigan. Rachel Kaplan is Professor of Environmental Psychology in the School of Natural Resources and in the Doctoral Program in Urban and Regional Planning, as well as Associate Professor of Psychology, at the University of Michigan.

The Kaplan's prior book, *Humanscape: Environment for People*, reflects their theoretical and empirical work in several of the topics discussed in the present volume. They have also contributed chapters to numerous volumes in this area, and their articles have appeared in *Environment and Behavior* and *Population and Environment*.

Both authors hold B.A. degrees from Oberlin College and received their Ph.D. degrees in psychology from the University of Michigan, Ann Arbor.

PREFACE

"Environment" and "cognition" are words that do not often appear together. This is certainly understandable since rather separate specialties are associated with each. It is also unreasonable. "Environment" would not be the problem area that it is were it not for what mind has achieved. Indeed, many seemingly appropriate solutions to environmental problems have turned out to be unworkable because the human element has been ignored.

On the other side of the fence, mind is not an abstract computing device. The human mind and its capacity for thought and action arose in the context of certain environments as a means of dealing with those environments, of discovering the resources, avoiding the hazards, and so on.

This book has two central themes: (1) environmental problems are people problems, requiring an understanding of how people think, what they care about, and the circumstances under which they behave in reasonable and constructive fashion; (2) human cognition makes more theoretical sense in the context of the environment, past and present. While it is true that people can process symbols, especially letters and numbers, with great facility, even these activities are more readily understood in the larger context of an environment extended in space and time, an environment that at one time defined the conditions for survival. In this perspective many otherwise unrelated pieces fall together into a coherent whole. How people perceive, what they prefer, how they struggle with adversity, and even what assistance they receive from their culture, all fit together as complementary aspects of a larger picture.

Thus this book is addressed to the student of cognition who wishes to consider the functioning of the mind in a larger context. It is addressed equally to the environmental designer/manager/planner who wishes to incorporate human needs and human input into environmental decision making. It is also addressed to a third group of potential readers. It is addressed to the concerned and thoughtful human, to the individual who recognizes that all is not well in the current relationship of mind and environment and who would like to explore some more constructive alternatives.

ix

This book can speak to these diverse interests because these interests actually share much in common, though specialization has progressed so far that this common portion has fallen into neglect. It is often easier to achieve insight in each of these areas from the perspective of this common core than in terms of a segregated, isolated, specialized body of knowledge. A brief sketch of some of the topics covered in this book might illustrate the essential interrelatedness of these apparently separate interests.

- Perception and cognition are intimately related processes; understanding them and their relationship is essential to understanding how people relate to their environment.
- What people prefer and care about both influences and is influenced by the thought process. People's comfort, their sense of feeling at home, and their confidence in any given setting are all inseparable from their knowledge of that environment and from how readily knowable that environment is.
- People are active, striving, often struggling as they attempt to deal with their environment. It is often easier to disrupt or undermine their efforts to cope than it is to help them. On the other hand, by focusing on the requirements for more supportive environments, it is possible to enhance people's capacity to help themselves.
- Problem solving and planning are vital expressions of the cognitive process, as far as environmental outcomes are concerned. Experts differ from the rest of us in the way they approach problems; it is essential that these differences be understood to take advantage of the expert's special skills and avoid potentially devastating errors.
- The frequent failure of various well-intended efforts at education and communication is readily understandable in a cognitive perspective. Sharing information can be far more effective given a grasp of a few simple but crucial principles.
- Research can be a way of relating to reality rather than an abstruse activity of the specialist. Properly approached, research is a widely available means of obtaining vital information concerning people/environment arrangements that are appropriate and satisfying.
- Participation need not be frustrating and counterproductive. Viewed in the context of the human thought process, it becomes a powerful way of relating people to what happens in the environment. It is a means of involving people in environmental design and decisions that can be constructive and stimulating for all concerned.

ACKNOWLEDGMENTS

Some years ago with the help and urging of our students we began work on a theoretically-based compilation of papers in the human/environment area. That project culminated in *Humanscape: Environments for People*. The same forces that led to *Humanscape*—a perceived need, a fascination with converging insights in different fields, a wealth of opportunities for application of theoretical concepts—have continued unabated. The students too continue to be as stimulating and helpful as ever. Both they, and many of the former students who are now active in this field, have contributed greatly to this effort.

In addition to the students, a number of colleagues have had a substantial impact on one or more portions of this volume. We are indebted to Niels Prak and Camille Wortman for stimulating discussions and helpful insights. Another person playing a key role in the intellectual development recorded here was Howard Deardorff; he and Douglas Kinsey also performed yeoman service in their creation of illustrations that not merely expressed but extended the meaning of the text. Extensive comments on a number of drafts by Daniel Stokols and Irving Altman played a major role in the restructuring and improving of the manuscript; their thoughtful and perceptive contribution is greatly appreciated.

Our cover is a small portion of a poster by Diane Schatz entitled, "Community alert: Preparing for energy emergencies." We first learned of this poster through an article by Joel Schatz in *Rain: Journal of Appropriate Technology*. The article describes the poster's remarkable success in interesting government officials and corporation executives in a decentralized approach to dealing with energy problems. Since the poster exemplifies such themes as understandable graphics, images of the future, and participation in dealing with environmental problems, it seemed uniquely suitable for a cover illustration. We are grateful to Diane and Joel Schatz for their interest and encouragement as well as for their permission to use a portion of their poster. For information on obtaining a full-color copy of this large poster, write Transition Graphics (P.O. Box 2185, Salem, OR 97308).

This volume has been under construction for some time. There came a critical point in its development when a rapid bringing together of the various threads was essential. This was achieved by putting the manuscript into a computer-based textediting system. Our various academic affiliations—the Department of Psychology, School of Natural Resources, and Program in Urban and Regional Planning—provided the necessary funds for computer time and even a terminal, vital and appreciated contributions. But even with that aid this volume would not have seen the light of day had we not found someone who could understand the computerese as well as type rapidly, accurately, and often under great pressure. It was our great good fortune to find someone who not only filled these requirements, but also made many helpful suggestions and took responsibility far beyond the call of duty. For these and other reasons we were delighted to include Abram Kaplan as a member of the project team. (In his spare time he also took many of the photographs that illustrate the text.)

Once again our involvement with this volume is conceptual and moral rather than financial; the royalties are being donated to the Environmental Defense Fund.

Stephen Kaplan
Rachel Kaplan

CONTENTS

COGNITION
AND
ENVIRONMENT

part one

INTRODUCTION

It has been an exhilarating time in cognitive psychology. The computer has provided a most interesting and stimulating analogy for studying what the mind does. In the process, the computer revolution also contributed to the concept of "information" as an abstract idea. The initial hopes were that information would provide a content-independent basis for measuring what the mind is doing. While this has not proved useful, the notion of information in a more intuitive sense has persisted and contributed to the great advance of research and theory in the past decade.

As is so often the case with scientific positions (Kuhn, 1962), the very success of the information-processing approach has begun to create strains. The mind/computer analogy has been pursued so thoroughly and extensively that it is becoming increasingly clear that there are a great many ways in which these two systems are not alike (Dreyfus, 1972). There has also been a growing appreciation of the fact that the human capacities for perception and thought are not neutral, general-purpose processes; rather, they are processes attuned to a particular environment. There is, in other words, a physical world in which this system must function. Further, the human system must have evolved in a world of this kind and hence must have become efficient at dealing with the sorts of challenges this world had to offer.

During the same era that has seen so much progress in the area of human information-processing, another area has also emerged: environmental psychology. Although there has not been much interplay between these two subdisciplines, there should be. Cognitive psychology must take the environment more seriously. Environmental psychology must take the mind more seriously. This volume provides a sketch of what such a joint venture might look like.

The interaction of these various trends yields a view of an organism utilizing facile mental processes in dealing with a complex and uncertain world. In particular, we shall be looking at the processes of recognition, prediction, evaluation, and action. These are viewed not only as areas of ability, but also as matters of great interest and concern to the organism. Humans like to recognize (hence, the familiar material in Chapter 1 of this book should be quite agreeable). Humans like to predict (you may like to try to figure out what this book is about from the table of contents and from what we have said so far). Humans like to evaluate and do so readily. Humans also like to act—in the broad sense that encompasses both the making of decisions and the behavior that results.

Hence these processes all become a part of how we react to the environment. The recognition of some patterns that are pervasive all around us, the prediction that continuing in our ways is likely to lead to certain consequences, and the evaluation that these may not be favorable compel us to take action. What we do—both as individuals and as groups—is greatly affected by our understanding. As a result, information is an inescapable commodity. We crave it, distrust it, exchange it, and, all too often, are overwhelmed by it.

chapter one

THE EXPERIENCE OF THE ENVIRONMENT

Imagine yourself perched comfortably on the limb of a tree, peering through dense foliage at the behavior of people crossing a stream below. There is no bridge, but there are a few rocks that, with a bit of imagination, could be thought of as stepping stones. Here comes someone now. He steps out onto the stone closest to the bank, balances precariously, looks around, tentatively places one foot on the next stone, withdraws it, tries it again, hesitates, and finally commits his full weight. Then more looking around, more hesitation, more testing, withdrawing, and testing again. Finally the stream is crossed, and our hero sits down on the bank for a little rest.

Now imagine another series of observations. An individual strides confidently up to the edge of the stream, steps onto the first stone with one foot, swings the other foot over to the second stone, and continues smoothly across with hardly a break in stride. There is not a trace of indecision or hesitation.

One might think that these two different observations involve vastly different people. In fact, since this is a book about psychology, one might assume that the two individuals differ in their attitudes, their approaches to life, their very personalities. But consider for a moment a quite different alternative. Could it be that these two sets of observations involve the same person at different times? What could make a person function so differently under apparently similar circumstances?

If the halting, groping performance came first and the smooth, efficient pattern was observed some time later, such a difference would hardly be surprising. We expect experience to make a difference. We expect someone who is familiar with an environment to be more effective in it than someone who is there for the first time.

With this explanation, the difference between the two stream-crossing events is not that surprising; in fact, it suggests that familiarity must be powerful stuff. And indeed the power of familiarity is demonstrated over and over again in our everyday experience. For example, one sometimes has an ailment that is a bit worrisome, leading one to consult a physician. The physician may do little more than give the condition a name, that is, put it in a category that makes it more familiar, and (unless it is a threatening category) one then feels much better. People visiting a foreign country can be heard making frequent comparisons with "how it is back home." They are making an effort to familiarize by analogy, to apply what they have knowledge about to areas they are ignorant about.

It may seem farfetched to drag one's prior familiarities with one on a trip. After all, is it not necessary to acquire knowledge directly, through the building up of experience after experience? Fortunately the answer is "no." Through fairy tales, children have for centuries come to be familiar with environments they have never seen. Adults have this capacity, too. At least that is the implication of the statement sometimes heard when strangers are introduced, "Oh, I've heard so much about you that I feel like I already know you."

Much of the contribution of familiarity we tend to take for granted. We move smoothly and confidently through our world, quite unaware that the smoothness and confidence are based on our familiarity. If something happens that fails to fit this familiar pattern, we can readily be disconcerted or confused or dismayed. Even a fairly minor departure from the familiar can bring our smoothly flowing behavior to an abrupt halt.

For an example of such a mild discrepancy, consider the individual who stumbles downstairs for breakfast, reaches for the coffee cup, and begins to drink. However, knowing of this individual's fondness for beer, a friend has filled the cup with cold beer rather than hot coffee. One can fairly safely predict a sudden disruption in ongoing behavior—not a mild, "Fancy that, the coffee is strange this morning," but probably something a good bit more dramatic.

A circumstance that does not match what we are familiar with can be extremely confusing and disruptive to thought. There is the story of the time the elephant escaped from a traveling circus. The police of a small town were looking all over for it when they received a phone call from a resident. "There is a huge beast in my garden," she complained, "and it is pulling up my vegetables with its tail." "What is it doing with them?" asked the puzzled police sergeant. "You wouldn't believe me if I told you," replied the distraught lady.

These examples are probably sufficient to make the point. Familiarity brings with it greater confidence and speed. The performance is better, and the individual may even be able to do more than one thing at a time. The feelings of the individual carrying out the performance are different, too; there is a sense of knowing what to expect, of being able to anticipate or predict what might happen next.

The person unfamiliar with an environment lacks these advantages. Smoothness is replaced by hesitation, efficiency by fumbling. However, the person who thought the setting was familiar and then finds it responding in an unfamiliar way, is no better off. Indeed, this is often more confusing than simply lacking familiarity.

What it Means to be Familiar

Clearly the person familiar with a setting possesses something useful and valuable. But what is this "something"? What does it mean to be familiar?

In a rough-and-ready fashion we can say that a person who is familiar with an environment acts as if the essentials of that environment were already stored in the head. Being familiar means being less dependent on information from the environment. One need not pay as close attention, one need not be as sensitive to feedback because one knows it is there, knows what to expect. Decisions can be made without waiting, without careful testing.

Stated simply, a person who is familiar with an environment acts as if there were a model, or map, of the environment stored in the head. This analogy is appealing because models and maps are conveniently compact relative to what they stand for and because they can be manipulated. One can play with a model, one can take an imaginary trip on a map. Both activities imply the capacity to anticipate, to check out possibilities that are not yet present in the real (i.e., physical) environment. (The terms "model" and "map," when used in this way, are usually modified by the terms "mental" or "cognitive" as reminders that they refer not to physical things in the world but to a pattern of stored information.)

The intuitive appeal of the cognitive map has not passed unnoticed, as this *New Yorker* cartoon illustrates. Understanding it depends upon sharing the assumption that people have (or at least can have) map-like conceptions of the environment in their heads. The cartoon also raises another pertinent issue—the difficulty of sharing cognitive maps. The policeman is attempting to transplant his good cognitive map into someone else's head. This is a classic frustration. What has come to seem so simple to someone familiar with a given environment cannot be transferred in its simplicity into the head of another. Of course it can be communicated—that is after all what education is about—but the process tends to be rather slow and tedious, often taxing the patience of donor and recipient alike.

Cognitive maps require experience, but at the same time, thinking of them is obviously different from thinking of the experience that one had in that particular setting. Thus the cognitive map must be a sort of accumulation or summary of that experience. It is, in other words, the schematic knowledge a person has about a familiar environment. Such

Drawing by Stevenson; © *1976. The New Yorker Magazine, Inc.*

stored knowledge is enormously helpful for making one's way through an environment and, of course, for giving directions to others. The stored information a person has about an environment necessarily influences how the environment "feels" to that person, what is noticed, what is ignored: in other words, the larger experience of the environment.

The cognitive map thus appears to be a promising concept in the study of environmental cognition. Since a person's reactions to and feelings about an environment are as much a function of how that environment is known—of the model one has of it—as they are a function of the environment itself, this concept would seem to be a vital link between the physical world and subjective experience. Conveniently enough, the concept is intuitively comfortable as well as promising in terms of potential usefulness.

There is, however, a fly in the ointment. While its intuitive character makes it easy to feel at home with, the cognitive map concept in its undeveloped, informal version is far more ambiguous than it perhaps appears on the surface. Essentially, the mental model as discussed so far is a rather loose analogy. How far does it extend? In what sense do people have maps in their heads? Are they multicolored like printed maps? Does north point up? Do they have to be unfolded to be read? Is there someone inside there to read them? How do we pull out the correct map and locate on it where we are right now?

Until we can answer these questions with confidence and with good reasons, we cannot consider ourselves very knowledgeable. We cannot consider ourselves in possession of a conception that is likely to be useful.

TOWARD A MORE RIGOROUS CONCEPTION

The development of this conception is the purpose of the initial portion of this book. In order to arrive at a useful and reasonably unambiguous conception, we must be clear about what we are looking for. The more successful we are at identifying criteria, at spelling out our specifications, the more directed our search can be. Let us explore, then, the requirements or constraints that might prove useful for this purpose.

There are two sources of criteria that are particularly pertinent and particularly helpful. One source is the environment. The cognitive map must be of the environment. Thus properties of the environment profoundly influence the map-making process.

On the other hand, there is no reason to believe that a cognitive map constitutes "pure" knowledge. It is, rather, knowledge for a purpose, knowledge with a function. Presumably that function is to guide the behavior of the "owner" of the map, to help the individual in whose head the map resides be effective in that particular environment.

The Environment: Diverse and Uncertain

Let us look first at the environment and the constraints it provides. Perhaps the most striking thing about what we find on the earth's crust— our environment—is the diversity and complexity of it all. There is a great deal of variety and a great deal going on. This is certainly the impression one gets from a rough overview, and taking a closer look does nothing to change this impression. One might assume that the complexity is only a matter of the multitude of ways that simple elements can be combined and recombined. As our resolving power improves, however, so does our awareness of complexity at finer and finer levels.

At least as basic in information-handling terms as the complexity of our environment is its uncertainty. There are many things on earth. At any given time, when one of these things is present it gives rise to certain patterns of energy which we know as light, sound, etc. While these patterns necessarily have some aspects in common from one time to the next, they characteristically vary widely. The crucial consequence of this variability, for our purposes, is that there is no simple signal upon which to base recognition of an object.

The uncertainty that permeates the environment arises not only in how objects present themselves, but also in the relations of objects and their patterns in time. Even in a familiar environment it can be difficult to predict what might happen. This is true in the long run—changes in a neighborhood over the course of a few years, for instance—but it is also true on a much shorter time scale. As one looks idly out the living room window, there is no telling what one might see in the next few minutes—a delivery truck, a fire engine, a warbler, a child in a fancy costume.

Yet another level of environmental uncertainty ranges from the dramatic occurrence of natural hazards at one extreme to the vagaries of weather at the other. This is not to say that fire, flood, earthquake, and other natural events big and small that intrude on human purposes are not caused, but they are not, by and large, predictable in any reliable fashion and are experienced by humans as part of the uncertainty of the environment.

Some Functional Properties

Now let us turn to function, to the requirements of a person behaving in the world, for additional criteria we would want a satisfactory conception of the cognitive map to meet.

Figuring out how something works is generally easier when one has some idea of what it does. In a very rough way, what a cognitive map "does" is obvious: it stores information about the environment so that a person can know what to expect and what to do in various circumstances. Immediately we know that we are dealing with a means of storing information and that, further, it must be possible to "get to," or access, that storage in relation to particular places in the environment. Further consideration of the requirements for functioning leads to three rather broad criteria:

Generality. People are constantly wandering into new situations or into old situations with new variations. Admittedly, many people complain of the same old grind day after day. But they are ignoring a great deal of variability in the process. Imagine if one were to measure every aspect of a particular situation on a particular day. It would be most unlikely that the identical values would show up at any two points in time. Situations rarely, if ever, repeat themselves. Thus the information we have about the environment must in some way be general rather than particular, or else it would apply only to the past. Information generated by similar circumstances must somehow be stored together; we must somehow be able to keep track of similarities and ignore idiosyncracies.

Economy. An individual is presented with a tremendous quantity of information each day. There is not only the danger of exceeding an individual's storage capacity; there is also the possibility that storing a huge amount of information could make it difficult to get out the appropriate portion when needed. Many of the technologies humans have devised for storing information and retrieving it would be totally inappropriate for handling the vast amount of information that is continously stored in the mind. Imagine any other filing system with the cross-referencing potential that the mental system possesses! Whatever explanations one finds for how the environment is coded in the mind must come to terms with the economy of that storage system.

Connectedness.   People often find themselves in environments that are only somewhat familiar to them. Yet they manage to get from one familiar place to another despite a lack of information about much that lies between. Somehow there need to be connections between known points, or else getting from place to place would generally be impossible: A cognitive map riddled with uncrossable gaps would rarely be useful.

SOME CONCLUDING COMMENTS

In understanding how humans experience the environment, the idea of a mental model or cognitive map seems intuitively promising and understandable. The map analogy seems useful in certain ways, but it can also be misleading. Surely the maps in the mind are not printed on plastic cards, and surely no green gremlin with yellow marking pen resides there to highlight the route to be taken. Granted, we want to find a framework for understanding environmental knowledge that retains some of the intuitive flavor of a map-like concept. Any such framework, however, must also be credible and consistent with current psychological and physiological knowledge. In addition, there are functional requirements that must also be met.

Essentially we have approached the problem of what a cognitive map is by asking what it must be able to do. Therefore our search for some constraints to place on the cognitive map idea has uncovered certain properties that seem essential to support effective functioning. Thus, to cope with the endless dissimilarities in environmental configurations, the model must be able to extract generalities. To make access to stored information speedy and reliable, the coding process must function economically despite great variability in the input. Finally, the map must function as if continuous despite enormous gaps in the information at hand.

The functional requirements that a framework must take into account are further complicated by some of the properties presented by the environment. The complexity and uncertainty of that environment compound an already difficult problem, that of handling vast amounts of information despite limited capacity for storage and limited time in which to act.

part two

COMPREHENSION OF THE ENVIRONMENT

A cognitive map is essentially made up of pieces that are connected to each other. The first chapter in this part talks about the pieces; the second deals with how they are connected. The pieces are not, of course, arbitrary pieces chopped out of our experience like parts of a jigsaw puzzle. Rather these pieces constitute the way we break up our experience into meaningful parts. Our goal here is to identify the basic unit of thought. This is a rather difficult problem; solving it turns out to require meeting two of the three criteria we discussed in Chapter 1: economy and generality. The third criterion, connectedness, is then the focus of Chapter 3.

The literature in environmental psychology not infrequently mentions "environmental perception." Often this concerns how people think about their environment (e.g., Saarinen and Sell, 1980). In other words, the distinction between perceiving and thinking is difficult to make and can often be misleading. The first chapter in this part, "Recognition and the Basic Building Block," is about perception. It is about how we come to recognize the things in our environment. We come to perceive things with great efficiency, not because it is easy—for the environment presents great obstacles to this process—but because of the power and ingenuity of the mechanisms involved.

Perceiving things is, however, only part of the story. Another central aspect of environmental perception is the space that surrounds and provides context for the things in our environment. The mechanisms whereby we comprehend both objects and spaces play a central role in the way we relate to our physical world.

While Chapter 2 is about perception, it is just as much about thought. This overlap is no coincidence. Recognizing objects is so challenging that it cannot be done efficiently without internal structures that stand for frequently encountered objects. These internal structures in turn go a long way toward providing a basis for thinking. Perceiving is inherently a cognitive process, and thinking in turn depends upon the structures that arise out of perception.

Although Chapter 2 takes us a large part of the way toward a framework for a cognitive map, it leaves a crucial gap. To function in the world, we must be able to go beyond what is directly in front of us. We must be able to contemplate future alternatives, to think about what might happen next. To bridge the gap from what is to what might be requires connectedness. It requires that there be a way to get from one basic building block to another. This is the central concern of Chapter 3, which deals with prediction, the going from what is perceived to what are possible subsequent events.

With the development of this predictive capacity, the requirements for a cognitive map have been met. Chapter 3 concludes with an analysis of various alternatives and with an examination of the cognitive map as a spatially derived factor in the thought process.

> There is no power to see in the eye itself. . . . We cannot see anything until we are possessed with the idea of it, take it into our heads—and then can hardly see anything else.
>
> Henry Thoreau

chapter two

RECOGNITION AND THE BASIC BUILDING BLOCK

The search is on for a way to explain how humans know the environment. If a cognitive map is not really a map, what is it? How does it "work?" If we could find some reasonable way to explain how humans comprehend their environment, such a finding would have far-reaching implications. Let's hold off on the implications until later in the book. The purpose of this chapter is to begin to develop an explanation of what a *cognitive* map might look like.

As we already mentioned, humans have the capacity to store a vast amount of information. They depend on the capacity to retrieve that information, often with no perceptible delay in time. The circumstances surrounding retrieval are often quite different from those of the initial encounter. We seem to be able to shift easily from thinking of a particular place to thinking of that place as a "point on the map." We can describe details as well as generalities. We can talk of places we have not seen in a long time. In a very meaningful way, the environment seems to be in our heads. Of course, not the real environment—but some form of that environment. We have a *model* of the environment, and this model has an important effect on what we do and how we cope.

To appreciate how impressive this internal model is, it might be useful to consider the approaches taken by some alternate storage/retrieval mechanisms, filing cabinets, say, or videotape systems, or computers. These devices handle the problem of storing information and retrieving it all the time. Are they in any way analogous to the internal model humans carry about?

The Filing Cabinet

The mind as a filing cabinet is an interesting analogy to consider. Granted, the mind's "hardware" must be miniaturized, and perhaps the storage medium is more like microfiche than like file folders, but the model here involves some drawers and some hierarchy of content categories. Things can be stored in the "proper place," and access is quite efficient when one goes to the "proper" location in the drawer. Misfiled information is a definite problem, as is information that does not readily fit the categories. Cross referencing is a particularly perplexing problem when one realizes that any information must be categorizable by numerous procedures. How to file the features of a place as well as its location? "Would you pull out the file on where vegetables are in Supermarket A, please. And now, the file on which supermarket carries brand W." We have not mentioned the drawers that store how we feel about certain places—or are the files color-coded to reflect preferences? It is probably not particularly useful to pursue this analogy further to sense its shortcomings. To the extent that it says that information is stored in the mind and that we have access to the information, it is acceptable. But is the filing cabinet necessary?

Videotape

For many people stored information has a stronger visual component than the filing cabinet analogy would suggest. Of course, one can put pictures in the files, but they do not retain some of the sequences of images that humans seem to carry with them. A videotape analogy, on the other hand, is appealing because it can put sound and vision together and also maintain the sequential information. Also, the "picture" is transformed from the real situation to a storable image—a process the mind must also master.

Is the mind much like a videotapedeck? Well, once again, to the extent that this analogy points to storage capabilities it has some utility. But consider the retrieval problem. If one had to run back through one's tapes each time one wanted to locate a bit of information, then the more experiences one has, the longer it would take. Even if it took only a thousandth of a second to scan each recorded minute of experience, an individual with only a single year's worth of 10 hours a day of experience would take more than three and a half minutes to run through the information accumulated. Clearly, retrieval based on even a fast rewind cannot approach the economy that the internal model must possess. The possibility of cross referencing seems even more difficult here since any one tape must include numerous content categories.

Though it is appealing to consider the videotape analogy as pertinent because it stores visual information, it is important to consider whether the recorded picture is akin to the picture in the mind. This brings up the often-used analogy that the eye is like a camera. The assumption in both cases is that the image as stored maintains a close relationship to the pattern of light that generated it. Although the eye has certain attributes that correspond to the camera, what is stored in the mind is strikingly different from the record produced photographically.

It takes a camera to demonstrate just how different the actual pattern of light is likely to be. Photographically, we can see that the identical picture rarely recurs. Humans, however, tend to respond to a given thing in a given way, no matter which of the possible light patterns the thing in question is presenting at any particular moment (Figure 2.1).

A Superb Computer

As computers have become ever more portable and ever faster, the analogy to brain function has become ever more enticing. And so one can think of the kinds of files computers have. As well-developed categories, such files avoid the problem of retrieval that is necessarily sequential; at the same time, they make such sequencing an option. With an efficient enough processing mechanism, multiple storage of information to handle cross referencing is less of a problem—except for limitations of total storage capacity.

Well, let us consider the problem of presenting the computer with patterns of light. What would we have to tell it in order for it to be able to recognize the things embedded in these patterns? What would it have

Figure 2.1 The identity of this object of perception is not obscured by variability in the pattern of light.
A. W. Kaplan

to know, what tricks would it have to use, what problems would it have to solve before the hazy image on the screen would lead it to the conclusion, "elephant"?

An obvious and tempting solution is in terms of pictures. That pattern of light is, after all, a picture. If the computer would simply store in its memory all the pictures it had ever seen, and if some way could be found to test whether they matched the image on the screen, then our problem would be solved. Except for a few awkward difficulties. As noted earlier, the identical picture practically never repeats. Thus one could have a great deal of experience with elephants and still not recognize an elephant approaching at a slightly different angle. Granted, one could fuzzy up the picture a bit so that little differences did not matter, but some little differences *do* matter. The difference between, for example, an elephant and a statue of an elephant is subtle perhaps, but important.

Recognizing things does not involve merely deciding that light patterns that differ slightly from each other are "identical." It also requires putting together patterns that are obviously not the same. An elephant viewed from the side is quite different from the same elephant, say, as it passes overhead. Somehow it is necessary to place a great variety of different patterns under a single heading, to treat them as members of a category or equivalence class.

Backgrounds present still a further problem. The other things going on at the same time are also part of the light pattern. Thus the pattern of stimulation generated by an elephant standing under a tree is different from that of an elephant standing next to a tree, which is again different from that of an elephant eating a tree. (Humans are so proficient at separating an object from its surroundings that it may be hard to comprehend that this is a problem. Not only do we take apart the pattern of stimulation into the important thing plus all the rest, we often eliminate the rest so effectively that we no longer realize it is there. Thus humans persist in taking photographs in which the camera somehow adds, growing out of someone's head, a tree or telephone pole that obviously was not there when the photograph was taken.)

THE CHALLENGE OF PERCEPTION

Even such a hasty analysis makes clear a few important points. First, although technological advances in information-handling have been incredible in recent years, they nonetheless pale in comparison to the capacity of the mind. Second, any explanation of how we know the environment must address the problem of how we perceive it in the first place. Before one can ascertain what might happen next, one must know what is happening and where one is in the environment. In other words, understanding environmental cognition requires a prior understanding of environmental perception. Although perception is in this sense basic, it does not follow that it is therefore simple.

Part of the complexity of the perceptual process arises from the necessity of dealing with two quite different problems. On the one hand, one must have some way of dealing with objects, of recognizing those vital packages of stimulation that appear again and again, in one form or another, in our environment. On the other hand, one must be able to deal with the remainder of the scene—that is, the background, the larger picture that surrounds these objects.

As far as recognizing objects is concerned, what seems to be required is not a multitude of stored pictures extracted from prior experience but some sort of summary of these many experiences (S. Kaplan, 1978a). Ideally, this summary would emphasize what tends to be common across experience rather than what has varied from one encounter to the next. It should be responsive to that varied class of stimulus patterns that can arise from the same object. Ideally, too, it should be a "confident" summary, confident in the sense that limited information of the right kind should lead to the conclusion that the object is indeed present. In other words, a trunk, a blur of gray, and a skinny tail should lead to the conclusion "elephant" without a lot of quibbling about not having noticed whether it had big feet or not. It would also be helpful if even a slight indication that there was an elephant in the environment would bring this summary to the fore, so that other information that would support or deny this possibility could be sought. In this way an object could be, as it were, pulled out of its background, separated from those aspects of the stimulus pattern that do not fit the previously developed summary.

When we turn our attention to the context for the object, or the larger picture, we find that what is involved is not one issue, but many. The separation of objects from background is essential, but just a beginning. We need to know how far the objects in the scene are from each other, as well as from us. We also need to know what kind of environment surrounds these objects—is it a large field or a small room? What is the terrain like? Is it rough and craggy or smooth and easy to traverse? There is a lot we need to know about the objects in our world; at the same time there is much to be understood about the setting in which we —and they—are located.

While the perception of objects is a central theme in traditional theories of perception, there is no comparable work on the perception of settings. The concept of space turns out to capture the idea of setting in a way that is quite powerful and general. Fortunately, there is considerable interest in the perception of space, especially in terms of depth cues. The discussion here, and the available literature, put heavy emphasis on visual perception. This is hardly arbitrary. Humans rely heavily on visual information (Posner, 1978; Posner and Rothbart, 1980; Rock and Harris, 1967) and, in fact, use visual imagery in many instances that are not actually visual (Freides, 1974). The "mind's eye" seems to favor vision, but the distinction between objects and space applies as well to the other senses. Being able to identify objects by smell, touch, taste, and sound is often critical. At the same time, knowing the object without being able to preserve information about location would be quite unsatisfactory. We are always concerned with locational information: where the sound or cry or odor is coming from, where the doorway is as one fumbles in a dark room, and so forth. Thus the *whatness* (object) and *whereness* (space) aspects are essential to perception regardless of which sense is involved.

The Location System

The first step in dealing with the challenges of perception is to take in appropriate information from the environment. Within the domain of visual perception one can distinguish between an ancient, rather primitive visual system that extracts certain basic locational information from the environment and another major visual system known as the contour system. Let us look first at the properties of the location system.

Consider some earthling making its way across the land. Basic to its survival is the virtually continuous assessment of surrounding conditions. Chances are high that top priority in the visual domain goes to anything that moves. Stimuli that move demand immediate attention, but motion information by itself is not enough. What one does with respect to a moving stimulus is largely a function of its size. Is the size increasing (coming closer)? Is the increasing size big relative to the earthling? Some rough notion of the form would also be a help. In other words, some very basic information involves relatively gross distinctions that code location, size, and rough form.

It is only relatively recently that scientists have considered the part of the visual system that is characterized by location processing (Chapter Note 1). From an evolutionary perspective, it must be an ancient system and one common to many species. A rough-and-ready assessment of "where" and "how big" and of changes in the location of potentially important stimuli (objects) must be made without delay. Never mind if one might err in deciding that the approaching blob is dangerous. At least one will still be there to appreciate it was an error!

Thus the location system not only provides some basic information about objects; it also provides information about the context in which the objects exist. At the same time, it is important to be able to perceive the spatial framework for itself and not just as a context for objects. It is in this spatial world that we move and function.

Our concept of space depends upon our capacity to perceive and think about distance. "Space" implies that everything is not piled together at one point but that it is—or can be—spread out. Different things can be different distances from each other and from us. In a space, some things are close together and others are far apart. Such distinctions can have a substantial effect on the way a scene is interpreted (Figure 2.2). Space does not require the actual existence of things as long as there is the possibility for things to be in different places (i.e., different distances from each other or from some fixed reference points).

There are two kinds of spatial information provided by the location system. One of these involves thinking of a scene as a *picture plane*, in other words, as having the axes up-down and right-left. Thus a very

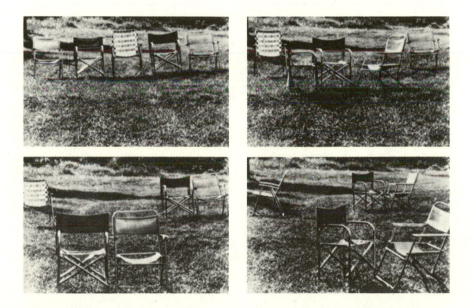

Figure 2.2 Objects by themselves do not determine a scene; distance and location also play a role.
A. W. Kaplan and S. Kaplan

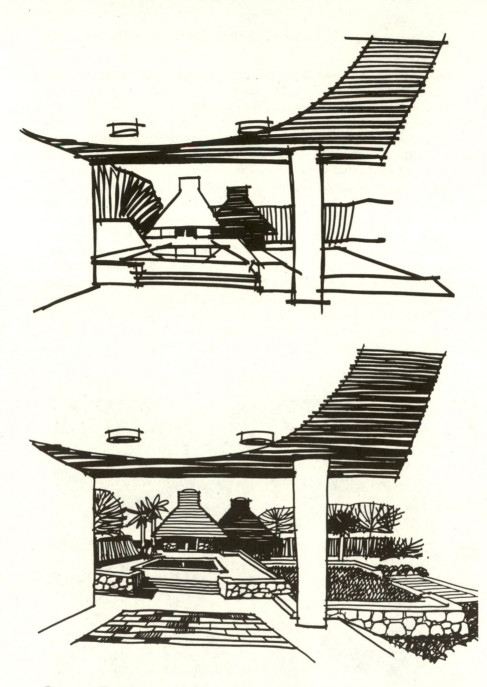

Figure 2.3 The top view, showing a designer's rough sketch, emphasizes the arrangement of elements on the picture plane; in such a rendering only minimal depth information is provided. The bottom view is a detailed drawing of the same scene. Note the many ways in which depth information has been provided.

H. L. Deardorff

quick glance at a scene may be enough to yield information such as that there are two small objects in the upper right of the scene and one large object in the lower left. Comprehending a scene may start with very basic distinctions of this kind (Figure 2.3).

Location system functioning is not restricted to the two-dimensional picture plane, however. This system is also ideally suited to a key source of information about the three-dimensional world. In his analysis of "the kind of distance perception required for flying" (part of a study carried out for the Air Force), Gibson (1946) emphasized the critical role of texture. *Texture* gradients provide information about depth through systematic variation in the *size* of the element. The nature of the element is of little importance. Hence the location system's capacity to provide information about size and location provides direct information about texture gradients (Figure 2.4).

A closely related form of spatial information is that of *surface*. Frequently a set of surfaces defines the space one is in. Here, too, the texture-reading capability of the location system provides direct access to vital spatial information.

Figure 2.4 The ferns in one photo and the tree tops in the other are examples of differences in size of element, varying with location. In this way, texture can be a compelling source of information about three-dimensional space. Also see Figure 2.2 for another example of how texture provides depth information.
A. W. Kaplan

The Contour System

In order to be able to tell different objects apart, one must know more than the distribution of patches of different sizes. The perception of *line* can be enormously helpful in discriminating different objects. "Location" turned out to be a rich and complex idea, and so too "line" is not a simple concept. The outline of something, for example, can be highly useful information. Here we are dealing with what is technically called *edge*, a line with surface on one side but not on the other (Figure 2.5).

Another important distinction with respect to line is its angle, or *orientation*. Here, too, is information that could be used to group like objects together and to discriminate among unlike objects. The contour system codes visual input for all these kinds of information—for line, for edge, and for orientation (Hubel, 1963; Hubel and Wiesel, 1968). In addition, it is sensitive to differences in wavelength, that is, to color (McCollough, 1965).

Such particular aspects of a visual pattern are often called *cues* since they give specific guidance as to what is present in the environment. Presumably such cues are not random, but have been selected for their usefulness in comprehending the environments our species has encountered throughout its evolution. This mechanism for extracting features thus provides an analysis of visual input. This analysis constitutes an interesting trade-off in information-handling. The benefits include a vast reduction in the complexity of the input. In other words, it provides a restricted language for characterizing a visual pattern. Out of the near infinity of possible configurations, only a comparatively limited set of cues is selected for further processing.

At the same time this arrangement is not without its costs. The cues thus extracted are so detailed and particular that, by themselves, they lack any meaning for the organism. Knowing that one is confronted by a certain number of lines of different orientation, a certain number of edges, and a certain number of colors tells one little about what is going on in the world. Thus the cue analysis provided by the contour system provides only a beginning to the problem of recognizing objects. The urgent task of organizing this potential clutter of details will be addressed in the next section of this chapter.

In addition to providing rich information about objects, contour-based information also plays a role in the perception of space. The contour system provides spatial information primarily in the form of distance cues. It can contribute to knowledge of distance through linear perspective—the convergence of parallel lines in the distance. This is particularly effective in environments with appropriately placed roads or

Figure 2.5 These portions taken from Figure 2.3 have been labeled to illustrate the distinction between line and edge.

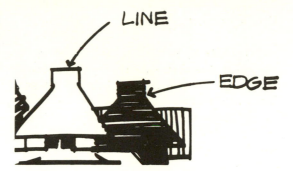

railroad tracks. Interposition also depends on contour information since it requires detection of which object is in front and therefore obscuring part of a farther one.

Cues of this kind play a central role in Renaissance painting; they also receive considerable attention in the typical basic psychology textbook. Despite their prominence in art museums and introductory courses, however, they may play a limited role in the perception of real environments. There are few circumstances that depend solely on these contour-based cues. Although a space can be defined in contour terms, the locational definition of space is probably of at least equal importance (Figure 2.6).

Location and Contour in Visual Perception

It is now possible to put together the various components of the perceptual process and see their contribution to a larger whole. Table 2.1 summarizes the contribution of the two hypothetical visual systems to the two essential aspects of visual perception: objects and space.

Figure 2.6 The top drawing defines a space using *line*, a contour-based cue. In the bottom drawing, *texture*, a locational component, has been added to give the same scene a sense of surface and depth. (In terms of locational processing, the "texture" in this scene would ideally be less dependent on lines, but it provides a good example of a designer's way of representing texture.)
H. L. Deardorff

Table 2.1

The Perception of Objects and Space

| VISUAL SYSTEM | ASPECTS OF VISUAL PERCEPTION | |
	Object	*Space*
Location	Size Locus Motion Rough form	Surface and distance via texture
Contour	Contour-based cues or feature information (line, edge, orientation)	Distance via contour cues

The location and contour systems thus play complementary roles in visual perception. The location system provides a holistic means of dealing with objects. In many respects it reflects the very properties of perception emphasized long ago by the Gestalt psychologists and more recently by Gibson (Chapter Note 2). It deals in wholes rather than parts; it is direct and immediate rather than inferential and mediated. It is not particularly precise; rather it is approximate and global. The information it provides is basic both in the sense of being relatively simple and in the sense of being essential for functioning.

The contour system, by contrast, is precise and analytic. Its particular strength is in providing a powerful basis for recognition of objects despite the many problems that make object recognition potentially so difficult. In many cases recognition of an object will occur independent of its size or location or motion. At the same time, these additional properties have enormous importance in the interpretation of the object's current status and in helping one decide what response (if any) is appropriate.

Three-dimensional space can be perceived on the basis of either locational or contour information. Although the combination seems to produce the strongest effect, the location system has the important advantage of preserving surfaces. It is also possible that there will exist a scene that lacks contour information concerning depth; however, except for cartoons and other line drawings, very few circumstances lack textural information.

(Attempting to relate perceptual processes to the realities of the physical environment has become a topic of considerable theoretical interest—and controversy! In his *Ecological Approach to Visual Perception*, Gibson (1979) has continued his broad-scale attack on the information-processing approach to perception. Since the issues Gibson and his followers have raised are important ones, and since the approach we have taken is a modified information-processing approach, some discussion of this controversy seems called for. As this would be something of a digression here, it appears as Chapter Note 2.)

OBJECT RECOGNITION

Despite the generous variety of locational and contour information that contributes to the perception of objects as well as of space, there remains a critical unresolved problem. The system as presented thus far lacks a means of recognizing objects. In other words, there still needs to be some way of developing a summary from a series of nonidentical experiences with a given object so that we recognize the object quite reliably even though only limited information is available at any given time. *Representation* is the name given such an internal summary of a class of stimulus patterns (Chapter Note 3). Its role is to take the place of— that is, to represent, or stand for—some object in the world. To understand how such representations come into existence, it is necessary to consider another aspect of the perceptual process. In particular, building on the insightful work of D. O. Hebb (1949), let us consider the perceptual process as comprising two aspects. First there is the dividing of the environment into properties so that the essential ones can be identified. We have seen how the location and contour systems have achieved just that. The second aspect of the process is the recombination, or synthesis, of the salient properties. In this way a composite, or summary, can be achieved.

From Elements to Representation

The problem of synthesis is a rather knotty one, largely due to the uncertainty that characterizes our commerce with the environment. The simplest solution would be to identify all features belonging to a given class of objects and to specify that when they are detected in the environment the object they characterize is indeed present. The difficulty here is in the definition of "belonging." There are a great many features that at one time or another can be found associated with an object (just as "pink" is sometimes associated with "elephant"). To require all such features to be present would be a substantial handicap. Some scheme must be derived to determine which and how many features will be necessary for the perception of an object. This scheme will necessarily be a compromise, for just as requiring too many features would lead to recognizing objects only under the rarest of circumstances, requiring too few would lead to too frequent recognition, at a frequency higher than the actual presence of that object in the immediate environment. Thus if "pink" were by itself a sufficient feature for the recognition of elephants, we would be "recognizing" elephants with a higher frequency than is consistent with even modest accuracy.

It is clear then that coming to conclusions about the presence of objects in the immediate environment requires some scheme for determining the adequacy of the available feature information. Several solutions to this problem have been proposed. One of the most popular solutions is based on the attractiveness of the computer as a model for human information-processing, and the facility of the computer in handling lists.

The List Model

This model is based on the idea that there are certain features that a pattern of stimulation *must have* if it is to be classified as a particular object. These critical features are, then, necessary and sufficient for perception of a given object. The approach of listing critical features has an appealing simplicity and a refreshing way of cutting to the heart of the problem of dealing with the presence of the class of patterns in question. There is, however, a serious drawback to this approach. Most of the objects in our environment do not have critical features. They have important or salient features, and often a good many of them, but they rarely have features whose presence is necessary for perception to occur. Let us consider the example of the elephant again. Surely a gray hulk and a wrinkled skin and the gleam of a tusk will yield the conclusion of having seen an elephant. But a white-washed animal of only moderate size with a long trunk and big ears must also be an elephant. This problem is, of course, not restricted to elephants. In general, objects viewed from different angles, under different patterns of illumination, and passing by us at different speeds yield quite different patterns of stimulation.

One solution to this difficulty of obtaining critical-feature information would be to suspend judgment until a thorough examination could be carried out. Unfortunately, the pressures of the environment are such that even a second look may be excessive, let alone a thorough examination. Suspending judgment about an object where the few available features are consistent with the hypothesis that the object is a lion (or an elephant) could be a grave error indeed. Those who feel that such arguments have no force in modern times might reflect on the experience of driving in traffic or crossing an urban street or of passing multitudes of faces in a crowd.

The critical features necessary for the list type of solution are thus rarely available, given environmental uncertainty and time constraints. A more satisfactory solution would involve deciding on the basis of some adequate sample of features characteristic of the object in question. If a subset of the salient features will be sufficient, some structure other than a list will be required. There is also the question of how a subset is to give the experience of a "whole," of a coherent "thing." How, in other words, is the necessary synthesis to take place? How can we put Humpty-Dumpty together again?

The Network Model

While the necessity of having critical features is the fatal flaw of the list model, a slightly weakened form of that assumption appears to be eminently reasonable. Certainly an object can be said to have *salient* features, that is, features that are likely to be detected when the object is present. If an individual could somehow learn that these features "go together," that they constitute a larger whole, then the goal of creating a summary of experience, a synthesis of the important elements, would be achieved.

Let us look then at what sort of learning would take place given experience with the various collections of features likely to be generated by some object. As a rule of learning, let us assume the most basic and most widely accepted principle, namely, *contiguity*. This principle states that two events that occur close to each other in time are likely to be associated. (Strictly speaking, it would be more accurate to say that if two events occur close to each other in time, the elements in the brain that represent them are likely to become associated. In the particular case under consideration, it would be the elements in the brain that stand for the various features an object can have that would tend to be associated.)

Given this rule, as an individual repeatedly experiences an object, the features of the object will tend to become associated with each other. It is unlikely that the resulting pattern of associations will constitute a list, since there is no single order in which an object exposes its features. Rather, the structure will be something of a tangle, with associations or connections going in many directions among the salient features. Such highly interconnected structures are more properly called *networks*.

Consider now what happens when a familiar object is encountered. Some of the features of the object are detected; in other words, the elements in the brain that correspond to certain features of the object go into an "active" state. In colloquial English, they turn "on." Being in an active, or on, state means, as far as elements of the nervous system are concerned, sending messages or impulses to those other elements with which one is associated. Thus the on elements will send messages to elements representing other features of the object. Receiving messages in turn influences those other elements so that they are more likely to themselves go into an active state (Figure 2.7).

Figure 2.7 In this schematic diagram, elements A and B are "on"; elements C and D are receiving messages from both A and B and are hence more readily turned on than are the other elements.

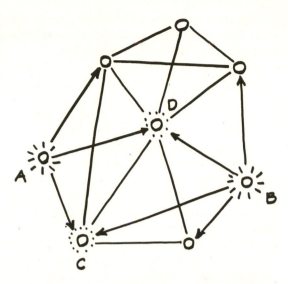

Thus, detecting a subset of features can result in a chain reaction within the network of feature elements representing the object. The entire network turns on, and the object is experienced as present. The network thus stands for the object in the experience of the individual. It constitutes an integration, or synthesis, of the salient-feature information, thus summarizing the communality among the innumerable "pictures" of the object previously experienced by the individual. The network, in other words, fulfills the essential requirement for a mechanism underlying the representation concept.

Recognizing with a Network

Recognition turns out to be no small achievement. Let us examine how the proposed mechanism for the representation comes to terms with the factors that are responsible for making recognition so difficult.

The first factor is the enormous variability in the patterns of stimulation that can arise from a single object (or, perhaps more appropriately, a single kind of object). The complexity and the uncertainty of the environment conspire to provide a dazzling array of possibilities and an awesome opportunity for confusion. Some of this variability is noise, that is, stimuli not correlated with the presence of the object. This part of the problem is handled when the individual analyzes the whole into elements, and so the elements bearing no *consistent* relationship to the object can be eliminated and ignored in the ultimate summary that represents the object.

Some of the variability, however, occurs within the very stimulation that characterizes the object. To say that there are rarely features that are critical is to acknowledge the presence of substantial variability even among salient features (Figure 2.8). Allowing subsets of the salient features to lead to activity in the entire network permits recognition despite this variability. Note that there is no requirement that particular subsets be present; many different possible combinations of detected features will be sufficient. This is not to say that all features are equal, however. More important feature elements (that is, those corresponding to features that are more reliably indicative of this object and less closely tied to other objects) will be more strongly associated with other elements in the network and will thus be more influential. In other words, such elements will require less help in moving the entire network into an active state.

To describe the representation as a collection of salient features, weighted in terms of their importance, is essentially the same as calling it an average, or summary, of the experience that led to it. Posner (1973) uses the term "prototype" to capture this sense of summary. The classic research of Posner and Keele (1968, 1970) nicely illustrates the power of this way of thinking about a representation. Their studies involved random patterns of dots. Several such patterns were selected, and each was given a name. Then each of these patterns was subjected to various distortions ("degraded" is the technical expression) using a computer procedure. In this way a number of degraded versions of each original pattern were produced. Participants in this research saw only these degraded versions. Each time they saw one, they were told its name. In time they learned to recognize these patterns despite their variability. A week later they were asked to identify the same material; however, now the original patterns were added to the collection. By this point the participants were not as effective at recognizing the degraded versions, but they unhesitatingly identified the original patterns correctly, even though they had never seen them before. Thus they must have constructed some sort of internal prototype out of the experience with the degraded versions.

Similar results have been found with verbal material. A sentence that does a good job of summarizing a story is identified with high confidence as having been in the story even though it was not (Bransford and Franks, 1971, 1972). Brown (1980) has taken this line of research one step further by using artificial patterns that have both critical and salient features. It turns out that people consider a pattern with many salient features of a category to be a good example of the category even though it lacks the critical feature. Conversely, patterns that have the critical feature of the category but few salient features are not consid-

Figure 2.8 Substantial variability in the patterns presented by an everyday (and readily recognizable) element of the urban environment.
A. W. Kaplan

ered to be examples of the category. Here again a statistical summary, or prototype, seems to be basic to the recognition process.

Variability, however, is not the only factor that makes recognition difficult. A second complicating factor is the separation of figure and background. Some patterns, a white cloud in a blue sky, for example, do not constitute much of a challenge. Many backgrounds are not that uniform, however, and many objects bear much more similarity to their backgrounds than do clouds to blue skies. The protective coloration of many animals (Figure 2.9) provides an interesting challenge. Although this example may not seem as crucial in the modern world as it was in earlier times, the modern world is not lacking in noisy, confusing backgrounds. Driving along a commercial strip development, for example, is probably every bit as challenging in terms of object recognition as sighting the spotted leopard amidst the spotted shade.

The network solution to this problem begins with the detection of various features in the stimulus pattern. Out of this diversity some of the features will belong to a common network. The corresponding elements will thus turn on and will begin sending signals to other elements in the network. Two things might happen next: (1) If there are enough elements on, their activity will be sufficient to turn on other associated elements, leading ultimately to widespread activity in the network. In such cases incomplete information will have led to perception of the object as complete and whole. (2) If there are fewer elements on, other elements will receive inputs, but in insufficient quantities to turn on themselves. They will then be in a state where they can readily be turned on given a small amount of additional input. Thus if present in the environment, even weakly or partially obscured, the features these elements stand for are likely to be detected. This process can be viewed as an automatic search for the missing information. In other words, to look at this process in less molecular terms, the existence of an internal prototype of a pattern allows one both to gather together the salient-feature information and to look for additional, related features when not enough information is available at first glance.

SOME CONCLUDING COMMENTS

The basic building block, the representation, combines a multitude of achievements into a simple process. It does what has to be done to recognize patterns. At the same time, however, the solution is not without a cost. The experience an individual has of the environment is structured and shaped by this mechanism. The way the world seems is in no small measure a function of how we process the information we receive from the environment. The transformation from incoming information to

Figure 2.9 For many animals, presenting a visual pattern that is easy to separate from the background could be maladaptive.
A. W. Kaplan

the turning on of the appropriate representation involves at least four different aspects that leave their mark on perception.

Simplicity. Information is discarded. There is far less information in a representation than in the many experiences that led to it. This does not mean that our experience is restricted to the information contained in the representation. The representation for "car," for example, presumably does not include size and color since these features are not characteristic of cars in general. Yet we do perceive size and color, and these features modify our experience of any particular car. At the same time, however, the car that we experience is much simpler than the stimulus pattern that it generates. Unless we paid particular attention, we can find ourselves hard pressed to provide any details of a car we saw only a short while ago.

Essence. The loss of information is not random, but highly systematic. What is retained is what tends to be reliable and characteristic. We thus are inclined to perceive in a stereotypic fashion. How something is experienced is greatly influenced by the prototype member of its category. Some adults, for example, seem to perceive all teenagers as fitting their, the adults', prototype of teenagers. Comparably, some teenagers perceive all adults as matching their stereotypes of what someone over 30 is like.

Discreteness. A representation involves the separation of experience into distinct categories. In the process of grouping different patterns into a single equivalence class, the continuity of experience is severed by category boundaries. Although the most familiar examples of discreteness are "good guys" and "bad guys" (or "us" versus "them"), such a separation need not involve an evaluative code. Things are perceived not only as distinct from each other, but as distinct from their surroundings as well. A landmark, although embedded in a context, stands apart in people's minds.

Unity. The representation tends to behave as a thing. It is no longer a collection of features but an entity that participates in thought as a substitute for what it stands for. This property enables one to recognize objects in confusing backgrounds or under conditions of ambiguity where definite information is lacking. It also makes it possible to jump to conclusions, to move promptly to a confident conclusion, well before all the pertinent information is available. Unity also serves to give imagined things their concreteness, their sense of reality.

Together these properties color the human experience of the environment. They shape not only what people perceive but what they do as well. They constitute a significant portion of what is sometimes referred to as "human nature." As such, they must also speak to the criteria that are essential for a cognitive map. In Chapter 1 we discussed three of

Table 2.2

How the Properties of a Representation Contribute to the Requirements for a Cognitive Map Mechanism

PROPERTIES OF A REPRESEN- TATION	REQURIEMENTS FOR A COGNITIVE MAP MECHANISM	
	Economy	*Generality*
Simplicity	Information that has low reliability is discarded.	By leaving out details, a representation "fits" many different instances.
Essence	A single prototype stands for many different instances.	That which is more characteristic, more reliable, will be more likely to fit the general case.
Discreteness	The elimination of continuity eliminates a great deal of information concerning what is "between" one thing and another.	The establishment of category boundaries aids generalization. Also, the separation of things from background allows generalization despite background variability.
Unity	Economy of experience— once a sense of unity exists, one needs fewer encounters with place to learn about it and understand it.	Unity allows one to conclude that something is present despite a great deal of missing information. This greatly broadens the circumstances under which one is willing to apply a given representation.

these—economy, generality, and connectedness. The representation relates to the first two; it is an economical means of coding experience that is sufficiently basic to have high generality. Table 2.2 provides a summary of the ways in which the characteristics of the representation relate to the requirements of a cognitive map.

Notes

1. Location Processing

Much of the research on this primitive visual mechanism has been carried out in the cat (Sterling and Wickelgren, 1969) and the hamster (Schneider, 1969). The extension of superior coliculus research to monkeys was pioneered by Wurtz and his colleagues; a recent review covers these and other primate studies (Wurtz and Albano, 1980). For some indication of the functions this mechanism might serve, see Held (1970), S. Kaplan (1970), Posner and Rothbart (1980), and

Trevarthen (1968). Bronson (1974) presents an ingenious analysis of the possible role of this mechanism as underlying the surprising competencies of visual perception in infants. A particularly readable discussion of location processing can be found in Lindsay and Norman (1977, pp. 75–80).

2.   A Critique of the Information-Processing Approach to Visual Perception

In the last several years a major attack on the information-processing position has been launched from the perspective of the Gibsonian position (see Haber, 1978, for a helpful discussion). This attack has raised a number of issues of considerable interest. Perhaps most noteworthy is the fact that Gibson takes the environment seriously. In contrast to most adherents of the information-processing position, Gibson (1966, 1979) is concerned with the effectiveness of visual perception in picking up the sort of information one might need to function in the physical environment. His descriptions are sensitive and thought provoking. Gibson's world is far removed from the letters and numbers that have for so long dominated the stimulus patterns of the information-processing researchers.

While the approach we have been taking is based on an information-processing point of view, this perspective has been modified in several important respects. It might be helpful to explore these differences before taking up the Gibsonian critique of information processing.

In its orientation to analysis and synthesis as basic to object recognition, the approach we have taken is closely aligned with the information-processing perspective. On the other hand, the biological dimension of our approach leads to some important differences. There are at least three ways in which the impact of this biological dimension has been decisive:

1.   Considerable attention has been devoted to the neural network activities assumed to underlie information processing.

2.   It is assumed that humans are a product of evolution and that they reflect that heritage in their information-handling patterns, in their biases, in their very nature. (More on this in Chapter 4.)

3.   The location system has received little attention in the information-processing literature. However, the physiological data and the fact that the location system provides answers for certain of the otherwise unsolved problems of perception make this possible mechanism seem most promising.

The information-processing position has tended to emphasize parts rather than wholes, the analytic rather than the synthetic. This is, in fact, a pervasive area of disagreement between Gibson and the information-processing perspective. It is therefore interesting to note that all three of the biologically based modifications that are central to our approach tend in a holistic direction. (1) Hebb's (1949, 1972, 1980) work with neural networks was in part an attempt to meet Gestalt concerns without abandoning the underlying ideas of element and association. The neural network standing for an object acts as a whole even though it is composed of discrete elements. (2) An organism trying to survive in a difficult world must hang together; it must function as a whole. This perspective tends to discourage getting lost in disconnected details. (3) The location system is inherently holistic in its operation. It provides a balance to the analytic inclinations of contour-processing.

The Gibsonian attack on information processing is broad-based, covering many issues. (It is, in fact, so broad that it approaches being diffuse.) For our purposes it will be helpful to group the most central arguments around three major themes: immediacy, memory, and sufficiency.

Immediacy. Gibson argues that no "processing" is needed; perception is "direct" and unmediated. This of course rules out anything as complex and devious as analysis and synthesis. In part the issue is semantic. At one time it was believed that the lens of the eye created an image on the retina and that this physical image was subsequently analyzed by some presumably "intelligent" agency in the brain. While this old language has been retained in modern information-processing theories, the meanings have shifted substantially. The "image" on the retina no longer plays an intermediary role. Rather, patterns of light stimulate receptors, leading to subsequent patterns of firing higher in the system. No one is required to "analyze" anything; the term "analysis" here refers to the results of this pattern of firing.

At the same time the emphasis on a direct, nonmediated process is strikingly parallel to the functioning of the location system. Here the essentially analog nature of the process makes possible the internal representation of scenes without the necessity of analysis and synthesis. Gibson in fact tends to emphasize scenes, and many of his illustrations are of scenes rather than objects. Certainly Gibson's ecological emphasis is consistent with a brain structure that has been characterized as an "ambient" visual system (Trevarthen, 1968), since one of its functions is to enable an organism to traverse uneven terrain. Likewise, Gibson's emphasis on surface is reflected in the basic structure of the location-processing system.

Memory. Gibson is famous (or notorious) for his disavowal of memory as playing a part in the process of perception. He is quite willing to admit the importance of perceptual learning, but not of memory. This is a strange position from the information-processing perspective, since there would seem to be no way to preserve the fruits of perceptual learning for future use without memory to store the appropriate information. Here again there is a semantic component to the argument, deriving from old terminology whose meaning has gradually shifted over the years. In fact, Gibson (1966) explicitly notes that the improvement of perception with experience does not involve "memory in the common-sense interpretive meaning of that term" (p. 277). He goes on to indicate that by memory he means "recalling or recollecting." Given this sense of memory, he must surely be correct. An individual looking at an object does not perceive that object by remembering a previous encounter with it. Perceiving involves the turning on of a structure based on many previous experiences, but it does not feel like (or resemble theoretically, for that matter) a reconstruction of a past

event. The use of the term "memory" has come to refer, at least among information-processing theorists, to durable changes in structure. In this meaning of the
term, the assertion that memory plays a role in perception should be not only
uncontroversial but hardly remarkable. If perceptual learning takes place and influences future perception (and there is general agreement on this), then it must
be maintained in the brain through some sort of structural alteration.

   Sufficiency.   Gibson argues that the information provided by the environment is in itself sufficient for perception, that no complex "inference" or "filling
in" by the brain is needed. This is a reflection of Gibson's peculiar brand of
functionalism. He is aware of the richness of the real-world physical environment that organisms live in. In contrast to laboratory stimulation, the environment is rich indeed. In this sense his functionalism is a great advance over the
traditional information-processing perspective. On the other hand, his rendition
of the organism's life in the real world is strikingly peaceful, tranquil, and safe.
There are no lurking dangers. There are no hidden predators. Speed is not a consideration. Information is never incomplete because of limited time or protective
coloration or the deviousness of potential enemies. Gibson's "ecological" approach applies to a peculiar ecology, one in which one is never in any danger of
being eaten.
   In the framework we have presented, the representation plays a vital role in
the recognition of objects. Perception of the space in which the objects exist requires a quite different sort of mechanism. The location-processing system fills
these requirements very well; it provides a means of dealing with spaces and
surfaces as well as additional object information that is simple but of enormous
functional value.
   This dual approach to perception meets many of the objections that Gibson
has raised concerning the traditional information-processing position. Other objections appear to be grounded in definitional problems. However, it must be
recognized that, for whatever reasons, Gibson has come to take a position that
essentially denies the usefulness of the representation concept (cf. R. Lachman
and J. L. Lachman, 1979). This is in many respects ironic. Gibson speaks of a
process of perceptual learning that leads one to know better what to pay attention to. He speaks of a "chunking" process, whereby with increasing experience
one can take in more at once. His affordance concept suggests stored information
that makes possible our appreciation of an object and its potential. He thus
comes about as close to having a representation as one could without acknowl-
edging it. A recurring weakness in Gibson's position is his failure to suggest any
mechanisms or structures that might underlie the functions he describes. And, in
denying the relevance of the representation, he once again lacks a mechanism for
what in this case is a remarkably coherent, familiar-sounding collection of ideas.

3.   Representation

   This concept has been the topic of active research and discussion in recent
years. Although neither terminology nor definition has been consistent, the central core of concern has remained recognizable. Among the terms used are "inter-

nal representation," "schema," "prototype," and, most recently, "natural category." Although early work by Bartlett (1932) and Attneave (1957) showed considerable insight into the issues, the concept did not receive widespread currency until Neisser's *Cognitive Psychology* was published in 1967. One of the most perceptive and useful discussions of this concept can be found in Chapter 3 of Posner's (1973) *Cognition: An Introduction*. The close connection between representation and object has been underscored by Rosch (1978); B. G. Campbell (1974) has focused on the object in cognition from an evolutionary perspective. Some of the flexibility of manipulation possible in using this "mental furniture" has been demonstrated by Shepard (1975). Useful general discussions of the role of this concept in cognition include Bransford (1979, Chapter 6) and Wickelgren (1979, Chapter 10).

The position we take in this chapter is largely in accord with the way the representation concept has come to be understood in the information-processing literature. We have, however, extended and broadened the concept. On the one hand we have made the assumption that the representation has an internal structure and internal dynamics that are worthy of study and exploration. This is the topic of the remainder of the chapter. We also see the representation as a vital element in an individual's models of the environment. These larger cognitive structures are discussed in Chapter 3.

chapter three

PREDICTION AND THE COGNITIVE MAP

The recognition of objects as well as the development of representations that make recognition possible, constitute no small achievement. By itself, however, this achievement is of only limited value. The capacity to recognize some familiar landmark, for example, helps very little if one does not have any other information connected to it. If one does not know what is near the landmark, if one cannot predict what will happen if one passes it and continues on in the same direction, then such recognition provides little in the way of assistance. Likewise, the capacity to recognize our old friend the elephant, even to recognize it from many angles, despite its being partially obscured by other objects, is of little value if one cannot anticipate what is likely to happen next.

A representation is, by itself, merely a building block. It cannot provide us with a conception of what is happening in time or of the arrangement of space. To comprehend patterns in time, that is, to be able to relate the present to possible next events, requires that one be able to anticipate, to predict. In terms of structure, anticipation implies some sort of continuity. It implies that one must get from one representation to other representations if one is to have any conception of what the future might bring.

Comprehending patterns in space places essentially identical requirements on cognitive structure. One must be able to anticipate what places come next. Again, one's representations must be at least somewhat continuous if one is to have a larger conception of what follows what.

It is this continuity issue that makes the difference between a collection of isolated representations and a coherent structure, a cognitive map of space or time. There must be some way to transcend the discreteness of our codes for things and events. There must be some way to overcome the separateness of representations in order to achieve that powerful cognitive tool, the internal model of the environment.

40

Our experience tends to support this emphasis on continuity. Intuitively our cognitive maps seem as continuous as the environments they represent. Between any two points there is another point. From any point it feels as if we are free to move in any imagined direction we choose. The very use of the term "map" suggests such continuity.

On the other hand, our intuition might be misleading us in this respect. The apparently continuous map has many gaps and discontinuities. On functional grounds, the requirement is not for continuity but merely for connectedness. In other words, to function, it is not necessary that one know all the possible points between place A and place B. It is only necessary that place A and place B be connected—that one can in general go from A to B. Thus connectedness would seem to be sufficient both as a functional requirement and as a means of approximating the experience of continuity.

The proposed means of achieving connectedness is an ancient one as far as psychology is concerned (see Voss, 1969). It undoubtedly dates back to Aristotle, and it has received no little attention since that time. It is a concept that has the advantage that a good deal is known about it. It also has the advantage of simplicity, although for many tastes it is undoubtedly too simple; it smacks of a certain austerity that might not seem well suited to describing the richness of cognitive life.

This ancient, familiar, austere mechanism is the *association*. Stated in simplest terms, a representation is assumed to be *associated* with the other representations that have tended to follow it in an individual's experience (S. Kaplan, 1973a). In this way connectedness is achieved, transforming what would otherwise be a mere collection of representations into a cognitive map (Chapter Note 1).

THE MAKING OF A COGNITIVE MAP

In attempting to understand the significance of this apparently simple-minded concept, let us look at what is required for the appropriate connections to arise. What sorts of experiences are necessary for representations to become associated with each other?

Objects or events or particular places are coded as representations. These are patterns that generate relatively reliable patterns of stimulation over repeated encounters. Early in life, representations develop that correspond to simple objects in the environment—a ball or bottle, for instance. With time, there are representations for "person" and then for particular persons, such as parents and siblings. With increased maturity, we develop representations for all sorts of patterns, many of them rather abstract. We develop representations for sunsets and celebrations, for baseball games and neighborhoods.

These kinds of objects and events and places do not arise as isolated experiences. They happen in various contexts and in relation to a variety of next experiences. *Each representation comes to be associated with those likely to follow it.* Since these associations are built up as the results of many experiences, representations will not generally have unique associations. Instead, each is likely to be associated with numerous others. Various of these will be the result of very different amounts of experience; they will thus vary considerably in their strength. Some of these associations will, in other words, seem far more probable than will others.

Let us consider a simple example. Imagine a hard-working, red-blooded, stalwart American citizen whom we shall call John. John goes directly to work five mornings a week, except in unusually bad weather, when he takes the kids to school even though this constitutes a detour from his customary route to work. On Saturday he often goes to the auto parts store, and on Sunday he sometimes goes to church. "Home" thus has not one, but at least four different places associated with it. Further, these associations are not all of the same strength.

Associations between representations are thus the result of sequences we have experienced. Underlying this assumption is the same simple rule of learning that was the basis for the formation of representations. This rule, called the *contiguity* learning rule, states that if one thing tends to follow another closely in time, the two will tend to become associated. Just as features were associated through this rule to form representations, so also do representations become associated.

You might be worried at this point about the many sequences that people carry around in their heads. If experiences tend to be sequential and if the contiguity rule leads to associations of whatever things follow one another, would not the result be that people tend to learn many isolated sequences? While this is the case to some degree, especially in new environments, it is a quite misleading picture of how cognitive maps are learned. Let us return to John's situation for a moment. Sometimes after work John drops by the friendly neighborhood tavern on his way home. (It is actually not exactly on the way home but well worth the extra distance as far as John is concerned.) On Friday John sometimes goes home from the tavern by way of the auto parts store, to save having to go there Saturday morning. One could imagine these various sequences being stored in John's head in the following form:

1. Home → work → home
2. Home → work → tavern → home

3. Home → work → tavern → auto parts → home
4. Home → auto parts → home

John is quite capable of recognizing "home" as a destination. It turns on the same representation as does "home" as a starting point. We thus have a modification of sequence 1 as follows:

Home ⟷ work

Since sequence 2 involves the representation of sequence 1 as a subset, we can rediagram the composite of 1 and 2 as follows:

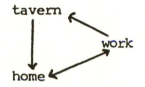

Likewise we can include sequences 3 and 4 as follows:

Thus what is experienced as independent sequences need not be stored that way. What makes this integrated and compact storage possible is the pattern recognition capability of the representation. As we noted previously, John is quite capable of recognizing "home." In other words, his various experiences with it turn on the same representation. So, too, for "work," for "tavern," etc. *Thus different sequences of experiences that pass through common places will share representations in common.* In this way different experiences with any given place are overlaid on top of each other.

These sequences of experiences are stored as overlapping patterns, yielding a whole network of associations. This network is not only an efficient way to store sequences of experiences; it even contains sequences that were never experienced before. Although this may sound a bit strange, it actually follows quite directly from what we have already discussed. Let us return to John's world. He has, as you no doubt recall, associations between his representations of home and work, work and tavern, and tavern and auto parts store. He also occasionally goes from the auto parts store to the grocery store when his wife asks him to pick up a loaf of bread for Saturday lunch. The composite diagram of John's experiences thus looks like this:

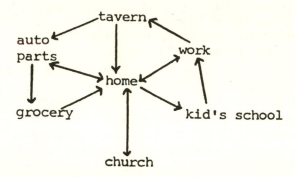

Remember that the experienced sequences include home-work-tavern-auto parts and home-auto parts-grocery. Although he has never experienced it, if John were asked to stop at the grocery on the way home from work, we would assume that he could carry out that sequence without difficulty (Figure 3.1). In this way the proposed mechanism is economical not only in the way it stores information, but also in the way it utilizes experiences (Table 2.2). First, the mechanism pulls together all experiences having to do with a given place. Everything one knows about that place is, as it were, under one heading. Second, this mechanism allows one to put together pieces of previously learned sequences

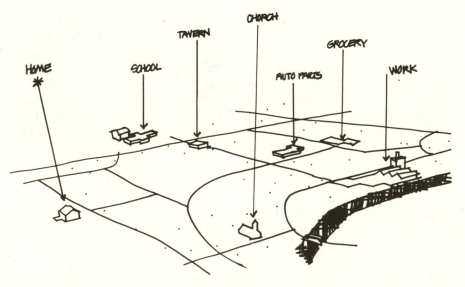

Figure 3.1 John's world.
H. L. Deardorff

in order to think about (and even carry out) novel sequences. In other words, it provides an orderly basis for innovation (S. Kaplan, 1976).

As an individual has more and more experiences that crisscross common things and places, the pattern of connections or associations in the brain becomes less and less like a collection of isolated sequences. Instead a more complicated structure begins to arise, a structure that has no good name but that increasingly resembles what we previously called a network. Here, of course, the points in the network are not elements, but representations. It is, if you will, a network of networks. And these representations are linked to each other by a pattern of connections.

Let us return for a moment to the distinction between continuity and connectedness. The existence of connections between representations of two different places does not retain the continuity between these places that exists in the environment. The connection does not carry any additional information concerning the intervening terrain. *The connection simply stands for the possibility of getting from one place to another.*

Some people will be tempted to challenge this description on intuitive grounds. It certainly *feels* as if one has continuous information. In part this may be the result of an illusion fostered by the connection pattern itself. It certainly feels as if one could provide a description of the route that so smoothly joins A and B in one's mind. In fact, though, people have trouble with such descriptions. Shortly after a new building has gone up, people often have trouble remembering what was there before, even when they are standing at the very spot in question.

In part, however, those who assert that they have more in their maps than mere connections between important places are undoubtedly correct. This is particularly the case for highly familiar material, but not because of any extra information carried by the connections. Rather, with increasing experience, new landmarks form between old ones, yielding a cognitive map of increasing density. Cognitive maps of highly familiar places are thus often packed with salient information. It might be for this reason that instructions from cab drivers, police officers, and other well-informed "old-timers" are often too detailed to be of use. It is interesting that the process of landmark learning is at least as much one of "filling in" as it is of "pushing on." Thus from very early in the learning process, there is a map that, although crude, is quite usable. There is an overall basis for guiding behavior even though much additional remains to be learned. Devlin's (1976) study of cognitive mapping in new arrivals to Idaho Falls shows essentially this same pattern (Figure 3.2).

It thus may be that a cognitive map intuitively feels continuous even though it is actually made up of connected, but discrete, representations. This view of a cognitive map places great emphasis on representations and hence on land-

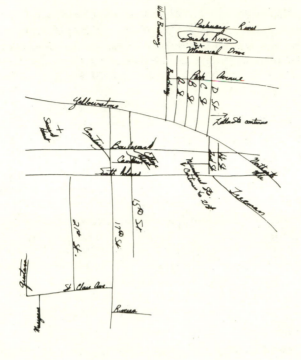

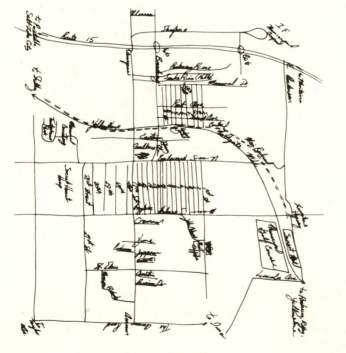

Figure 3.2 These sketch maps were drawn about three months apart by a participant in Devlin's study of new arrivals in Idaho Falls. Note that the later map is more an elaboration than a change, relative to the initial map.

From "The small town 'cognitive map: Adjusting to a new environment'" in *Environmental Knowing*, edited by G. T. Moore and R. G. Golledge. Copyright © 1976 by Dowden, Hutchinson & Ross, Inc., reprinted by permission of the publisher and author.

marks in the environment that the representations stand for. If environmental information is coded in this way, it should have a substantial influence on the way one remembers and thinks of portions of the environment one has experienced, suggesting hypotheses such as these:

1.   Landmarks tend to move to choice points. If there is no landmark where a route changes direction or a decision has to be made, a landmark in the general vicinity will be remembered as being at the critical point.

2.   Landmarks will be recalled as more prominent (in size or distinctiveness) than they actually are.

3.   Landmarks may be remembered as being in line of sight from the prior landmark when actually they are only the next memorable thing after the prior landmark.

4.   Landmarks provide information about distance. In some rough, general way the more landmarks between any two points in one's cognitive map, the greater the perceived distance is likely to be. This can lead to certain distortions. It would suggest that, other things being equal, the more landmarks a route has for a given individual, the longer it will be remembered as being (Chapter Note 2).

On functional grounds this conception of the cognitive map appears to do all that is required of it. It provides a satisfactory basis for decisions even when a great deal of information is missing. Further, it provides a basis for innovation since the connections can relate to each other representations that may have never been experienced together before. Finally, this structure constitutes a basis for anticipation, for prediction of what might be next. Indeed, it forms the basis for a quite substantial *lookahead*, for calculating some distance into potential futures.

Hierarchies and Generic Maps

It is most unlikely that there is one single cognitive map that contains all of the information an individual has. Rather, each of us must have many different cognitive maps that are distinct but at the same time somehow related. This suggests that there might be some sort of hierarchical relationship among the different maps that reside in a single head.

A closely related problem is that of scale. Some maps deal with small areas in considerable detail; others deal with vast areas where the detail is necessarily much more limited. A scale shift in the cognitive map is comparable to a shift to a totally different cartographic map. A city that might be represented by a street map at one scale might merit only a small dot on a map of the world.

Representations are not necessarily directly linked to environmental features. Some of them are based on input from other representations. In fact such a *higher-level* representation might itself be based on a group of interconnected representations that constitute a cognitive map. Take the idea of "neighborhood," for example. This concept acts as a "thing," an entity. Yet it is itself a summary of many separate things from a lower level. It stands for a grouping of particular houses, streets, stores, school buildings, etc. The cognitive map of a particular neighborhood, which comprises these (and many more) representations of objects and places, can in time lead to a new representation of a larger entity—a town, sub-urb, city, or whatever. These differences correspond to different scales: the capacity to shift from a room to building, to a neighborhood, to a city, and so on. In each case, it is still meaningful to speak of the representations making up the cognitive map as well as of the cognitive maps at the different scales.

Thus there are many circumstances where a cognitive map is in some sense a part of another cognitive map. We can call up parts, if needed; we can also call up the larger map without considering each of the parts. One can think of a town or city one knows well without the mental image including the very detailed knowledge one has of a particular neighborhood within that city. One could report on the location of a particular fire hydrant, but when considering the fastest way to get through town the detail of the fire hydrant will not be included. One could certainly place one's neighborhood cognitive map "in" the cognitive map of the town, but the former is not a part of the latter in the sense that one would be unable to think of them separately from each other.

Consider, for example, the straightforward, routine set of activities entailed in instructing someone to find a particular book on the book-shelf. First, the person is told to go to the study. This presumably requires a cognitive map of the house, or at least of a particular floor of the house. Next, "the bookshelf is on the left, behind the chair." This necessitates a scale shift to a map of a particular room. Then, the instruction is to go to the third shelf from the bottom—calling for another scale shift. Finally, the book is described as a "small paperback with a bright green cover in the middle-right region." Here pattern recognition is needed, in the context of yet another map, at the scale of a particular shelf.

The structure that corresponds to this description is a *hierarchical* one. "Hierarchical" refers to an arrangement that has multiple levels. Thus we might think of a higher-level cognitive map as one that is more abstract or at a larger scale. It would be a mistake, however, to think of such a hierarchical arrangement as being neat and orderly, with more detailed information available "below" each node of a higher-level map. Rather it is a patchwork, characterized by thorough knowledge here and there, surrounded by large areas of incomplete information, reminiscent of C. Alexander's (1965) "A city is not a tree." (Chapter Note 3 deals with some of the more technical issues raised by the hierarchical concept.)

Such a hierarchical arrangement has a number of other advantages in addition to this basic one of economy of thought. An important one is the filling in of gaps in one's information. If one is somewhere that is unfamiliar but identifiable in terms of a higher-level category, one might be able to decide what to do on the basis of analogy. In fact, it is not at all unusual to use even very limited prior experience as the basis for action in a novel situation. Say one is visiting a friend at a large convalescent center. One has never been to such a facility before but has been at a large university health service. By categorizing them both as "hospitals" it is possible to use the map of what one knows to help one in the new setting. Here a shift of levels is necessary to come up with the appropriate information. The classification "hospital" is a higher-level one than the way-finding information one is seeking, but by moving up to this higher level it is then possible to move back down to a particular cognitive map that might be suitable. Essentially this makes it possible to locate a substitute for the cognitive map that is missing because of insufficient prior experience with the new situation.

In many cases a new or unfamiliar situation calls upon information at a more abstract level where there are well-developed cognitive maps. Such *generic maps* can apply to many different situations, even to some that have not yet been encountered. Thus one might have maps of a "typical college campus" and a "small town with courthouse on the central square" and of "expressway interchanges" as well. These allow us to know how to behave and what to look for in new and unfamiliar situations.

Several observers of the built environment have talked about ways of seeing urban development in terms that sound strikingly like generic maps. Jackson (1970) describes the "traveler's way," a characteristic urban pattern leading from the bus station to downtown. Clay (1973) identifies areas such as "beats" and "turf" and provides some generic information about each. Whyte (1980), although focusing primarily upon sitting and pedestrian behavior, points to comparable generic patterns. These are undoubtedly very general forms that make our cities easier to perceive, to comprehend, and even to appreciate. C. Alexander, Ishikawa, and Silverstein (1977) have developed what they call a "pattern language," an ambitious and far-reaching set of generic concepts intended to serve as a guide to design and planning at all scales, from the individual dwelling to city and region. These patterns can be combined in different groupings and different ways, thus emphasizing the flexibility inherent in the generic.

Sometimes a generic map biases the way one structures one's experience. A study of the sketch maps that people drew of their apartments found that the errors tended to be in the direction of making the drawing more like the typical apartment (i.e., the generic map) than was in fact the case (Mayer, 1977, p. 104). Comparably, J. M. Mandler and Parker (1976) looked at the impact of what they called "real-world schemata" on people's memories after they were shown pictures of complex scenes. They define these schemata as "real-world knowledge of the way things are supposed to be" (p. 47). These generic maps were so powerful that people who had not originally seen the picture but were given the elements to arrange did almost as well as people trying to arrange the elements based on their having seen the picture a week earlier. Apparently much "seeing" is largely a check to be sure that the pattern doesn't deviate too far from one's generic map.

Generic maps are, of course, no more limited to the physical environment than are any other cognitive maps. Members of our culture have generic maps of basic cultural forms (a love story, say, or a church service, or a cocktail party). Cultures also provide generic maps of time. Agriculturally oriented cultures are known for their celebrations to mark the seasons; even in our culture landmarks in time can be identified. There are also generic maps of linguistic patterns; one of the great insights of learning a foreign language involves discovering how much these generic maps can vary from one language to another. People who are good at fixing things have a generic "fixing" map that can be applied to something they have never fixed before.

COGNITION AND SPACE

Space is central to the way we think. It is even possible that there are two distinct, but related, modes of spatial thinking. One is based on the cognitive map. Such structures code a great deal of spatial information, not only about patterns that are in fact spatial, but also about patterns where space is not a physical component of the situation. In addition, much of our thinking is carried out in a spatial context that is not necessarily part of the cognitive map structure. The location mechanism described in Chapter 2 might play a role here. Let us take a look at the pervasiveness of spatial thinking in these two contexts.

Spatial Component of Cognitive Maps

It can be quite upsetting to discover that something is not where we are sure we left it. How often one returns to that location to double and triple check because "it just has to be there"! Worse yet, one has directed someone else to fetch something, having provided the necessary directions, and the object is simply not there. It is at times like this that one can be vividly aware of the extent to which we count on spatial information being in the maps we have: where in the drawer the masking tape should be, where in the store the crackers are located, where in the garage the snow tires are stored, etc.

A similar sense of surprise (and dismay) can accompany the "mislocation" of entities that lack the concreteness of physical objects. We talk of a thought "coming back" or "returning." We have a sense for where in a story certain things should be happening, and their not occurring can have a strong impact on our decision whether or not to continue with the story. We accuse officials of wrongdoing when they do not follow agreed-upon patterns of action. We might recognize a bird by its sequence of actions and would be surprised to see it behave differently.

Cognitive maps code proximity and distance, order and sequence. There are paths between some things and not others. There are regions and levels, allowing one to deal with the same domain at different scales. In other words, cognitive maps have a set of relational spatial properties that constitute what we call structure. Spatial information is therefore intrinsic to the cognitive map. Without the relational properties one would be unlikely to anticipate next events and could hardly be surprised at the way the events unfold.

A person who is working on a way-finding problem and has thereby called up a cognitive map is quite obviously functioning within a spatial framework. A telling example of this is provided by Porteous (1971), who describes the perplexity created by a planner presenting a map of a town with north oriented upward, as is traditional. The townspeople, however, were accustomed to thinking of their town in a different orientation and found the map quite uninterpretable.

Way-finding provides, as one might suspect, an ideal context for observing the cognitive map in operation. R. Kaplan (1976) has studied this process in the context of the natural environment. She demonstrated that prior orientation designed to aid way-finding significantly enhanced the enjoyment of the subsequent outdoor experience. Weisman (1981), studying way-finding in university buildings, found that the single most effective predictor of disorientation was the *structure* of the building. Judges rated geometric patterns that corresponded to the corridor structure of the buildings on a simplicity scale. Those buildings corresponding to the patterns rated relatively simple were the least likely to cause disorientation. Since such overall structures are not something that building users tend to see all at once, this study points to the importance of the cognitive map built over many experiences as well as to the underlying structure that makes learning the cognitive map more or less difficult.

Another variable in Weisman's study was signage. Posted directions providing information would certainly seem, on intuitive grounds, to be an appropriate aid to way-finding. Contrary to expectation, however, the buildings with the most signs were the most disorienting. This apparent paradox was resolved when it was discovered that the buildings with the most confusing structures were the ones with the most signs. It appears that signs were used in an attempt to compensate for way-finding difficulties that were already present. This may be a quite general phenomenon; much of the built environment appears to depend on signs to correct pre-existing illegibility.

As we have seen, however, the usefulness of a spatial framework extends far beyond the interpretation of spatial information. Many patterns of information that are not obviously spatial have strong spatial components in the way people think of them. Text, for example, is ordinarily regarded as verbal as opposed to spatial. Yet many are the students who can remember where on the page the answer is—but not what it is. As we have seen, the "position on the page" phenomenon has its parallel in the "position on the bookshelf" phenomenon. Likewise, when comparing notes on the people at some meeting one has just attended, where the person in question was sitting is often the most communicative of various possible means of identification. As Thomas (1977) has pointed out, the memory of the wild berries one has foraged is accompanied by strong spatial codes. Comparably, one is likely to remember quite vividly where one saw an unusual bird. People seem to handle space so readily that it crops up in areas that do not on the face of it seem primarily spatial. This human facility turns out to make good sense in the context of human evolution (see Peters and Mech, 1975), a topic that will be discussed in Chapter 4.

The close relationship between the spatial and the structural is nicely illustrated by a study (Van Kreveld and Zajonc, 1966) in which the task was to learn pairs of items and their relationship. For one group, the elements (capital letters) were nonsense syllables and the relationship between them was "plus" or "minus." For the other group, the elements were countries and the relationship was "influences." While the information was formally identical, it seems possible that people might think of the material quite differently in the two cases. When one thinks of countries that influence each other, one might be inclined to think of a whole pattern of relationships. By contrast, neither capital letters nor pluses and minuses would incline one to think beyond each individual pairing. The results of the study indicate that such a differential effect was, in fact, operating. The group dealing with countries and influences differed in their memory for the material in two respects: (1) their performance was substantially superior and (2) the errors they made involved confusing countries at the same level of influence. Together these findings indicate that the superior group had constructed a cognitive map of the material. The pattern of errors underscores the spatial nature of this structure.

Examples of Spatial Imagery

To be up front
To have something behind one
To be behind in work
To be behind a candidate or issue
To cross the river to the other side
To cross the bridge
To put someone in her or his place
To have one's things in their place
To be on top of things
To be under it
To be on top of the world
To have a come down
To be feeling high or low
To stand by someone
To be beside oneself
"Back up a minute"
"I won't get ahead at this rate"
"The eventual solution surfaced early"
The course of life

Evidence for the importance of space in matters not primarily spatial may be surprising to those who have not thought of cognition as exhibiting a spatial bias. Even more striking perhaps are those cases where information without any spatial component is coded in a spatial framework. Research on this topic has focused on ordered syllogisms, a type of problem in which multiple comparisons are made. For example, an individual might be asked the following question: "Lisa is richer than Tom. George is poorer than Lisa. Who is richest?" Problems of this kind tend to be solved by creating imagined spatial arrays where, for example, the richest person is at the top (Huttenlocher, 1976, p. 268; also, Attneave, 1972, p. 305).

This type of research provides a particularly interesting example because it calls on two quite different forms of spatial functioning. It is unlikely that an individual attempting to solve a problem of this kind already has a ready-made map of the individuals in the story. On the other hand, with experience, problems of this kind become increasingly easy to handle. This suggests the development of generic cognitive maps for relationships of this kind. Such a generic map makes it possible to place the different individuals in different spatial *locations*. Let us turn to this distinctly different form of functioning.

Locational Aspects of Thought

Imagine a room: there is a narrow bed along the left edge, and along the opposite wall is a simple wooden desk. The chair in front of the desk is positioned so that one can look out of the only window in the room. A few feet to the right of the desk is a chest of drawers with a small mirror above it. On the far wall there is a watercolor landscape painting above a well-used armchair.

How can one accomplish a task such as this? Unlike the perceptual process described in Chapter 2, the situation here is not physically present. The pieces of furniture are not actually there to be seen, and the space they occupy is also only imagined. Yet, even with a brief description, it is likely that this task presents no difficulties and that, if several people were asked to draw a rough sketch of the room, different renditions would have much in common.

Imagining the room calls upon many representations: bed, desk, chair, window, chest, mirror, painting, and armchair. The concepts of "well-used" and of a "landscape" drawn by a particular procedure also require some higher-level representations. Chances are, some generic cognitive map of a room is also used to help one group the pieces. After all, if the description had included a cash register, let us say, that would have come as a surprise. A lamp on the desk is so likely to be part of one's generic map of such a setting that it might have been included in your image even though it was not mentioned.

In addition to using these various representations, however, the task also requires putting these things in places, that is, some notion of a space and of locations in the space. Different objects are to the *right or left* of others; the chair is *in front of* the desk, and the picture *above* the armchair. The process of imagining the room requires using some kind of mental "scratch pad" that provides a space for locating the elements.

Much as cognitive maps code proximity and distance, the locational aspects of thought also involve these properties. We have seen how the capacity to recognize objects has made it possible to think of them, to represent them mentally even when they are not present. (Thus, for example, one may think of a lion when the only pertinent stimulus was the crack of a twig.) In this way perception forms the basis for cognition. This may be the case not only for objects, but for spaces as well. The same location system that was discussed in the context of perception in Chapter 2 may have powerful and profound implications as a basis for "spatializing" thought. (Note: The role of spatial factors in the thought process has only recently been acknowledged; the probable mechanisms are not well worked out. The discussion of locational factors in thought is particularly speculative.)

Some idea of the contribution that this primitive location system might be able to make to the thought process is suggested by the kinds of spatial relationships that develop very early (Bronson, 1974). Piaget and Inhelder (1967) identify five such relationships, which are well described in a discussion of the "conception of space" by Robinson and Petchenik (1976, p. 89):

> First is the idea of propinquity, or *proximity*. . . . A second idea that develops is that of *separation*. In early perception two nearby elements may be partly blended and confused. An act of separation is required to dissociate them. A third spatial relationship present in elementary perception is that of surrounding or *enclosure*.

Another fundamental relationship (p. 7) "is established when two neighboring though separate elements are ranged one before another. This is the relation of *order* (or spatial succession)." Moreover, there appears to be one particularly important variant in the relationship of order: the idea of symmetry, or double order. Finally, there is the relationship of *continuity*, though it appears to be some time before the perceptual field may be considered a continuous whole. For a long time in infancy, the spaces that are qualitatively experienced (whether by tactile, visual, or other means) are not coordinated among themselves, and it may be that continuity has a different character at different levels of development.

Note that each of these properties is appropriate to the operation of the location system. These are also pervasive characteristics of human thought. Robinson and Petchenik argue that "one's understanding of spatial relationships has its foundation in the early development of spatial perception" (p. 89). As we have seen, the location system seems to be the earliest mode of visual perception available to the infant. There is thus at least circumstantial evidence for looking to this system as a factor in the spatialization of the thought process.

When people talk, and particularly when they explain something, they provide additional indication of the role of space in the thought process. The gestures people use often seem to be establishing, or perhaps pointing to, the spatial framework being used in organizing whatever is being explained. "On this hand" is, of course, on the opposite side of the space from "on the other hand." "Wow" is very large, something unimportant is dismissed to some lower corner, and so on. People with academic backgrounds often seem to use the blackboard in the same way. It serves a spatial, organizing function even though the actual content might be of little consequence. In other instances where the content may not be spatial in nature, the use of spatial arrays—such as tables and matrices—provides a spatial framework for communicating material that is difficult to envision otherwise.

The process of communicating one's thoughts is particularly dependent on the use of the scratch pad or the spatial array. While the speaker is "reading" an existing cognitive map, the listener is trying to combine the pieces into something that makes sense, where a structure might emerge out of disparate parts. Eye movements suggest that one is trying to follow such a spatial array, that one is shifting one's focus from one locus to another in the "mind's eye" (Chapter Note 4).

The importance of space in communicating is particularly evident in the richness of spatial imagery in verbal expression. Although such usage does not rely exclusively on a locational processing mode, or on generic cognitive maps, it nonetheless exemplifies our reliance on spatial context for circumstances that are not intrinsically spatial. Many situations are expressed in terms of *proximity or distance*, as in "that answer is not correct, but you are getting closer" and "that was a close call" and "why has she been so distant lately?" Others involve *order*, as in "you are way ahead of where one would expect for your age" or "she is a front-running candidate." Still other spatial analogies depend on the concept of *sequence* or route, as in the "road to hell," the "true path to salvation," "back on track," and so on. Also, the notion of *location* itself is pervasive in our usage: more concrete material is referred to as "lower" whereas the more abstract is "higher"; ministers speak of "higher" thoughts, which, while more virtuous than "lower" thoughts, also tend to be more abstract. Computer programmers contrast "top-down" approaches, which start with one's abstract goals, and "bottom-up" approaches, which start with specific details. There is the "bottom line," and there is the utterly important point that is "above all" others. To be lost is definitely an undesirable state; little wonder we provide each other with so much spatial guidance to stay on track.

ANOTHER VIEW OF THE COGNITIVE MAP

The topic of environmental cognition has been approached from a variety of perspectives. Theorists have different ideas about how cognitive maps work and even about what constitutes a cognitive map. A number of the divergent perspectives are discussed in Chapter Note 5. Perhaps the most stimulating and influential of these alternative views is that of Lynch (1960). Although the cognitive map idea was introduced by Tolman (1948), it was little appreciated or used until its reintroduction in Lynch's brilliant little book, *The image of the city*. Through the use of sketch maps and interviews, Lynch studied what people knew of their physical/spatial environment. People in three cities—Boston, Jersey City, and Los Angeles—participated in his research. The maps and descriptions they provided strongly suggest discreteness rather than continuity. Likewise, the five categories of content that Lynch identified are explicitly discrete. He refers to paths, edges, districts, nodes, and landmarks as types of elements.

Lynch's position provides a useful comparison to the network point of view. His five categories present a challenge to the scheme we have proposed: is the simple point-and-connection framework really enough? Let us take a look at how this theory deals with each of the elements Lynch proposes:

Nodes and Landmarks. Lynch distinguishes between nodes, which he sees as junctions or concentrations of function, and landmarks, which he describes as physical objects seen more from the outside (often at a distance) than entered into. However, both sorts of notions involve things or places. They both are coded by representations and serve as a point in the cognitive map, if they correspond to repeated experiences that have some importance to the individual. A street intersection might not, for example, create a place that is important if there is nothing to remember. Appleyard (1969), in a perceptive discussion of how buildings are known, points to the importance of striking sensory qualities in determining what will be remembered—what will, in effect, be a good candidate to become a landmark.

Visual distinctiveness is not the only important factor. In some environments there is little that is distinctive, but people must nontheless find means to remember their way. DeJonge (1962) reports that a lack of environmental differentiation in one area of Delft led residents to rely on such subtle cues as the color of the curtains in the window of a certain house. Devlin (1976) discusses the role of "functional landmarks" in her study of Idaho Falls. These are likely to be more personal, based on the choice points in the individual's commerce with the environment. Appleyard found parallel influences in his study. Buildings at decision points tended to be remembered, even if they were not otherwise striking. He also found that buildings that fell in the line of vision along major pathways were better known. Thus, in Lynch's terms, people strive to find landmarks—practically create them—to make nodes (in the sense of functions) "imageable" (Figure 3.3).

Nodes and landmarks in the environment are surely important to people's way-finding, but whether such places are mentally represented in a way that differentiates between them is a separate issue. The likelihood of a place or object being coded in one's mental map is a function of a great range of attributes that would seem to cut across this distinction.

Several studies have pointed to the importance of landmarks in the formation of cognitive maps. They point to the importance of patterned and distinctive environmental arrangements in spatial learning. Acredolo (1977) studied the ability of children to relate to a large-scale space. The task was to find a trinket placed either to the right or to the left. When

Figure 3.3 Top: An intersection that lacks notable features. Bottom: Intersection with prominent landmark—presumably easier to remember.
A. W. Kaplan and S. Kaplan

the child's position was changed so that the view of space was reversed, three- and four-year-olds needed landmarks to be able to function effectively, but five-year-olds were able to do the task even when landmarks were not used. In a similar vein, Acredolo, Pick, and Olsen (1975) found that differentiation was an even more profound factor than familiarity in children's memory for spatial location. (See Acredolo, 1981, for a discussion of related studies.)

At the other end of the age spectrum, Weber, Brown, and Weldon (1978) found that nursing home patients were more helped by distinctiveness than by familiarity in their ability to orient to the nursing home environment. If we assume that visual distinctiveness is central to learnable landmarks, then the results of this study support this general theme.

In an ingenious series of studies on the behavior of chimpanzees, Menzel (1969, 1973) has provided insight into the cognitive-mapping inclinations of some of our fellow primates. His description of reactions to a 1,000-foot by 400-foot fenced compound that each chimpanzee had 36 hours to explore underscores the central role of landmarks in their exploration and their performance:

> Chimpanzees travelled from one structure or object to the next, apportioning their time at each place roughly in accordance with the prominence of that feature. There was considerable focus on the edges of a feature. . . . Space is always structured in terms of prominent objects. (Menzel, 1969, p. 78)

Edges and Districts.   A district, in Lynch's scheme, is a portion of a larger map that has a coherence, a character of its own. In our terms, it is a region, that is, a point in the network, but at a higher level of abstraction than individual places or objects. (We prefer the use of "region" largely because of its generality. The word "district" has urban connotations that might tend to limit its usefulness in other contexts.)

Regions in this sense can involve whole neighborhoods, or they might encompass a much smaller setting that nonetheless serves as a higher-level landmark. In studying maps of interior environments drawn by kindergarten-age children, Schadler and Siegel (cited in Siegel and White, 1975) found what they called "mini-spatial representations." These included coherent clusters of furniture whose relation to other areas or clusters was not accurately indicated. This idea is similar to what O'Keefe and Nadel (1978) call "place representation." They suggest that the place representation "can be taken as a part of a cognitive map, while conversely a map can be viewed as a set of ordered, connected places" (p. 93). Such regions may be developed in the process of learning an area or in later recognition of the coherent subparts of the whole.

An edge, too, from a network perspective, is at a higher level of abstraction than points and connections. On the one hand, an edge serves as a boundary of a region; at other times, an edge becomes a region in its own right. Thus the edge between pasture and forest helps demarcate these two regions. The mountain range or skyline that helps people's orientation constitutes both an edge and a region (Figure 3.4).

Paths.   While a path might seem to translate directly into what we have called a connection or an association, there are several important differences. Lynch's paths are channels of activity. They are rich in content. The connection concept, by contrast, is on an entirely different scale. Lynch's channel of activity would presumably be composed of whole sequences of connected representations. The richness of content, in other words, resides in the representations. The connections, as we view them, serve merely to link the representations. They have no content in themselves. It is here, as we have seen, that an important economy in the storage of information is achieved. There is much missing from one's map, but one gets from place to place nonetheless.

If "path" is used in this special sense of a link between distinctive places, people would be expected to have little information about por-

Figure 3.4 Railroad tracks are well-known boundaries. Waterfronts, by contrast, while also serving as an edge, constitute a region as well.
Lower drawing by H. L. Deardorff

tions of the environment coded in their maps as paths. The importance of landmarks in people's way-finding tends to support this hypothesis. Suggestive evidence also comes from a study of spatial information that students have of their own campus (Weisman, unpublished). Photographs of paths received very low recognition scores despite the fact that these were portions of the environment traversed every day.

A critical theoretical issue as far as landmarks are concerned is whether they precede paths in the learning process. Two recent overviews of the cognitive-mapping area tend to indicate that they do. Siegel and White (1975) make a strong case for the precedence of landmarks, and Evans (1980), although finding the evidence somewhat mixed, tends to agree. From a developmental point of view, landmarks are the anchor points and "the child's acts and 'route knowledge' are registered and accessed with reference to these anchor points" (Siegel and White, 1975, p. 40).

From a network point of view, then, it would seem that the notion of points (representations that correspond to places or objects or events) and connections (associations linking the points) is sufficient to form the building blocks of cognitive maps. The addition of a hierarchical structure that permits "points" to designate increasingly abstract representations provides the basis for discussing both the features of the environment and our constructions of these features into shared concepts. Although the significant elements to be negotiated in the environment are many and intricate, the environment as represented in the mind can be characterized in terms of relatively few different kinds of elements.

Generalizing the Cognitive Map

As we have seen, the cognitive map is not restricted to recording the landmarks, paths, and districts of the physical environment. In fact, there are several reasons for suspecting that the cognitive map is a highly general cognitive structure, pertinent to much, if not all, of the information that humans perceive, process, and store.

The theoretical perspectives we have just examined are all tied directly to ways of understanding environmental cognition. However, the idea of cognitive maps has been used by people representing a variety of disciplines as well as to refer to a variety of contents. The concept has made an appearance in anthropology (Fischer, 1971), planning (Greenbie, 1975), education (Reif, 1974), and sociology (Suttles, 1972). Of course, its use in design was initiated by Lynch's work and has not stopped there (e.g., Green et al., 1975). It lends itself to discussions of the future, to the structure of organizations, and to conceptual structures of all kinds (Chapter Note 6).

The widespread use of the idea of cognitive maps does not, of course, imply that its users share an explicit formulation of how such structures are formed, of whether a point-and-path notion is sufficient, or of whether the paths themselves code content or not. Nonetheless, the adoption of the expression by people representing such a diversity of discipline suggests at least an intuitive appeal to the concept.

From a more rigorous perspective, there are also several reasons for suspecting a potentially wide applicability for this concept.

1. The constituents are general. The representation, which is the basis for each of the points of the map, is probably the most generally useful and widely applicable concept in cognitive psychology. It need not refer to places and indeed is not typically used in a spatial context. Connections, likewise, are not in any sense particular to spatial settings. In other words, the cognitive map is a way of converting sequences of thought into flexible patterns of relationships.

2. The current thinking among students of cognition and memory tends to support the generality and usefulness of cognitive maps. One position emphasizes groups of features or properties as defining a concept (E. E. Smith, Shoben, and Rips, 1974). According to this position, the meaning of something is what it is composed of. A contrasting position argues for the importance of a network of associations in determining meaning (Collins and Loftus, 1975).* From this point of view the definition of a concept is based on what the concept is associated with. Clearly there must be truth in both these positions. The question is how to incorporate within the same framework both the features that make up a concept and its various associations. Since the cognitive map is made up of feature-based representations connected to one another by a network of associations, accounting for both positions within this framework is hardly a challenge (Chapter Note 7).

3. In recent years there has been considerable emphasis on the idea of a "system." A great many different processes and activities can be interpreted in such terms. A system, in turn, is defined as a set of elements and the relations between them. This of course describes the cognitive map as well.

Where does this lead? What is the importance of this generality? Let us step back (an analogy, to be sure) for a moment and take a look at the larger (!) perspective.

People cannot and do not know the world in its every detail. Rather, they tend to remember the essentials and how these are related. In this way they can preserve in simplified fashion the essential relation-

---

*The network under discussion here, it should be noted, is a *semantic* network. However, with recent work pointing to the necessity that semantic material derive its meaning through connections to nonsemantic material (Bransford and Johnson, 1973), it is probably wise to think of these networks as cognitive rather than specifically semantic.

ship that existed in reality (see S. Kaplan, 1978b). Such an arrangement of ideas is often referred to as a *model*. The concept of model is an exciting one not only because it suggests how, out of the many different possibilities, people tend to store information, to structure their knowledge. It is exciting also because the actions people take, the decisions they make, their hopes, their fears, their aspirations are all based on their conceptions, on their models of the world. Forrester (1971, p. 54) captured very effectively the impact people's models have on their choices and actions:

> Each of us uses models constantly. Every person in his private life and in his business life instinctively uses models for decision making. The mental image of the world around you which you carry in your head is a model. One does not have a city or a government or a country in his head. He has only selected concepts and relationships which he uses to represent the real system. A mental image is a model. All of our decisions are taken on the basis of models. All of our laws are passed on the basis of models. All executive actions are taken on the basis of models. The question is not to use or ignore models. The question is only a choice among alternative models.

SOME CONCLUDING COMMENTS

Back in Chapter 1 we explored some of the ways in which familiarity makes a difference. The behavior of the person in a familiar environment was smoother, more confident. It was also less distracted, less preoccupied with the details of the situation. It should now be possible to see why familiarity has so powerful an influence. To be familiar is to have a cognitive map.

A cognitive map is a compact, orderly collection of knowledge. It contains more information than one can generally perceive at once, thus permitting one to anticipate, to react, to consider possible next events. When one does not know what might happen next, the number of possibilities one can imagine can grow at an alarming rate. Thus having a more concrete conception of future possibilities tends to simplify one's cognitive processing, and to contribute substantially to one's confidence.

Anticipation is also a factor in the smoothness of behavior people show in familiar settings. By knowing what is coming next, one knows what to do next. Otherwise one may have to wait after each act to see what happens before knowing what action to take next. Not only does such dependence on feedback produce hesitant, halting behavior; it also forces the individual to pay attention, to think constantly about what is going on. While being aware of everything one does, being "totally conscious," has been considered a desirable goal by some psychoactive groups, constantly thinking about what one is doing is a distraction relative to everything else. Being preoccupied is not compatible with being alert, and there are times when being alert is essential. (William James, 1892, showed his appreciation for the limitation of how much can be thought about at one time when he praised habit for its role in freeing the mind for other things; for a thoughtful discussion on this topic, see Bateson, 1972.)

There are thus many payoffs to familiarity, to having a cognitive map, an internal model of the situation in which one finds oneself. The British psychologist K. J. W. Craik (1943, p. 61) clearly recognized many of these advantages:

> If the organism carries a "small-scale model" of external reality and of its own possible actions within its head, it is able to try out various alternatives, conclude which is the best of them, react to future situations before they arise, utilize the knowledge of past events in dealing with the present and future, and in every way to react in a much fuller, easier, and more competent manner to the emergencies which face it.

NOTES

1. The Cognitive Map

With the growing interest in and acceptance of the cognitive map concept, the literature has grown apace. There are two classic references, Downs and Stea (1973) and G. T. Moore and Golledge (1976). A more recent and lighter treatment of the topic can be found in Downs and Stea (1977). Some recent texts on cognition (e.g., Neisser, 1976) explicitly deal with this topic.

Specific mention should be made of the burgeoning literature on cognitive maps in children. There is evidence that cognitive-mapping capabilities are present as early as three years old (Blaut and Stea, 1974). Studies have looked at real towns (Sperling, 1965) and model towns (Herman and Siegel, 1978), at topics as concrete as barriers (Kosslyn, Pick, and Fariello, 1974) and as abstract as the acquisition of visual information (Day, 1975). Since the mapping process turns out to show systematic changes with age across a wide variety of dimensions, this has been an unusually fruitful area of research.

Implicit in this discussion of cognitive maps is the assumption that they do not constitute some peculiar preoccupation of Western culture, but are an activity and concern characteristic of the species as a whole. There has by now been some cross-cultural research on this topic (for example, Altman and Chemers, 1980; Pick, 1980; Rapoport, 1976; Saarinen, 1976; Tuan, 1974, 1977); what data there are lend no support to the notion that Western culture has any monopoly in this area. Wong (1979) finds cognitive maps in Hong Kong to be essentially similar to those described in Western studies.

The cross-cultural study of cognitive-mapping is particularly challenging in environments devoid of visual differentiation. Carpenter (1955), for example, describes the topography of Southhampton Island, where he studied the Aivilik

Eskimos: "For the most part it rolls away, mile after empty mile, featureless and undifferentiated, save for quiet island pools that blue-spangle its monotonous expanse" (p. 131). Though visibility is often seriously impaired by weather conditions, way-finding seems confident over miles of land. The Aivilik knowledge of distance and route seems to be based on subtle variation in topography and winds, for which they have an extensive vocabulary.

A similar, apparently undifferentiated expanse that has been studied extensively is the sea. Puluwat, an island in the Pacific Ocean that is not in sight of any other island, has become famous for its navigators. Although the trackless ocean might seem a poor setting for establishing a cognitive map, quite the opposite is the case, as is evident from Gladwin's (1970, p. 34) description:

> No longer is it simply a great body of water which, encountering Puluwat, shoves around it and reforms on the other side to flow on to an empty eternity. Instead the ocean becomes a thoroughfare over which one can think of oneself moving, other islands left behind to right and left, toward a particular island of destination which as one comes up upon it will be waiting, as it always waits, right where it is supposed to be. When a Puluwatan speaks of the ocean the words he uses refer not to an amorphous expanse of water but rather to the assemblage of seaways which lie between the various islands. Together these seaways constitute the ocean he knows and understands. . . . [Thus] Puluwat ceases to be a solitary spot of dry land; it takes its place in a familiar constellation of islands linked together by pathways on the ocean.

In reviewing the cross-cultural data on spatial orientation, Hallowell (1955, p. 186) comes down on the side of universality:

> From the standpoint of human mobility and spatial orientation this practice would appear to have a generic human function. When integrated with individual knowledge and experience of the terrain it affords a schema of reference points for topographic orientation. Such points are not only a guide to action but, once known, can be mentally manipulated and organized in the form of "mental maps," and the spatial schema inherent in them communicated.

2. Landmarks and Distance

A study by Sadalla and Staplin (1980) provides direct support for this hypothesis. Indirect support is provided by studies showing greater perceived distance toward the center city than away from it—presumably because there are more landmarks in the downtown direction. (Saarinen, 1976, discusses some of these studies; they have not yielded conclusive results, possibly because of the methodological difficulties inherent in studying perceived distance [cf. Cadwallader, 1976, and Briggs, 1976].) Stevens (unpublished) has proposed that the route to an unfamiliar place seems much longer than the route back because of the many potential landmarks one identifies on the way there. The study she carried out lends support to this ingenious interpretation.

3. Hierarchical Structure

In terms of the network idea, the hierarchical structure could be said to involve vertical as opposed to horizontal connections (see Wickelgren, 1979, for a similar usage). One way to think of this is in terms of an arrangement in which there are different *levels* of cognitive structure. The level that receives information from the sensory analyzers would be the locus of representations of concrete objects. Horizontal connections within this level would yield cognitive maps. At this low level the maps would presumably be of particular places.

The next higher level would receive its input not only from sensory analyzers, but from the preceding level as well. At this next level we would expect to find representations that are somewhat more abstract, forming the basis for cognitive maps that are less detailed and that cover larger areas. The representations at this level might stand not for a place but for a *region*. A compression of information has occurred; there is necessarily a loss of information in this transformation and at the same time a gain in economy. The vertical connections here would tie the detailed maps to the more general ones, allowing one to describe in detail how to get from one's home to the expressway, then in general terms where the expressway goes, and then, returning to the greater detail, how to get from the expressway exit to one's favorite boating site.

Hierarchical arrangements of this kind are often thought of in terms of "trees." At each successive level what were many branches the level before now become one. It is easy to think of the head as ultimately coming to a point as summaries of summaries make the content of the next level simpler than the one before. Such a conception is so neat and convenient that it would be attractive indeed were it not so totally misleading. It is based on the assumption that each representation at a given level participates in only a single point at the next level. This assumption is certainly not justified. A given object falls into many categories, just as a given feature is characteristic of many objects. An elephant, for example, can be a four-legged animal, a threatening beast, and a vital element of a circus. Comparably, one can think of a particular state as part of New England, part of the North (as opposed to the South), and one of the original thirteen.

4. The Mind's Eye

There have been a number of studies that lend support to the existence of a "mind's eye" distinct from the direction of gaze. In general these studies involve looking at a fixation point placed somewhere within an array of information. A signal for changing the direction of gaze to some other point within the field is then presented. The uniform finding has been that there is a change in internal attention to that new point *prior* to the beginning of the eye movement (Jonides, 1980, 1982; Posner, 1978). This would seem to indicate a shift in focus within what we have called the locational scratch pad. Supporting this locational interpretation, Wurtz and his colleagues (e.g., Goldberg and Wurtz, 1972; Wurtz and Mohler, 1976) have reported a parallel covert attentional shift reflected in a change in receptivity of superior colliculus neurons. Another indication of the meaningfulness of this analog locational framework in attention comes from a study by Kosslyn, Ball, and Reiser (1978) dealing with visual images of previously presented material. They found that scanning visual images takes more time when further distance within the visual image is involved.

5.   How Much Structure is Enough?

The various perspectives in environmental cognition all deal in one way or another with the issue of structure. The critical issue distinguishing them is that of how much structure representing the environment is stored in the individual's head. Gibson's position (1979) ostensibly does without the representation concept altogether (R. Lachman and J. L. Lachman, 1979). He emphasizes immediacy and directness, characteristics that well describe location-system functioning (Note 2 in Chapter 2). Gibson makes it clear, however, that he intends these descriptions to apply to all perception. In other words, he argues that there is sufficient information in the environmment to make internal structures unnecessary.

Upon close examination, however, there is reason to believe that, despite his assertion to the contrary, Gibson is relying on a representation concept. He acknowledges that perceptual learning occurs, that it leads to increasing compactness and chunking, and that in the process the individual comes to know better what to look for. The representation is one of the few concepts (and perhaps the only one) able to provide a mechanism for all these aspects of the way humans come to know objects. Further, Gibson speaks of *affordances*—the perception of anything in the environment automatically involves the perception of what it offers or affords with respect to one's own actions and purposes. It is hard to see how such an assessment is possible without any cognitive structure. Consider two objects of about the same size and color. One is a rock, the other a milkweed pod. Their affordances are totally different. This information, however, is not available merely by looking at the objects; even looking very hard. The visual patterns they provide do not tell the whole story. After one has touched them, squeezed them, tossed them, and so on, there will be much more useful information to go on. This information will become associated with the appearance of these respective objects so that in the future a glimpse will be sufficient to call up one's store of knowledge about them. Thus, far from constituting a challenge to the idea of cognitive structure, the affordance idea constitutes an interesting example of "going beyond the information given," Bruner's (1957) description of one of the ways in which having a representation of something provides an adaptive advantage. (Baron, 1981, also discusses the necessity of positing an inferential process to enhance the usefulness of the concepts Gibson proposes.)

Wohlwill (1973) has raised a related issue in his forceful statement that "the environment is not in the head!" This is an important point. What is in the head is not the environment. It is a representation of it, selective, sketchy, probably somewhat idiosyncratic. It may indeed constitute an "image" of the environment (that is often what it feels like), but it must not be mistaken for a "picture" of the environment. Pictures are characterized by such properties as continuity and detail, which make them quite distinct from images. While it is a mistake to believe that the environment is in the head, however, it is equally a mistake to believe that what is in the head is irrelevant to how people experience the environment. What is in the head is distinctly different from what is in the environment, and it is this very fact that makes the interaction between the two so fascinating and so essential to an understanding of behavior.

Another domain of difference between the perspective we have discussed and that of certain others working in this area involves the assumption of continuity. Actually this assumption tends not to be explicitly stated. Rather, data are collected concerning spatial information under the implicit assumption that there is something like a continuous map in the head that corresponds to some degree to the physical reality.

Many such studies in the cognitive-mapping area involve estimates of distances and direction, using various procedures. Sometimes these values are estimated directly. Alternatively, sketch maps may be used to obtain an indication of how participants view their neighborhood, their city, the world, or whatever. Although such maps show a great deal of individuality, they also characteristically reflect greater size for the map representing the area the participant is most familiar with. Thus students in the United States often show their country as disproportionately large. Students in Europe, by contrast, drawing "their world," will have Europe as a dominant feature, with the United States quite small. It is not unusual for investigators to conclude that these distorted sketches represent the cognitive maps of the given space. The implication is that people have a distorted space in their heads that stands for the real space.

It is not hard to see how one might fall into such an assumption, and, on the face of it, it seems innocent enough. However, the continuity that is one of the most striking aspects of physical reality—and of physical maps, for that matter—is not necessarily a part of our mutual models of these spaces. We have seen how enormously inefficient a cognitive map that is actually continuous would be. It is for this reason that the idea of *connectedness* (see Downs, 1970) as an approximation to continuity was developed. This allows an associative knowledge structure to contain *map-like* information while at the same time being very different from a physical map in important respects. The concept of connectedness means that with increasing experience one's accuracy gets better and better; at the same time one can function with only distant but connected points.

Research emphasizing distance estimates tends to assume an underlying continuity in the way people conceptualize space. Certainly people can make such estimates; from a network point of view, however, what these estimates involve is by no means a direct reading of some internal map. If people do indeed code their spatial experience in terms of structures of interconnected elements, the distance estimates are necessarily rather complicated inferences. Such inferences would be influenced by such factors as the strength of connection between the points, the number of points in the estimated segment, and the scale on which the estimated distance is described.

From this perspective it is hardly surprising that the results of research on perceived subjective distance are complex, often confusing, and sometimes apparently contradictory. Goodchild (1976) has attributed recent progress in research on cognitive maps using multidimensional scaling to the abandonment of a continuity assumption in favor of what he calls "a discrete view of space" (p. 179). It is also understandable that a number of studies on subjective distance carried out on college campuses have yielded exceptionally high accuracy. This is a space with which the participants tend to be highly familiar, a space that is filled with landmarks that provide structure.

The assumption of continuity is an unexamined issue in these approaches. Although the concept of schema and representation is playing an increasingly important role in research on thinking, studies on cognitive maps have generally ignored the matter of the generality and economy afforded by representations. Instead they have interpreted the renditions of the internal model provided them in rather literal fashion.

6. Maps and Conceptual Structure

Scott and Wertheimer (1962, p. 12) use the map analogy in describing the way partial information can be pieced together into a rough totality which, although inexact, "may offer better understanding of the territory than no map at all." The larger process they are referring to is that of developing a construct through multiple imperfect measures, a process known in psychology as construct validation (Cronbach and Meehl, 1955) or discriminant and convergent validation (D. T. Campbell and Fiske, 1959). This will be discussed further in Chapter 9.

7. The Propositional and the Analog

Considerable recent debate has focused on the issue of whether knowledge is stored in a propositional (based on abstract statements) or an analog (mirroring some of the properties of the world) fashion (see Evans, 1980). Since a cognitive map has some structural relationship to what it represents, it could certainly be considered analog. Unfortunately, there has been a tendency on the part of those favoring the propositional position to caricature the analog position, treating it as if it referred to a *picture* in the mind (e.g., Pylyshyn, 1973). In a thoughtful analysis of these two positions, Norman (1976) distinguishes the propositional from the analog on the grounds that it is *generic* and *relational*. However, as we have seen, the cognitive map is based on representations (which are necessarily generic) and associations (which constitute the paradigm relation). Hence cognitive maps must be analog and generic and relational.

part three

WHAT MATTERS IN THE ENVIRONMENT

This is the part that would be called "Motivation" in a traditional textbook. Not in an environmentally oriented text, however, since the sorts of motivation traditionally discussed in psychology have very little connection with the environment. This is not to say that motivation and the environment have no connection; only that the connection is far from obvious given the prevailing theories in both areas.

The situation as far as cognition is concerned is not much better. Abelson (1963) has written about "hot" cognition, that is, cognition dealing with emotionally laden material. However, most cognition must be to some degree hot in this sense. Most of what people think about matters in some way. As we have seen, people relate what they perceive to their past experience, and that past experience presumably "mattered" when it happened. In other words, there were, in varying degrees, good events and bad events. If one is to be able to call on experience as a guide to action, one's memory for an experience must be coded for how one felt about that experience when it happened. Memories must, in other words, carry with them the appropriate evaluative code.

However, cognition is intimately tied to motivation not only because of the goods and bads of our experience. The very process of using the cognitive mechanism has—and must have—motivational implications. When we recognize something hard to recognize, when we make a successful prediction, when we figure out a difficult problem, it feels good! And it had better feel good. If we did not care one way or another about such matters, we might opt for going back to bed when confronted by a cognitive challenge of some sort. It works the other way, too. Not being able to recognize or predict or comprehend is not taken lightly. Such events can be disturbing and even painful.

This intimate tie between what we can do (cognition) and what we want to do (motivation) expresses itself not only in the pains and pleasures per se, but also in the environments we seek and prefer. Environments differ in how readily understood they are and in how much interest they hold for us. Since we have a need to be cognitively effective, we tend to prefer environments that help make this possible.

71

One reason then for devoting a part of a book on environmental cognition to motivational issues is the intimate tie between motivation and cognition as they function in the real world. Another reason derives from why many practical people are interested in environmental cognition in the first place. They want to know how people "experience the environment." While what they have in mind usually does not include preference, this component of people's reaction to the environment is essential if the true scope of the experience is to be understood.

Ironically it is often the very individuals who wish to learn how people experience the environment who are most opposed to taking preference into account. It is not unusual among environmental design professionals to find the nagging fear that people will turn out to prefer the wrong things. Another commonly expressed concern is that "everybody likes different things." The implication is that preference is highly idiosyncratic and that attempting to study it will only lead to chaos. Although this may be true at surface level, one does not have to go far below the surface to find a great deal of consistency in what people prefer.

The first chapter in this part examines human needs in an informational context. These needs—for making sense and for involvement—depend on the environment for their fulfillment. The environmental properties that support these needs can be identified and provide a basis for understanding consistent patterns of environmental preference.

The second chapter in this part begins by examining the appropriateness of this notion of human needs (and of the pattern of preferences that serve these needs). How realistic is this conception in a world that is composed not of a sequence to choose from, but a multitude of overlapping, conflicting events that are distracting and even bewildering? This leads to a consideration of attention, of the possibility that out of all the potential chaos of the everyday environment one can still achieve clarity. Through attention, the human informational needs discussed in Chapter 4 can be met despite the challenges of an uncooperative reality. It turns out, however, that there are two quite distinct kinds of attention, and they have very different implications in terms of their duration of effectiveness and in terms of the costs involved. The ultimate cost, if one forces attention too long, is an incapacity to fend off cognitive chaos, a state of mind peculiarly terrifying to members of our species.

chapter four

EVALUATION, PREFERENCE, AND HUMAN NEEDS

Recognition, as we have seen, is difficult but essential. Without it there is no basis for knowing where one is or what is going on. By itself, however, recognition buys very little. One needs to know what might happen as well. One needs to be able to anticipate, to predict. The preceding chapters have been devoted to exploring how these requirements are met, to developing mechanisms for recognizing and predicting. But even this is not enough. The purpose of the thought process is to make action possible, and being able to recognize and to predict rarely provides sufficient basis for deciding what to do.

To see the insufficiency of recognition and prediction alone as bases for action, let us consider the following hypothetical example. Imagine an individual applying the recognition process to the scene before him: "large grassy open area, a few trees here and there, elephant on the far right." The prediction then might run something like this: "trees and grass likely to remain in present position, elephant pointing this way and likely to come closer. If I continue in my present direction, I am likely to get closer to trees and to elephant." There is obviously something wrong here. One is tempted to shout, "Good grief, don't just stand there, run!" But an important ingredient has not yet been included in the thought process of our hypothetical individual. Our reaction, and the advice we are tempted to provide, are both premised on our *evaluation* of the situation in general and of the elephant in particular. We have an evaluation associated not only with a possible future event (i.e., being stepped on) but also with the potential perpetrator of that event (i.e., the elephant). Clearly our behavior is mediated in vital ways not only by our recognition of things and our prediction of sequels but also by the evaluations that both things and sequels give rise to in our minds.

The basic concept of evaluation is a simple one. It is assumed that experiences with objects and events in the world leave in the individual's head positive and negative codes. These codes are further assumed to be associated with the appropriate internal representations. In other words, objects associated with pleasurable outcomes will tend to give a feeling of pleasure when they are again perceived. Likewise, objects associated with pain will give pain when they are perceived. The decisions to approach or to avoid, to seek or to flee, to venture or to retreat, are thus strongly tied to the evaluation of the situation. Although this is far from a complete picture, it at least provides reassurance that our hypothetical person need not stand there looking at a large and potentially dangerous animal without any notion of what to do.

The idea that representations have evaluative codes also has implications for prediction or anticipation. We have seen how representations permit *lookahead*, a running ahead in the mind of possible outcomes that have not yet occurred. Since representations are assumed to have evaluative codes, they will bring with them the signals of pleasure and pain even when they are turned on not in reaction to things in the environment but purely in anticipation of things that might happen. In this way people come to live in the future, in a world of possibility rather than actuality, a world that includes hopes and fears, anticipated pleasures and possible hurts. This may seem farfetched, but examples are not hard to come by. People in dire circumstances can be overjoyed despite their current conditions if they are anticipating great improvements. Likewise, people in the most favorable environment but anticipating bad news have no difficulty feeling miserable. Humans have the capacity to separate themselves from their current environment not only in terms of thoughts but in terms of feelings as well. Indeed, these patterns raise doubts as to the appropriateness of any sharp distinctions between thoughts and feelings.

Evaluative codes, then, guide our appraisal of the moment and color our images of the future. They are part and parcel of the cognitive maps we use in choosing our way and deciding what to do. They code our preferences, making it possible to anticipate what we would like and what we would rather avoid. This chapter will explore the preferences and needs that people have for informational aspects of their world.

What sorts of things do people need and want in order to make decision-making possible? It would seem reasonable that people should prefer the kinds of situations and patterns that make their survival more likely. They should opt for conditions that increase their comfort and sense of competence. While this seems reasonable enough, we generally do not think of our own needs from such a stance. Let us step back a moment and take a quick look at human evolution as a source of insight into the conditions that humans have had to contend with. An examination of the environment in which humans evolved may help clarify the question of human preference and needs.

TERRA INCOGNITA

Of particular interest in considering the origins of our species are the requirements that may have led to the capacity to make and use cognitive maps. The evolution of humans as a distinct species is believed to have occurred when our ancestors left the safety of the trees and attempted to make a go of it on the African savanna. The creatures who began this transition several million years ago were small-brained apes. Something that happened subsequently must have created the evolutionary pressure for a larger brain. Information handling on a larger scale must have become more urgent as far as survival was concerned than it had been for the tree-dwelling ancestors of these early humans (Chapter Note 1).

It must be remembered that those creatures attempting to cope with life on the ground, with the rigors of the African savanna, were not undifferentiated mammals, but insect-eating tree-dwellers with highly developed adaptations for that particular niche. The near-upright posture and the grasping hand (with opposed thumb) are well-known examples. Equally important for our purposes are not only the extensive development of the visual capacity but also the development of the capacity to separate object from environment, to perceive and react to *things* (see B. G. Campbell, 1974). An animal with perceptual assets such as these has the capability of seeing things well before their impact is felt. Seeing at a distance is not the same as being able to anticipate, but it is an important first step. Since the survival pressures of the savanna made anticipation enormously valuable, this capacity will figure prominently in the ensuing discussion.

Relative to life in the trees, the ground is a dangerous place. The savanna was well supplied with predators to which our ancestors were not automatically immune. Early humans were neither large and threatening nor small and unobtrusive. They were equipped neither with impressive fang and claw nor with armor or shell. Although their versatility in modes of locomotion was exceptional, in raw speed they could hardly match the prominent predators. Under these circumstances, figuring out what might happen well before it did happen was not merely useful; it was essential.

Hand in hand with anticipation is the matter of how fast information can be processed. Seeing at a distance is of little help unless all the cognitive steps between the seeing and the doing take place rapidly. Or, to put it in a slightly different perspective, the faster the information is processed and the faster the appropriate action is selected, the greater the distance that will remain between the organism and the potential danger.

Making a living on the savanna must have presented a serious problem to our ancestors. They were intruding upon an environment already well populated. The good niches were long since taken. Opportunities for obtaining sustenance were neither reliable nor lacking in hazards. They could, for example, gather food that was attractive to other animals, too, but they would have to somehow get there first. Such a procedure was highly risky and presumably would require covering considerable ground to make up in extent what was lacking in certainty. Anticipation is also a vital factor here, although the time scale is longer. A great deal of knowledge must be employed in the process (see Flannery, 1955).

Another opportunity for obtaining sustenance involved finding a niche that was not already crowded within the ecology of the African savanna. The hunting of big game presented an opportunity of this kind. The evidence suggests that this approach, or niche, was heavily exploited by early humans (Lee and DeVore, 1968; Pfeiffer, 1978). The inherent danger in this activity is obvious, but the ways in which it places heavy demands on information handling is perhaps less evident. One of the most striking of these is the matter of space. Big game are highly mobile, and keeping them in range required covering a lot of ground. It is estimated that the territory of the early humans was large, probably covering some 100 square miles. The informational requirement here is considerable—this is a great deal of geography to be familiar with. A related informational requirement involves the importance of returning home after the hunt. Humans were home-based animals. Because of their limited effectiveness as hunters, they often only wounded their prey and had to follow it until it expired (Laughlin, 1968). They must have often found themselves far from home. Thus for a variety of reasons our ancestors found themselves contending with space on a scale unknown to their primate brethren.

Big game hunting brought with it many additional pressures on information-handling ability besides comprehension of extended spatial areas. Strategy and planning must have been essential (Peters and Mech, 1975). Both anticipation and speed are vital in this context, too, as they are when contending with danger. The capacity to function in an information-based fashion seems to involve certain basic requirements whatever the setting. Although the evolutionary perspective highlights these requirements, they are probably no less pertinent to meeting humanity's information-handling pressures in any era.

Thus we see that the uncertainty and diversity of the environment that figured prominently in our earlier discussion were a central feature of human evolution as well. This suggests that the functional requirements, the importance of being able to recognize and to anticipate, were at least as incumbent on our ancestors as they are on us today (S. Kaplan, 1972). Certainly in the light of all this it is understandable that humans became proficient at extracting information from the environment and storing it in the form of cognitive maps. However, if an evolutionary perspective points to the urgency, even the necessity, of becoming a cognitive-map-building animal, it at the same time underscores the inadequacy of possessing this capacity in isolation. The capacity to build cognitive maps is simply not enough.

Imagine this version of our earlier tale: a mythical, earth-bound primate, a candidate for being our ancestor, is lolling in the shade of one of the occasional trees that dot the African savanna. A distant twig snaps. "I could probably figure out what that was," thinks our potential ancestor. "I could call upon my rich conception of the environment based on the adroit integration of vast experience and at least make a good guess as to what might be going on. But," it continues, "I never bothered to build a cognitive map in the first place, and at the moment I could care less whether I know what is going on or not." Knowing just this much about this mythical primate and its concerns, we can be pretty sure that it could not have been our ancestor. With an attitude like that, one might easily be eaten.

COGNITIVE MAPS AND HUMAN NEEDS

The capacity to build cognitive maps will do little good if it is not developed and used. Unless this awesome capability of map-building is put to use, it is unlikely that the capability will be maintained. In addition to having this ability, humans must be strongly motivated to use and extend it; they must prefer environments and situations that enable these activities to take place (S. Kaplan, 1973b).

Given this perspective, it seems reasonable that familiarity plays such an important part in cognition. It is well known that people prefer what they know, what they are familiar with. In the same vein, the fear of the unknown and the cautious reaction to the stranger are understandable. Familiarity increases one's confidence, one's facility; it provides opportunities to use the cognitive maps that have already been developed. We propose that the concern to *make sense* out of the environment is one of the most pervasive of human needs.

The motive to make sense inclines people to devote considerable effort to finding which of their cognitive maps applies to a given situation. It also ensures that people will be most uncomfortable in circumstances where *no* previously learned map is pertinent.

It is said, however, that familiarity breeds contempt. People like variety and get tired of the same old thing. We seem to have a paradox on our hands. It is not simply that familiarity has nothing to do with preference; rather it is that the relationship is not straightforward. The matrix shown in Table 4.1, using the folk utterances of a culture well known to many readers, suggests that we can, in fact, think of examples of familiar and unfamiliar situations that might be favored or disliked.

Table 4.1

Familiarity × Preference Matrix

	LOW PREFERENCE	HIGH PREFERENCE
LOW FAMILIARITY	That's weird	I've never seen anything like that before! Wow! That's neat!
HIGH FAMILIARITY	That old stuff again	No place like home

The opportunity to make sense of the environment seems not to be enough. People also prefer circumstances that require them to expand their horizons or at least circumstances where such enrichment is a possibility. People feel that, if they are to utilize their time and capacity fully, they must be exposed to circumstances that take all the capacity they have. Although people do not prefer to be overloaded or overwhelmed, they are usually at their best (and happiest) when the challenges they face fall just short of that. It must be in other words, that it is inherent in people to seek and cherish *involvement*.

There is a twofold advantage of being a seeker of involvement. First of all, it entails practicing one's informational capabilities. People will be more effective at recognizing and predicting in uncertain circumstances if they have had previous experience doing this. Such practice requires that there be uncertainty present, that there always be something that one can get involved with. This means that a human having no urgent biological need pressing is most likely to simply go to sleep until the next need arises. As a matter of fact, in our species having nothing to do is considered not a blessed state, but something to be corrected. It is a sign that one had better go out and find something to do. We would, on these grounds, expect humans to be rather restless creatures, often looking for trouble when they are not busy avoiding it.

The other advantage of being motivated to seek involvement is quite similar to the advantage of getting in plenty of practice. The familiar environment can become too undemanding. Involvement requires something more difficult, such as an unfamiliar environment can provide. Thus there is the inclination to explore, to enter new settings, to extend one's cognitive map. Here practice and increased knowledge go hand in hand. Note also some clues as to the human reaction to the familiar. The familiar offers little opportunity for involvement; at the same time the search for involvement gradually makes more and more of the environment familiar.

Involvement, then, plays an important role in keeping the organism prepared for what might happen in the future. Sudden danger and sudden opportunity alike are far more easily handled by an organism with well-practiced capabilities and lots of knowledge about the environment. A well-prepared human is one with a good supply of cognitive maps and a highly developed capacity to utilize them swiftly when necessary.

On the other hand, to be motivated by involvement alone would be a disaster. The search for challenge, excitement, and novelty could readily lead one beyond one's capacities, beyond the excitement that one knows how to deal with. Indeed, carried to its logical extreme, seeking involvement translates into a search for danger.

Involvement and making sense thus emerge as simultaneous needs. In fact, it seems less paradoxical that both the familiar and the unfamiliar may be preferred given the continuous trading off between the excitement of the new and the comfort of the known. For many people involvement is a much more visible, believable aspect of human motivation than is making sense. That people can be driven wild by boredom is a well-known phenomenon. We all have observed the hunger for experiences of a teenager with "nothing to do." But making sense matters to people, too—and not only to the "intellectual." It would make little adaptive sense for humans to abandon their hard-won facility and competence acquired in a familiar setting. People care about the order in their world at a local as well as a global level. The failure to comprehend even relatively inconsequential things can be quite discomforting. In fact, the concern to have things make sense and arrangements that increase the likelihood that the world is understandable are so important and pervasive that they will come up again in later chapters.

HUMAN NEEDS AND ENVIRONMENTAL PREFERENCE

So far we have looked at involvement and making sense as two rather pervasive human needs. They are essential to an individual's effective functioning and psychological health. As with other basic needs, one does not take care of them once and for all.

Just as with one's need for food or for affection, involvement and making sense are continuing concerns throughout one's lifetime. Indeed, one can extend the parallel still further. One's choices are greatly influenced by the alternatives that make it more likely that one's needs will be met. We are more likely to favor a situation where there will be enough to eat, where we will be received with affection, and so on. In this way we have *preference* for environments that are more likely to enable us to meet our needs in the future. Preferences are different from needs in their future referent and hence in their lack of immediate urgency. To fail to meet one's needs is painful and disruptive. To fail to meet one's needs is to be hungry or unloved or otherwise to experience a deficit in something essential. To fail to obtain one's preference may be regretful, but it does not itself undermine one's functioning. On the other hand, if one's choices are blocked, if one's preferences are not realized time after time, the likelihood of being able to fulfill one's needs will steadily decline.

The capacity to make choices in terms of future possibilities is, of course, one of the greatest advantages of being a cognitive animal. Quick calculation of what the future possibilities might be makes it far more likely that present choices will serve future needs. In other words, one would expect that humans, with their exceptional cognitive facility, would reflect the outcome of such rapid calculations in their preferences.

As pervasive and far-reaching human needs, making sense and involvement are important components in preference. These needs profoundly influence human preference for patterns of information. These preferences express themselves not only in relatively abstract situations (as, for example, people's reactions to written or oral messages), but in people's reactions to the physical environment as well. People prefer, in other words, both landscapes and books, interiors and organizations, that offer promise of being involving and of making sense.

Preference, then, can be viewed as an expression of the evaluation of one's possibilities. Although preference is a guide to choice, the assessment involved in preference is assumed to take place whether one actually has a choice or not. Thus one has feelings about landscapes one passes even though there is no choice to be made about them. Likewise, people look in store windows or at catalogs and decide what they do and don't like without necessarily planning to act on their preferences. To have preferences is a prompt, often automatic reaction. It is an extension of the perceptual process; like prediction, it enhances one's readiness to act even though no action may be called for at that particular moment.

The emphasis in this analysis of preference has been on its relationship to one's possibilities. It may be useful to differentiate two degrees of anticipation with respect to these. One is the rather immediate, the outcome of a comparatively simple, direct assessment. It is as if one asks oneself, "Is this a situation I could comprehend? Is there enough order, enough regularity so that I could figure it out without too much difficulty?'' This sort of assessment, of course, deals with the making-sense is-sues. There would have to be a parallel ''immediate future'' assessment in terms of involvement. In that case, the concern would be with wheth-er there seems to be enough going on to be worth further exploration, whether there is enough variety to maintain one's interest.

Just as it is possible to identify a making-sense and an involvement component of preference as far as the immediate future is concerned, there are comparable assessments possible with respect to a future that is somewhat more long-range. This longer-range perspective goes beyond what is direct and immediate. It concerns not what one can directly per-ceive, but what might happen if one were to spend more time in that setting. Could one learn more? Could one discover new things? If so, the environment is involving in terms of this longer-run assessment. Could one find one's way? Would one be able to maintain one's bearings? If so, the environment scores high as far as making sense in the longer run is concerned.

This framework for looking at preference is reasonable from an evo-lutionary point of view. It also makes good theoretical sense in the con-text of an informational approach to human functioning. While it is applicable to a wide range of informational circumstances, our focus here is on the application of these components to the environment. In fact, it was in the context of studying environmental preference that the frame-work evolved. By now, after a long series of studies examining a great diversity of environments, we feel the framework has been effective in enhancing our understanding of people's preferences for particular land-scapes and scenes (Chapter Note 2).

INFORMATIONAL FACTORS IN ENVIRONMENTAL PREFERENCE

The preference framework, up to this point, has been concerned with the two basic informational needs—making sense and involvement —and with a time dimension that focuses on the immediate and the longer-term possibilities. The combination of these two components yields four distinct combinations, or patterns, shown in Table 4.2.

Table 4.2

Preference Framework

	MAKING SENSE	INVOLVEMENT
PRESENT OR IMMEDIATE	Coherence	Complexity
FUTURE OR PROMISED	Legibility	Mystery

In looking at people's preferences for different kinds of environments, perhaps the most striking characteristic is the central role of space. A scene or landscape or setting is not merely something to perceive, but something to enter into. Implicitly at least, one must imagine oneself in the situation. One must consider how one would function if one were to enter into the space and move around in it. Thus the longer-range, or more future, aspect of preference depends upon the analysis of the inferred three-dimensional space. The more immediate aspect of preference seems to involve the two-dimensional qualities of the scene, or what we previously referred to as the "picture plane."

The Immediate Environment in a Spatial Context

As we have seen, this aspect of the preference model deals with the rapid assessment of "what's right there." There is a concern to grasp the main elements and relationships of the scene, of the picture plane.

Coherence. The issue here is how easy it is to organize, to structure. Being able to organize what one sees into a relatively few identifiable units, or chunks, is crucial here. The "fittingness" of an element in a setting (see Wohlwill and Harris, 1980) is thus an aspect of coherence. Redundancy, which makes it possible to treat a whole area of the scene as the same, is another important component. This interacts with identifiability, the ease of figuring out what these major units are. Thus if one corner of the scene contains a pine tree, a cow, and a parked car, there is identifiability but not redundancy. If that corner contained a forest of pine trees (or a herd of cattle or a parking lot full of cars), then there would be both identifiability and redundancy. If there were some sort of configuration of twigs and car parts with brown eyes and horns, there would be neither.

Another aspect of redundancy is repeating elements. Both scenes in Figure 4.1 gain coherence from the presence of the same basic visual unit repeated many times with slight variations. Here again, the cognitive organization of the scene is facilitated; it can be achieved on the basis of less total information. (Note that both scenes also benefit from having whole areas that can be interpreted as essentially the same; they thus are examples of both kinds of redundancy.)

Complexity. The involvement component of this relatively immediate assessment concerns whether there is enough present in the scene to keep one occupied. It is, in effect, an evaluation of whether there is enough going on to be worth one's making a map of it. Complexity is a factor with a long history. In the past, researchers working in the area of experimental aesthetics focused on complexity as a central explanatory

Figure 4.1 Examples of coherence.
A. W. Kaplan

concept (Berlyne, 1960). The results of experiments (most often using artificial material) indicated that there was some intermediate amount of complexity that would be most preferred. Too little complexity would suggest a boring situation; too much would also be undesirable. Subsequently, environmental psychology has taken research on aesthetics out of the narrow confines of randomly generated material, and the prediction of preference has become more complicated (see S. Kaplan, 1975, 1979b; Wohlwill, 1976, 1980).

This more recent research suggests that, while complexity is undoubtedly necessary for preference, it is probably a mistake to lean too heavily on this factor. In part this may stem from the conception of complexity as based on the number of different countable things. It may be useful to think of it rather as the visual "richness," or diversity, of the scene and to be careful to maintain coherence within this richness if preference is to be enhanced. It is all too easy to have complexity at the expense of coherence (Figure 4.2). What the preference framework suggests, however, is that each of the components plays a role (Figure 4.3).

Figure 4.2 Scenes high in complexity.
A. W. Kaplan and S. Kaplan

The Longer-Range Future in a Spatial Context

Just as one assesses one's possibilities as far as the picture plane is concerned, one is also concerned about the possibilities for a cognitive map of the three-dimensional space represented by the scene. This involves a longer-range future, an inference about what would happen if one were to walk some distance into the scene. This inference of the third dimension seems to be rapid and automatic: it occurs as much when one looks at a photograph as when one looks out the window, as well as when one is actually moving along a path and anticipating what will happen next.

Mystery. Of all the factors involved in the prediction of preference, mystery is the easiest to see when photographs within a given content grouping are arranged in order of preference. The more preferred scenes are very likely to give the impression that one could acquire new information if one were to travel deeper into the scene. They provide partial information concerning what might lie ahead (Figure 4.4). Mystery involves the inference that one could learn more through locomotion and exploration; it is a factor of great power in predicting preference for scenes of the outdoor environment (R. Kaplan, 1973b, 1975).

Although this is a familiar concept in the context of landscape architecture and has long been used in the designs of Japanese gardens, it is somewhat unexpected in the context of psychology. Perhaps for this reason there has been an inclination to translate it into some more familiar concept, such as "surprise." A critical difference between mystery and surprise, however, is that in a surprise the new information is present and it is sudden. In the case of mystery, the new information is not present; it is only suggested or implied. Rather than being sudden, there is a strong element of continuity. The bend in the road, the brightly lighted field seen through a screen of foliage—these settings imply that the new information will be continuous with, and related to, that which has gone before. Given this continuity one can usually think of several

Figure 4.3 These scenes show that settings that are high in complexity can be high in coherence as well.
Top: W. E. Hammitt; Bottom: M. J. Waits

Figure 4.4 Scenes high in mystery.
A. W. Kaplan and S. Kaplan

alternative hypotheses as to what one might discover. The mind-filling, or involving, experiences of entertaining a few fairly strong alternatives at once should yield a high level of preference; research by Crandall (1967) suggests that this is in fact the case.

Another important way in which the degree of surprise is controlled is the self-paced character of the discovery. The additional information will be obtained as one goes deeper into the scene. Thus the rate at which one experiences the new information is determined by one's direction and rate of travel. It is an informational opportunity, and a gradual one at that. With its promise of more to think about, mystery provides the involvement component for the longer-range, future aspect of preference.

Legibility. Just as one can imagine oneself somewhere in a scene acquiring new information, one can imagine oneself somewhere in a scene getting lost. Legibility, of course, is at the opposite pole. It is characteristic of an environment that looks as if one could explore extensively *without* getting lost. Environments high in legibility are those that look as if they would be easy to make sense of as one wandered farther and farther into them. Enough openness to see where one is going, as well as distinctive enough elements to serve as landmarks, are important here (Figure 4.5). Many recently constructed portions of the built environment are plagued by low legibility. Cartoons often depict the sprawling suburban development where locating one's home amidst the undifferentiated sameness is at best difficult. Shopping malls may be high in mystery, but they provide less support for one's overall sense of orientation. Campus buildings and libraries unfortunately also tend to suffer from lower levels of legibility (Weisman, 1981).

The significance of legibility is clearly evident in this plowman's description of the British landscape:

> There are about 400 acres of corn-land and I plow it all. All the fields are different. They have their names and they feel to be different places. It is how it should be. I wouldn't like the village to become a Tannington where the hedges have gone and the ploughman doesn't know where he is. A well-kept hedge is a good sight and tells you where you are. The hedges belong to the village. You get so used to seeing them standing there—they

Figure 4.5 Scenes high in legibility.
A. W. Kaplan and S. Kaplan

are like buildings and you miss them when they are knocked down. Some hedges are important and when they go you feel as bad as if a wood had been taken away. I think there are certain hedges which the farmers shouldn't touch without asking the people—although I can't see this happening. (Blythe, 1969, p. 238)

The Role of Content

The discussion thus far has emphasized informational factors, such as coherence and mystery. These process issues should not blind one to the powerful role of content, that is, the subject matter of the scene. One of the most powerful types of content is provided by the natural environment. Although it may seem obvious that there is a preference for nature, until a short time ago there were few studies dealing with this issue. Our first study dealing with this issue found an overwhelming preference for the unspectacular, nearby natural environment over both urban and residential scenes (S. Kaplan, R. Kaplan, and Wendt, 1972; see also R. Kaplan, 1978a). This research was promptly replicated in a study in which the preference for nature was, if anything, even greater (Wohlwill, 1976). Zube (1976) has also reported increased preference for more natural settings (Chapter Note 3).

One insight that grew out of this research concerned the role of *primary* landscape elements. These are components whose very presence is likely to raise preference substantially. The existence of water in the landscape is frequently found to enhance preference. In several studies, we also found that the presence of trees is a strong preference predictor (e.g., Gallagher, 1977; Herzog, Kaplan, and Kaplan, 1982; R. Kaplan, 1983).

Just as the informational factors can be interpreted in terms of the adaptiveness of preference for the kinds of environments in which humans can function well, these content issues can also be interpreted in evolutionary terms. Animals frequently show a preference for the sorts of environments that contain the elements needed for their survival (Hilden, 1965; Partridge, 1978), and humans may function similarly. Certainly a bias toward an environment containing such components as trees and water would be a positive step in terms of enhancing survival.

Affordance, Shelter, and Prospect

Our discussion of preference has led us to a conception of humans as spatial animals constantly assessing the possibilities presented to them by the environment, and making their choices accordingly. This is not a traditional conception; in fact, there is probably not a single introductory textbook that mentions it. On the other hand, there are some striking parallels in the literature. Of particular interest are two scholars who have paid close attention to the relationship between people and environments. One of these is the psychologist J. J. Gibson, who has placed so much emphasis on the role of the pattern of the environment in determining what people perceive. The other is the geographer Jay Appleton, who claims to be an amateur with respect to his topic, landscape preference. Appleton concentrates particularly on landscape painting as an expression of preference at various points in history.

Gibson (1979) has contributed a variety of insights and perspectives to the study of perception. While his emphasis on the relation between the patterns of the environment and the adaptive requirements of the organism is consonant with the position we have taken, his commitment to the idea that memory plays no role in perception is quite contrary to the cognitive perspective outlined in the preceding chapters (Note 5 in Chapter 3). However, his concept of particular interest in the context of preference is his *affordance* concept. As we have seen, what an object affords an individual is what that individual might be able to do with that object. In other words, the affordances of an object are its potential uses. Gibson argues that assessing the affordances of an object is an automatic process, an integral part of perception; people routinely perceive things at least in part in terms of what they could do with them.

In terms of preference for environments, the concept of affordance needs to be extended. When one thinks of an environment, one is likely to have an image of the scene rather than of a single object. A scene is not merely a collection of objects; the larger spatial context must also be considered. In addition, as Gibson (1966) pointed out many years ago, there are gradients, textures, and surfaces. These qualities play a central role in defining that larger spatial framework within which individuals perceive and act.

There has been careful study of the many factors involved in the perception of the spatial framework. From the perspective of preference, of evaluating environments, however, the issue is not how people manage to perceive depth, but what difference having this information makes. Unlike the affordances offered by objects, the issue with respect to space is what we can do not *with* it, but *in* it (Figure 4.6). Gibson in fact begins his analysis of space in these terms. He speaks of locomotion over the ground surface in terms of "negative affordances," such as obstacles and barriers. He also discusses the larger-scale space in his consideration of "the affording of concealment," the possibility of finding a hiding place. As we have seen, obstacles and barriers are not the only factors in assessing one's possibilities for locomotion. Even more important, one's feeling about an environment is greatly influenced by what

Figure 4.6 A setting affording the opportunity to play in the water and to test one's balance. Others may see it as a place for quiet reflection. But it is also possible that some would see it as an impediment rather than an attraction.
A. W. Kaplan

might be called "cognitive affordances," that is, whether one sees possibilities for maintaining one's bearings and for acquiring new information. Nonetheless, Gibson's idea of an automatic, routine assessment of one's possibilities is strikingly parallel to the conclusions we have been led to through the study of landscape preference.

Further clues as to the kinds of assessment people make of outdoor environments are provided by Appleton (1975) in his provocative book, *The experience of landscape.* Here he attempts to identify what makes certain landscape configurations pleasurable to people. He approaches this problem in a functional way, that is, in terms of those aspects of the environment that would tend to support human functioning and hence make survival more likely. The two central concepts he proposes are *shelter* and *prospect.* Shelter he views as a place to hide in, a place where one can see without being seen. This, of course, is directly parallel to Gibson's concealment. By contrast, prospect emphasizes the opportunity for unhindered seeing.

Here we have two significant candidates for the affordances of the environment. An environment should be preferred, in Appleton's framework, if one has a chance to hide, to find refuge, and if one has the chance to seek, to look into the distance. To cast Appleton's two principles in informational terms, an environment supportive of human functioning is one where one can gain information about what is going on and at the same time be able to prevent others from obtaining information about oneself (Figure 4.7).

How, then, does all this tie back to the proposed matrix of factors that predict preference? In the case of prospect, the connection is straightforward. Prospect, by ensuring visual access to the surrounding environment, suggests a setting in which learning can take place. It thus provides a striking parallel to mystery.

The tie between shelter and making sense is not so direct and obvious. The common denominator here is safety. An environment one can make sense of may not be exciting (although it can be), but it is likely to be one where one knows what to watch out for and what to do. It is a setting one is familiar with; close to home, one might say. It thus offers shelter in the metaphorical sense.

This is not to say that shelter is important only in the metaphorical sense, however. Rather, both senses—metaphorical and literal—are undoubtedly factors in people's preference; both are general, far-reaching informational components of the way people perceive the large-scale environment.

Familiarity and Preference—Once Again

Earlier in the chapter we considered the complexity of the relationship between familiarity and preference. Let us return to this issue now that we have a more extensive framework for considering the various components that play a role in determining preference. It is now possible

Figure 4.7 Two scenes from Woodcock's (1982) study of biome preference. The scene on the top, showing a mixed hardwood forest, is high in refuge, while the scene below, representing a savanna, is high in prospect.
Top: W. H. Wagner; Bottom: J. H. Falk

to see why familiarity seems both to help and to hinder preference. Familiarity influences both of the major factors in preference. It enhances the making-sense component; at the same time it tends to undermine involvement. This dual influence is readily understandable in terms of the way familiarity relates to the operation of the cognitive process.

Familiarity describes the relationship between an individual and something that individual has had considerable experience with. In theoretical terms, we assume that the experience is sufficient to have led to the development of an internal model of that something. And models, as we have seen, constitute a simplification, an economical means of coding information. Such a simplification is likely to aid the making-sense process. It provides a way of concentrating on essentials and ignoring irrelevant and potentially distracting details (Figure 4.8).

At the same time the compactness of the coding means that less cognitive capacity is involved; what once filled the mind no longer does so. It is, in other words, no longer involving. This is an adaptive mechanism, encouraging the individual to cease spending time with what is already familiar. On the other hand, this creates problems as far as preference is concerned. What was involving before it became familiar now no longer is. A portion of the environment is, as it were, "used up." The way people feel about environments would constantly change even if the environments did not. Given human preference and human cognitive processes, the preference for commerce with the unfamiliar is a necessary consequence. Although some texts treat curiosity as an extra,

Figure 4.8 A potentially confusing scene unless, of course, you have prior knowledge about beaver lodges.
A. W. Kaplan

added-on property of human motivation, it seems more appropriate to consider it a natural outcome of the way humans experience their environment.

Another expression of the tendency for involvement to decline with increasing familiarity is the "grass is greener" phenomenon. That the grass looks greener on the other side of the fence is another way of saying that anticipation is often more desirable than realization. Anticipation, of course, suggests the role the future plays in positive evaluation. Future events can promise new information (mystery) and competence (legibility). As one becomes familiar with these realities, there is no longer an unrealized future to aid the evaluative balance sheet.

However, this pattern of dissatisfaction and restlessness with increasing familiarity is a possible, not a necessary outcome. Sometimes familiarity, by simplifying a previously confusing situation, enhances the making-sense component sufficiently to produce an overall gain in preference. Also, mystery can remain despite familiarity. The bend in the road continues to draw one despite having frequently traveled the road. One's relationship to a special other person can retain a sense of wonder and mystery despite a substantial familiarity that many years of knowing one another brings. Highly experienced computer programmers still find substantial mystery in contemplating what the computer is doing with their latest program.

The trade-off between making sense and involvement can be a subtle one. While familiarity may lower preference and lead to a yearning for new pastures, it might also lead to a shift of level within the same situation. Since familiarity simplifies, it becomes possible to take in more at once, to treat what once filled the mind as a part of something else. In this way the focus of exploration shifts, leading to an ever-deepening knowledge. Thus there can be highly familiar situations in which one feels one is constantly seeing new things.

A related way in which involvement is sustained despite increasing familiarity is through a shift from exploration to play. Familiarity, the outcome of exploration, is also the starting point for play. In play the focus is not "what is this?" but "what can I do with this?" It is as if the identity of the elements was achieved through exploration and the way the elements can be arranged and rearranged is achieved through play. Although manipulation is central to play, the manipulation need not be of concrete objects. With increasing familiarity, the mental entities become increasingly compact, increasingly discrete, and increasingly responsive to activation in the absence of what they represent. They become, in a word, manipulable. Thus familiarity is essential to the playful rearrangement and recombination of the elements of thought that we tend to associate with insight and creativity.

SOME CONCLUDING COMMENTS

Cognitive maps require evaluative codes in order to be effective guides to action. Embedding evaluative codes in cognitive maps, however, not only facilitates decision-making; it also permits people to have feelings right now about things that have not yet, and might never, happen. It allows the future to color present feelings and, occasionally, to dominate them.

The picture is further complicated by the fact that processes, too, make their claim on evaluative codes. One would expect certain contents to be tied to evaluative codes. Food objects and sex objects, for example, must be tied to pleasurable codes; injury must be tied to pain. It is perhaps less obvious that circumstances that do not directly help or harm but that support or hinder certain processes also have affective consequences. Making sense and involvement, as we have seen, are factors in people's feelings about things that are independent of specific content.

It is important to recognize that, while desirable content and desirable process often go together, this need not be the case. One can find working on a problem or puzzle rewarding even though the resulting solution is neither tasty nor beautiful nor desirable in any other way. Just as there can be positively evaluated process without correspondingly positive content, the converse can also be true. One can find a lollipop enjoyable even though obtaining it involved no ingenuity, adventure, or other valued process.

The combination of these two distinctions—present/future and content/process—suggests an interesting table of possibilities. For each of the four cells of Table 4.3, there is the possibility of an event that is coded positively ($+$) or of one with a negative code ($-$). As far as *content* is concerned, these $+$'s and $-$'s come from innate reactions (e.g., to

Table 4.3

Preference, Type of Material, and the Time Dimension

		CONTENT	PROCESS
PRESENT	−	I'm afraid of that elephant.	I don't know what to do and I hate it.
	+	I like this lollipop.	I like doing this puzzle.
FUTURE	−	I'm afraid we'll meet an elephant.	I'm afraid I'll not know what to do.
	+	I can't wait to eat my lollipop.	I can't wait to work on this puzzle.

sweet things) and from the evaluative codes built into one's cognitive map. As far as *process* is concerned, the informational factors that determine preference (and presumably have a basis in innate structures) are assumed to account for both the positive and negative reactions. It should be remembered that any such table tends to isolate extremes; in the typical case a person's feelings are likely to be influenced to some degree by all of these factors.

The present–content cell is the traditional focus of discussion of . motivation, and the future–process cell is the one most often neglected. Yet the environmental implications of the affect associated with future process are particularly pervasive. People unfamiliar with a given environment may fear becoming lost or disoriented and thus not even enter it. This influences how far people are willing to venture beyond their home in the urban environment and how they react to the opportunity (or, in their eyes, threat) of visiting a natural environment ("Go to the woods? Not me!"). The attitude toward the future (and the willingness to accept reassuring utopias) similarly reflect this evaluation of processes that have not yet happened.

NOTES

1. Human Evolution

For readers interested in extending their knowledge of the fascinating topic of human evolution, Pfeiffer's (1978) *The emergence of Man* is a good choice. It is enjoyable reading. In addition it has the advantage of being sensitive to many of the psychological and information-processing issues involved. B. G. Campbell's (1974) *Human evolution* is one of the best texts in the area. A compact source of useful material on evolution and information-processing is *Humanscape* (S. Kaplan and R. Kaplan, 1978). For the most part, the information-processing wing of cognitive psychology has tended to ignore the entire domain of human evolution; for an encouraging indication of a changing perspective, see J. L. Lachman and R. Lachman (1979).

Probably the best-known current approach to human behavior emphasizing evolution is sociobiology. For a brief and thoughtful presentation of some central issues in this area, see E. O. Wilson (1978). Among other recent works in this area, the volume by Barash (1979) is noteworthy for its ingenuity. R. D. Alexander (1979) provides a more scholarly perspective. The strength of all these works lies in their recognition of the significant role of evolution and hence genetics in human behavior. Their weakness lies in several interrelated difficulties:

☐ They have a preoccupation with altruism, that is, with the question of whether people are ever *really* selfless in their assistance of others. To reduce so many human interactions serving so many multiple functions to an issue of

whether one's genes benefit more or less directly is a caricature of human relationships.

☐ There is a tendency to ignore psychology, to jump directly from genetics to sociology. As such, there is no reality attributed to psychological processes
and mechanisms. Thus, in the sociobiologists's perspective, an individual caught
cheating on the group may put on a show of guilt and shame in order to remain
in the good graces of the group. To anyone who has experienced these emotions,
however, they are clearly not a pretense but a vivid, and often difficult to shake,
reality.

☐ A related issue is the tendency to adopt what might be called an implicit rationality theory. Individuals are assumed to be attempting to maximize certain outcomes, namely, those in which their genes stand to benefit. Thus the
picture is painted of individuals who are both calculating and conscious of what
they are doing. The fallacy of such a view of how humans make choices is
adroitly illustrated by Hebb's (1972, p. 131) comments on why people engage in
sexual behavior: "The primary reason . . . is not to produce another generation
of troublemakers in this troubled world but because human beings like sex behavior." Much human action is comparably based more on preference than on
rational calculation with an eye to maximizing outcomes. Preference in turn has
been shown to be a process that occurs at great speed and without consciousness
(G. Mandler, 1975a; Zajonc, 1980). People often do what is adaptive because
their preferences and inclinations show the impact of evolution, not because the
fate of their genes is a conscious priority coloring all their actions.

☐ There is an insensitivity to the profound role of information in human
adaptation. As we shall see in the next chapter, humans are deeply concerned
with making sense of the world, with comprehending the forces that make
things happen. This is an overwhelmingly difficult task to carry out alone. Humans depend on each other for aid in this struggle toward comprehension. Thus
much human interaction is not an exchange of favors toward some possible future gain for one's genes. It is a mutual effort to achieve a level of understanding
that is central to the functioning of each participating individual.

For help in unraveling these and other issues relating to genetics, psychology, and culture, an excellent source is Midgley's (1978) *Beast and man*. In recognizing the importance of genetic factors *and* the limitations of sociobiology,
Midgley skillfully places evolutionary issues in the context of psychology and
philosophy. All three domains benefit from her wise and witty treatment.

2. Research on Environmental Preference

The broad area of environmental aesthetics is an active one as far as research is concerned. Designers, understandably enough, are interested in the environmental patterns that people appreciate. Planners, too, may become
concerned with the scenic and its preservation. A critical issue is whether there
is any research evidence that the scenic is more than a matter of individual
whim (Bufford, 1973). Laws governing scenic protection have in recent years
been upheld in court, despite widespread uncertainty as to their legal viability

(see Bufford, 1980; Wohlwill, 1976). Probably the most pervasive interest in environmental aesthetics (often called "scenic beauty" in this context) has been on the part of federal agencies charged with the management of land and natural resources. Decisions about "harvesting" forests, about conserving soil, about developing parks, about siting electric transmission towers, all impinge to some degree on scenic values. (*Proceedings of Our National Landscape Conference*, 1979, provides a useful source of both the kinds of issues and the range of agencies that are pertinent.) In some cases enhancing scenic beauty is the primary goal; in others, identifying, measuring, and making predictions about what will be preferred is a major concern.

Our own studies in this area have tended to have strong links to these applied concerns. At the same time, the pattern of results has again and again contributed to our theoretical education, ultimately leading to the framework presented in this chapter. Although these studies have had different contexts and purposes, the basic procedure has remained much the same. In order to see how the theory evolved from a series of studies of this kind, it may be helpful to discuss the basic procedure this research has followed.

Two central issues that research in this area must confront are (1) how the environment is to be presented and (2) the format for participants' reactions. In terms of the first topic, it would seem most appropriate to present the environment by taking people to it. As it turns out, however, not only are the costs of doing this high and the logistics complicated, the benefits are questionable. Numerous studies have demonstrated that visual substitutes of the real environment (e.g., slides and photographs) are entirely satisfactory (S. Shuttleworth, 1980; Ulrich, 1979) and, in fact, provide distinct advantages. (These are discussed further in Chapter 9.)

There are a variety of possible reactions one might obtain from people; a simple preference rating (using a five-point scale) seems to have certain advantages. It is something people enjoy doing and do quickly, and the data so produced have proved to be meaningful and relatively resistant to extraneous factors. From a theoretical point of view, as we have seen, preference appears to tap a deep, underlying facet of the organism's makeup; it functions as a highly efficient and largely unconscious process.

The basic experimental procedure, then, involves individuals rating photographs in terms of preference. These may be presented as slides or as a photoquestionnaire that the participants may fill out at home or in a field setting. As it takes only a few minutes to complete these ratings, the environment can be sampled quite extensively.

In Chapter 9 we discuss the use of certain statistical procedures that lead to the grouping of photographs in terms of similar patterns of ratings. Thus, the results of the ratings permit analysis both in terms of the average preference for the various photographs and in terms of the groupings as well. Since the photographs within a particular grouping can vary substantially in how preferred they are, examining these relationships leads to further insight into the basis for these patterns. In a situation of this kind, the statistical procedure provides not an answer but an opportunity for discovery. It is in this way that a series of factors was discovered which play a role in understanding environmental preference (R. Kaplan, 1975; S. Kaplan, 1975). Over the years, the framework we discuss here has undergone a number of changes as new results have led to further insights (R. Kaplan, 1979b; S. Kaplan, 1979b).

3.   Natural Environments and Well-Being

Demonstrating the substantial preference for nature scenes was an important first step in understanding the psychological relationship between people and the natural environment. Recently another important step in this process has been taken with analysis of the impact of nearby natural environments on the people who encounter them on a daily basis. In a study of multiple-family housing complexes, R. Kaplan (1983) found that people who had a more natural, more desirable view out of their window experienced substantially higher neighborhood satisfaction. In a rather different context, E. O. Moore (1981) studied the role of the environment in the lives of the inmates of a federal penitentiary. His measure of well-being was the demand for health-care services. Inmates whose view was of farms and forests utilized health-care services at a significantly lower rate than inmates whose view was of less preferred content.

chapter five

COGNITIVE CHAOS: ATTENTION AND STRESS

In the real world the major concerns have little to do with lollipops and elephants. The analysis of preference and evaluation in the previous chapter may well be accurate, but perhaps it is too neat. Involvement and making sense are important, to be sure, but the world that rushes by is much more complicated. Sometimes we have the luxury of exploring things one at a time; more often, however, it seems that everything is going on at once.

Right now, for instance, you are presumably reading. At the same time, however, any number of things may also be going on nearby: the radio is playing, the phone rings, someone walks into the room accompanied by a friend whose voice catches your fancy. In addition, lots of things are going on in your head without apparent external provocation: your mind wanders, you think of the 25 other things that need to be done, you wonder what time you were going to meet your friend tonight. Suddenly a great urge to visit the refrigerator takes priority. And all this might be in a relatively quiet setting where concentration is at least possible.

In this chapter the focus is on this more usual state of affairs, where so much is happening so much of the time. Confusion is easy to come by. Urban stress is often attributed to this characteristic level of stimulation. In fact, the term "overload" is often applied to it. We want to examine what kinds of patterns constitute this all too usual situation and what the consequences are. It is also appropriate to wonder whether the framework developed up to this point applies to these conditions after all.

Let us first look at a few typical moments that depict this pervasive confusion:

Supermarket shopping. Ted needs some cereal, and he is looking for it where he has found it before. But the aisles have just been rearranged and the cereals moved. They are in aisle 7, and he is in aisle 2. While passing the pickles, he looks over the relishes. Four kinds, three brands, three sizes, and a special on one of them. Is it a better buy? Olives.

Haven't had any in a long time. Ted can't remember if there still are any in the pantry. Maybe it would be better not to buy them today. The store seems to have added a house-plant section! Some flowering plants catch Ted's eye, but he is determined to get to the cereals. Well, fancy meeting a long-lost friend here! Ted chats awhile and decides to invite the friend over for Saturday dinner. Better buy something special for that. May as well look over the meat even if the price is out of sight. No, he can't get himself to buy any after all. Chicken? There is that new recipe somebody just gave him. Cereal. Finally. They are out of the one Ted wanted. His daughter encourages a different brand. Ted tells her again that just because it's on TV doesn't mean he has to buy it. Well, finally Ted gets to stand in line at the checkout. He notices the cigarettes that look like the ones that were advertised as having such a low tar content. On second thought, maybe that wasn't the brand, and Ted puts it back. Daughter finds a lollipop and is about to open it. Ted yanks it away, knowing what will happen. He wonders why they keep all the candy at child-height right there where there is trouble every time. He offers her a piece of fruit from his purchases. The chicken is leaking out of its wrapper. He remembers something else he should have bought. And so it goes.

The trip to work. It's a nice morning, and the three blocks to the bus stop are a pleasure. Sue notices that the Browns have put in a new bush in front, and suddenly all the forsythia is flowering on the block. Looks like people are moving in around the corner. Sue wonders if their children will be better behaved than the bunch that used to be in that house. No one else is at the bus stop this morning, and while she waits, Sue tidies the planter there, removing a few weeds and a little trash. Then she looks at the newspaper in the rack, but the headline is just the same as what she heard on the radio before she left home. The bus is visible now, and she positions herself by the sign that indicates which buses stop there. Well, Sue is lucky this morning and gets a seat on the bus. They've changed some of the advertising. Some never seems to change. Forgot to ask for a transfer. Sue goes and gets one, and soon she gets off this bus and gets in line to wait for the next one. This is at a crowded intersection with lots of people making their way to everywhere. Lots of advertising of many sizes, colors, and contents on buildings, passing buses, and trucks. The stream of traffic is hard not to notice. Cars are honking, cabs are whizzing by, people are trying to cross regardless of what color the traffic light shows. The newsstand is doing a brisk business. Sue tries to figure out who seems to be stopping to buy a newspaper. She is surprised at how many people also pick up a candy bar in the morning. A bus arrives. It's the wrong one. Some people get off, and for a moment there is a real crowd scene, but soon things are back to a reasonable line waiting some more. Finally, her bus comes. It is full, and she is lucky to get on. A sea of faces—too many to relate to or to think about as individuals. She worries she'll be late today. She tries to think about work, but her mind wanders to other things. She'll have to rush home from work tonight.

A visit to a college campus. Bob is a senior in high school and has just arrived on the campus of a college he is considering for next year. He doesn't know anyone there right now, but his sister used to know some people who went there. It's not a very big campus, but right at the moment it seems enormous. His appointment with the admissions people isn't for another hour, and he decides to just roam around and try to get a feeling for the place. Maybe he can stop thinking about the interview that way. The buildings don't seem to have names on them. He tries to figure out whether they are dorms or classroom buildings or what. Some have names, but they don't help. People's names; why do they do that? He asks somebody if there is a snack bar someplace. That was a good move because suddenly he finds himself in a building with lots of people and bulletin boards and information and food, too. It all feels really strange. There are so many things he has never seen before. He would like to talk to some of these students—after all, next year he may be one of them—but he doesn't quite know what to say to them. He is sure he looks very different and they know he is just in high school still. There is a bookstore right inside this building (he hasn't ever seen that arrangement before), and he decides to look it over. What a lot of neat-sounding courses, judging by the books they are using. Bob worries whether he can make it in college. He thinks of buying his kid brother a souvenir, but then he isn't sure where to put it while he has his interview later. He is surprised the time has gone by so fast; suddenly he better start heading for the admissions office. He isn't sure at all how to get there, however. He remembers that its name is another one of those people names. Crane Hall or Crone or something like that. He really doesn't want to ask how to get there because that just makes it clear he is in high school. He finds a campus map posted on the wall, and it even says, "You are here." That helps a lot. And they have the building names in alphabetic order and indicate what they are about. So, it's Krell Hall he is looking for. That is the building with the tower on one side. Off he goes, map in mind, without noticing that he is right by an exit that faces his destination.

These are all slices of "real-world experience," yet they involve relatively controlled amounts of confusion. Although Bob is in a strange situation, he knows he will be there only for a short time. Should he return next year, he will know much more about the situation. In these scenarios there is none of the uncertainty of the public-housing resident

who is concerned about the declining neighborhood and the poor maintenance of the building, of the citizen of a less-developed country who
has been forced to relocate because of the construction of a new dam, of
the person with an illness in the family, or whose business is failing, or
who has just lost a job. Still, in each case there is a great deal of confusion and uncertainty and a vast array of information to be processed
somehow.

Even in these relatively benign situations there is so much going on
at once, there is so much stimulation, that one gets the impression of
overload. There are many external patterns competing for one's attention; at the same time, there are many thoughts and internal patterns requiring attention, too. It is reminiscent of the cartoon of a man standing
outside his house watching Santa Claus and a baby-bearing stork head
for his chimney simultaneously. He is waving his fist and shouting,
"One thing at a time, dammit, one thing at a time!"

We do not do well handling too much at once. This limitation does
not refer to our capacity to store information. Although that, too, must
be limited, it is clear that we can store a tremendous amount of knowledge. We cannot, however, use it all at once. In fact, we can use only a
small fraction of it at any one time. What we can actively work with at
a given moment is severely restricted. This is what the term *limited capacity* refers to in the context of human information-processing (Chapter
Note 1).

The overloading of this limited capacity stems in part from the
wealth of stimulation surrounding us—the lights, the sounds, the diversity. Part of it, however, comes from what might be rather than what is.
Part of the problem, in other words, arises out of uncertainty. While
only one thing happens at a given time and place, a great many things
might happen. This uncertainty contributes to the sense of overload.

While the confusion and amount of stimulation indeed feel like an
overload, this intuitive concept does not explain the problem adequately.
If we examine this idea a bit more closely, we discover that the presence
of lots of stimulation need not be overwhelming at all. The library
stacks are simply bursting with information; yet many find this a quiet,
peaceful place to study. Then, too, it is not unusual to seek what would
seem like an overload—to go out on the town looking for excitement
and bustle even at a time when one feels like one has too much to handle.

A person is not a passive recipient of stimulation. Rather, people are
selective in what they perceive, in what information they attend to. The
issue, then, may be described better in terms of the requirements of attention, the demands to be selective in the face of a vast array of stimulation. This may seem like a contradiction: if attention involves the
possibility of being selective, would this not preclude the possibility of

being overwhelmed? However, the very possibility of selectivity, of some patterns holding one's attention and others being ignored, implies the possibility of being distracted as far as any given task is concerned. When one is attending to an interesting member of the opposite sex who happens to be passing by, one is by the same token distracted from whatever it was one had previously been doing. Thus while the possibility of attending selectively applies in many instances, some stimuli have such high salience that ignoring them requires considerable effort.

Another way, then, to think of excessive amount and variety of stimulation is in terms of distraction. In each of the short scenarios we described above, there is a wealth of distractions, both external and internal. While one is successfully selecting part of the environment, there is still plenty left that can be distracting. The problem of attention and selection must then account for the sense of overload, the constant distractions, and also for the fact that similar patterns at different times and for different people have such different effects.

INTEREST AND EFFORT

Selection in human information processing refers not to one process but to many. Being able to focus on what is pertinent is so important that people have at their disposal a variety of ways to achieve it. While some of these ways may be more appropriate to one sort of problem than to another, at a given moment many of these processes are likely to be operating simultaneously. In our effort to understand how an individual may be distracted in many different directions and why such experiences can be unpleasant and even stressful, we shall concentrate on two of these mechanisms of attention. One of these is based on interest; the other, called into play when interest is lacking, depends instead on effort. Both are based on a distinction William James proposed many years ago.

Involuntary Attention

The pattern of attention based on interest James called involuntary attention. It involves patterns that are difficult not to attend to. Placing the lollipops and candy where a child can easily spot them at the supermarket checkout handily captures this type of attention. In fact, many of the patterns that children are captivated by are good examples of involuntary attention: soap bubbles and balloons, butterflies and bouncing balls. James's illustrations include similar categories: "strange things, moving things, wild animals, bright things, pretty things, words, blows, blood, etc. etc. etc." (1892, p 231).

Involuntary attention makes a great deal of sense in an evolutionary context. While it would be extremely dangerous for an animal as cognitive as a human to have reflexive reactions to important stimuli, having automatic attention would ensure that the cognitive apparatus was not off somewhere in the clouds but was concerned with the urgent issues at hand. Thus fires, loud sounds, and many other specific contents hold our attention. James calls such fascinations "direct" or "instinctive."

James also discusses instances of involuntary attention that are "derived" from previous experience—the things we notice in areas of great familiarity and expertise, for example. Thus a photographer is intrigued by patterns that others may not see at all, and an English teacher can't help but notice grammatical errors. We all sometimes find ourselves with ears perked at the mention of our name, and we seem to sense when a dull conversation has turned to a brighter moment of joke-telling.

Interest is such an agreeable basis for attention that it may not seem to involve attention at all. When the patterns of stimulation that we require from the environment are the ones that are attractive to us in their own right, selection is no problem. The very possibility of such a congenial state of affairs, however, brings with it the basis for a far less comfortable set of circumstances. If it is possible for there to be interesting patterns that match our purposes, then it must also be possible for there to be interesting patterns that do not. It is possible, in other words, for there to be attractions in the environment that are distractions as far as our purposes are concerned. Advertisers exploit this concept every day. Advertising attracts our attention for the purposes of the advertiser, not for our purposes. From our perspective, the fact that one's attention is so readily drawn to such material is a well-planned distraction. Certainly the impact of commercial strip development is in no small degree because of this. The banning of billboards in certain areas may be a reaction to this systematic coercion of our attention.

The possibility of being overwhelmed by distraction is, in these terms, a function of the interest or attraction of the environment. There might be too many competing sources of attraction (for example, the proverbial country mouse's first experience in the city). Alternatively, there might be a conflict between interest and purpose. The discomfort and stress created by such situations may be related to the necessity of exerting considerable effort to focus one's attention.

Voluntary Attention

James used the term "voluntary attention" to describe attention that requires effort since it arises not out of the way we react to certain environmental patterns but out of our volition, that is, out of our intentions and purposes. As such, voluntary attention is necessarily "derived." When interest fails, one may have to force oneself to pay attention. Such an expenditure of mental effort may be necessary when the stimulus patterns we require to carry out our purposes are not interesting. Such mental effort will surely be required when other patterns, irrelevant to our purpose, are interesting and therefore interfering. Voluntary attention fills the need for a means of supporting an ongoing train of thought by blocking potential distractions.

James describes the various circumstances that entail voluntary attention in these terms:

> We get it in the sensorial sphere whenever we seek to catch an impression of extreme *faintness*, be it of sight, hearing, taste, smell, or touch; we get it whenever we seek to *discriminate* a sensation merged in a mass of others that are similar; we get it whenever we *resist the attractions* of more potent stimuli and keep our mind occupied with some object that is naturally unimpressive. We get it in the intellectual sphere under exactly similar conditions: as when we strive to sharpen and make more distinct an idea which we but vaguely seem to have; or painfully discriminate a shade of meaning from its similars; or resolutely hold fast to a thought so discordant with our impulses that, if left unaided, it would quickly yield place to images of an exciting and impassioned kind. All forms of attentive effort would be exercised at once by one whom we might suppose at a dinner-party resolutely to listen to a neighbor give him insipid and unwelcome advice in a low voice, whilst all around the guests were loudly laughing and talking about exciting and interesting things. (1892, p. 234)

Voluntary attention presents a sharp contrast to the involuntary variety. It is used when an individual so decides rather than when particular sorts of stimuli appear on the scene. It is used in circumstances where the stimulus lacks fascination but must be attended to anyway. Some days, it seems as if that's all one is doing. Unlike the patterns that were important and seemed to have the capacity to hold attention in evolutionary times, the modern world seems to present many patterns that are important to heed but fail to hold interest. In addition, many of the patterns that are difficult to ignore—the hubbub of traffic and milling crowds, the advertising calling out from all over—could hardly be considered of great importance. Thus there is no longer a harmony between what is interesting and what is important.

Fending off Distraction: Fatigue and Recovery

In a world where there is no longer a match between the interesting and the important, the opportunities for the "best" attention are few and far between. The "best attention," James told us, is effortless. Most of the time, however, we find ourselves in situations that require mental effort, in other words, in situations that call for voluntary attention. The mind is occupied with unimpressive details, we strain to remember innumerable items, we discover our attention wandering many times to topics demanding less effort.

It would seem that such exertion would take its toll, that there is a price to be paid for so much mental effort. Yet each of us is heeding, and discriminating, and resisting the various patterns around us all the time. Even if Bob's efforts to make sense of the new campus were straining, we can be sure he was going to put everything into that interview anyway, thus exerting yet more voluntary attention. We stay polite and hospitable, we keep with the demands of the job, and we seem to rise to each occasion that presents itself.

Clearly there are costs. Mental fatigue is perhaps the most obvious one; its most obvious effect is a decline in the capacity to force oneself to attend. Such fatigue is certainly a manifestation of the cumulative effect of distractions. One gets to the point where it is too much to rise to yet another demand. It is especially when one has approached this level of fatigue that one becomes aware of the effort that so many tasks require.

We could imagine some baseline amount of voluntary attention that is required for usual functioning. This involves inhibition of some of the distraction that goes on much of the time. When somewhat more distraction threatens, the inhibition would be raised above the baseline level and one would limit the amount of additional cognitive activity in the head. The more urgent one's central purpose and the stronger (e.g., bigger, louder, brighter) the distractions, the higher one would set one's inhibitory level. When, by contrast, the interesting aspects of the environment are supportive of one's purposes, one could function at a substantially lower level of inhibition. There would, in other words, be far less mental effort required (Chapter Note 2).

Mental fatigue, then, might be an indication that the inhibitory mechanism is fatigued, forcing one to operate at a lower-than-normal inhibitory level. This would presumably not be a problem when interest and purpose coincide. In a crowded and confusing world, however, such a concordance is increasingly rare. As circumstances require a level of voluntary attention that is not forthcoming, one's relation to the environment begins to deteriorate. There is a sense of declining effectiveness and rising frustration as one's purposes are repeatedly shunted. There is the tendency to overreact as inhibition becomes insufficient to deflect what would normally be ignored. From an observer's perspective, these effects would show up as irritability rather than as fatigue per se.

Irritability may in fact be one of the most pervasive costs of the prolonged exertion of voluntary attention. The striking thing about irritability is that it is frequently a hidden cost. Admittedly much of the time when voluntary attention is necessary we seem to function adequately. However, the cumulative effect of fatiguing the inhibitory mechanism takes its toll later. People in crowds, in traffic, in confusing situations do not tend to show striking irritability. Fatigue does not appear immediately. This makes it possible for people to rise to occasions, to function despite difficulty, and to "pay" later. Thus people make it in crowds and traffic and manage to save their irritability for home. The scene in many a household in the late afternoon is testimony to the irritability that has built up in the course of the day for each of the members. The increased levels of tensions in the home, not to mention homicide among friends and relatives, may also be related to this phenomenon.

Some interesting research has been carried out to show the delayed costs of voluntary attention. Most of these studies require participants to carry out tasks in the presence of loud, uncontrollable random noise. People are able to do this remarkably effectively. Subsequently, however, the costs begin to show. Various tasks performed under quiet, peaceful conditions but following the experience with noise show marked deficits. What the various tasks that reveal these problems have in common is their requirement for close, sustained attention (see Cohen, 1978).

In other recent studies it has been shown that this delayed, fatigue-like effect does not require noise to produce it. Attention-demanding tasks are also effective. Perhaps more important, it has been established that the effect has implications for various other kinds of situations, not just ones where one must pay close attention (Cohen, 1980). In one study participants leaving the experiment after working problems in the face of distraction were confronted by another individual, ostensibly another participant, asking for help. Those who had experienced random uncontrollable noise were the least likely to be willing to offer help (Sherrod and Downs, 1974). There is thus beginning to be evidence that points to a deficit in attentional capacity as relating to a psychological state characterized by irritability, reduced effectiveness, and a less positive relationship to other people.

Let us turn to the issue of recovery; how can one get the baseline level back? If there were but one kind of attention and it were to fatigue under too heavy demands,* then the only means of recovery available would be to rest. Rest is indeed an important factor here. We have all experienced how much better able we are to attend to things after a good night's sleep. Most students, however, have also experienced attention too fatigued to be restored by a mere night's sleep. Exam periods

---

*This seems to be the position taken by Cohen (1978) in a paper whose approach is otherwise quite parallel to that taken here.

provide an all too vivid example of such fatigue for some people. Since there seems to be a limit to how much one can sleep, a unitary attention concept is bad news for any of us so careless as to become more fatigued than can be restored through sleep.

As we have seen, however, there is reason to suspect that there are two distinct sorts of attention and that of these only voluntary attention requires mental effort. It would thus be possible to avoid the effort of attention (while awake) if only one could surround oneself with enough things that are involuntarily interesting. One could, in other words, rest the voluntary attention mechanism even when one is not sleeping if one could find a setting where it is possible to function primarily in the involuntary mode (S. Kaplan, 1978c).

This possibility has not escaped people's attention; they often seek environments that are involuntarily interesting when they feel in need of a rest. Vacation settings are characteristically high in such stimuli, although people seem to differ in terms of the particular aspects of involuntary interest they emphasize. Some people favor experiencing—or at least watching—danger. Others are oriented to challenge, or to risk. Some people prefer to spend their vacations mountain-climbing; others prefer the same element of risk, but unadulterated by the necessity of physical effort. This latter group is more likely to be found in Las Vegas than on some remote mountain peak. For many people the involuntary hold of natural environments, of wild animals, of rough topography, of green things, of lakes and streams and oceans provides an essential part of any vacation plan. (Some indication for the fascination inherent in aspects of the natural environment has been obtained in the context of gardening, R. Kaplan, 1973a, 1983, and wilderness, S. Kaplan, 1977b, 1982.)

As these various examples illustrate, there is indeed attention without effort. Involuntary attention is powerful and effective; it is no wonder that such patterns can be powerful distractions when one cannot afford to attend to them. It may be that the fatigue of voluntary attention would be slower to cumulate if spelled with periods of involuntary attention during the day. The flight to one's fantasy no doubt accomplishes some of that. Perhaps eating lunch under the shade of a tree rather than in the lunchroom with one's coworkers might also.

THE FEAR OF COGNITIVE CHAOS

Overload, as we have seen, can be viewed in terms of the distractions that abound in daily life. *Not only do distractions necessitate constant attention and discipline; they also make it hard to have a focus.* Without a focus it is difficult to carry out one's purposes. Furthermore, being able to focus plays a central role in one's feelings. Having a focus to one's thought feels good; lacking mental focus can feel terrible. People prefer to be focused, to know what is going on and what needs to be done.

The fact that focus is important to people does not mean that it is necessarily easy to achieve. The very complexity of the human cognitive apparatus means that there are many different possible reasons for lacking focus. There are many more ways to be confused than to be clear. If one cannot recognize the objects in one's environment, one is confused. Indeed, even if there is only one fairly prominent object in the environment that one cannot comprehend, it can be a most disturbing experience. It might seem that recognizing objects is so straightforward that it is not worth mentioning. We have seen, however, that the uncertainty and complexity of the environment make object recognition a challenging task. Failures to recognize are of course more common in unfamiliar settings, but we have all experienced errors in dealing with familiar things whose identity momentarily escapes us. Such experiences can be most upsetting.

Confusion can take place at the cognitive-map level even if object recognition has been fully successful. One can recognize the entities that surround one as cars, buses, taxicabs, buildings, and people—and still be lost. One can even have a feeling of familiarity about the various lawnmower parts that surround one and still not remember how to put them back together. One can feel lost in the middle of a forest, or of an explanation, or of a translation one is attempting. It is not an enjoyable experience in any context.

Figure 5.1 This picture lends itself to a number of alternate interpretations. Appearances to the contrary, however, it is neither a floating log, nor a pile of dirt showing above the water, but a largely submerged alligator.
A. W. Kaplan

The basic capability of comprehending things and their relationships can generalize in a number of directions. So, too, can the potential to be confused. One dimension of such generalization is in the direction of abstraction, of functioning at a higher level of one's cognitive apparatus. People have long been concerned with rather abstract issues, such as where the universe came from, the nature of causation, or the source of power in the universe. Humans throughout history have been storytellers, and frequently stories deal with concerns of this kind.

A fascinating example of the passionate concern to find order in a potentially confusing world is provided by Lévy-Bruhl's (1923) *Primitive mentality*. His slightly condescending discussion of the "unreflective" but not incapable "primitive mind" points to the imposition of a tight causal structure onto the uncertainty inherent in the universe. The headings from the first chapter of his book give some of the flavor of this determined effort to keep potential confusion under tight control:

1.   Primitive mentality attributes everything that happens to mystic and occult agencies.
2.   Disease and death are never "natural"—examples drawn from Australia and from South, Central, West, and East Africa.
3.   There is no such thing as accident; a misfortune is never a matter of chance.
4.   How such a mind accounts for the crime of the witch-crocodiles.
5.   How it explains everything unusual.

It must not be concluded, however, that the passionate concern to live in an orderly world is restricted to "primitives" or, for that matter, to any other special group. An analysis of the performance of mutual funds discussed in *Fortune* (1976) provides an example of this concern in a modern, urbane population. There is, it turns out, a relationship between the performance of a mutual fund and the amount of money the fund spends on research. This relationship, however, is negative. The more a fund spends on research, the less they have to invest and the worse their performance. This of course raises the question of why they spend money on research when it has no positive impact on earnings. Jensen, who carried out the analysis, proposes that investors cannot tolerate the uncertainty involved. They seek explanations on the part of experts, stories that ease their discomfort even though they totally lack predictive value. Jensen refers to this as the "religious theory of the demand for security analysis."

These examples provide some sense of the commitment people have to making sense of their experiences at a level beyond the immediate and the concrete. Indeed, we frequently observe actions that present no conceptual problems as far as the objects and relationships right in front of us are concerned but make no sense at some higher level. It can be very disturbing, for example, to see buildings constructed on a flood-plain or to watch people waste food in a hungry world. An interesting example from the recent past involves the rejection of the teaching of evolution in the schools in many southern states. In a perceptive discussion of this period in our history, Grabiner and Miller (1974, p. 836) point to the central role of the fear of being overwhelmed by confusion and change.

> But there were other forces generating a distrust of science in the 1920's, forces not limited to the South. World War I was followed by a wave of isolationism, coupled with a desire to return to what was essentially American: the old, tried and true ways. But the 1920's were not a conservative age. Science and technology seemed to be revolutionizing the way people lived. As technology changed the nature of farming, and as more factories were built, people felt that they had left something important behind. Radio then, like television now, brought the world into people's homes, giving them a sense of events beyond their control and passing them by. It is not surprising that, in a relatively conservative region subject to rapid change, people might have wanted a way to vote against the modern world and all its undesirable changes.

Clarity and the Future

There is, as we have seen, substantial indication that the cognitive domains in which people seek clarity and avoid confusion include matters that are quite abstract. Another domain of generalization that has a large impact on people is the future. People often utilize their cognitive maps in an effort to gain some conception of the future. What is anticipated, what it is thought might happen, is of vital concern. Sometimes the future in question is a rather abstract future. Thus one might make sense out of one's persisting but unappreciated efforts by relating them to a reward in a better world to come or to an increase in human happiness at some distant future time. (Some ramifications of this way of making sense out of otherwise perplexing experiences are explored in the next chapter, which deals with cognition and coping.)

While the potential future can be a powerful and positive influence, it, like abstraction, brings with it the possibility of confusion. Being scheduled to give an address to a large number of people or to meet an important person in the near future can render an individual distraught and even incompetent, although the situation of not knowing what to do, or confusion, is still many hours or even days away. Comparably, awaiting the outcome of an important uncertainty, such as news of whether one got the job one applied for or of how a medical test came out, can place one in a state of near paralysis.

BROOM-HILDA by R. Myers

Reprinted by permission of the Chicago Tribune-New York News Syndicate, Inc.

These relatively concrete instances of lack of clarity in the future can be devastating. The *abstract* future, however, is peculiarly susceptible to certain kinds of confusion. One of these involves the relation of one's own competence, one's ability to influence the environment, to one's expectations about the future. If the possible futures one can envision are undesirable and if there is no means one can think of to avoid them, one is afflicted with an insidious condition called *helplessness.* In his stimulating treatment of this topic, Seligman (1975) has shown how damaging it is to perceive oneself as helpless. Seligman feels that experiences of this kind readily generalize, influencing an individual's entire outlook. The damage comes both in the quality of the individual's experience—depression is a possible consequence—and in the effectiveness of the individual in dealing with the environment. In such cases there is no overlap between what one feels competent to do and what needs to be done to influence the future. It is a failure of focus with pervasive consequences.

A second way in which the abstract future is capable of disrupting focus rather than fostering it involves the realities of the human lifespan. The future serves to justify many things people do. It gives meaning to activities people might otherwise not even carry out. However, the human power of abstraction makes possible an unwelcome insight. Most people, at some point in their life, come to the concrete, personal, vivid realization that all people eventually die. It is only a small step from this insight to the realization that one is likely not to be around to benefit from many activities that are justified in terms of a future payoff. For some philosophers the inevitability of death makes all human action absurd. Clearly this insight has the potential for being enormously disruptive. E. Becker (1973), in his thoughtful and moving *The denial of death*, has argued that much of human civilization can be understood as a means of insulating people from this disruptive potential. Certainly issues of mortality and immortality are central to many religious positions. There is no denying that humans over the centuries have devoted enormous effort and ingenuity to dealing with what is in many respects a rather abstract matter.

On the other hand, it may be that Becker overstates his case. Many of his examples concern what he terms a "fear of chaos." While he sees this as a metaphorical fear of death, it may be that the fear is literally of cognitive chaos, of a state in which one's thoughts will be unable to focus. Certainly the fear of death is capable of instigating a state of cognitive chaos, but it is by no means the only way of achieving such a state. There are many ways to be confused, to be unable to figure out what to think and what to do. People find these situations painful and will go to considerable effort to avoid them. In a similar vein, Halle (1977) views the development of human civilization as concerned, first and foremost, with the achievement of order. Maslow and Díaz-Guerrero (1971) argue that people crave a "conceptual grip on the universe" or a "system of understanding" so strongly that "any . . . system, good or bad, is preferred to the lack of system, i.e., to chaos" (p. 377).

SOME CONCLUDING COMMENTS

The very pervasiveness of the concern for clarity suggests that not having it must make a difference. Although little research has been directed to this issue, every indication suggests that cognitive chaos is a painful state of mind. People who are well fed, well clothed, and well supplied with physical comforts but who are confused about "who they are and where they are going and what it all means" have been known to suffer so severely that they jump out of windows. Proposing alternatives to belief systems that help make sense of the world (an activity technically known as heresy) has been considered sufficient grounds for extermination at several points in human history. Modern Americans have been known to give up worldly comforts and even a large measure of their freedom in exchange for membership in a group that promises to end all confusion.

Despite—or perhaps because of—the high level of affluence in the United States today, there are indications that confusion about such basic matters as identity and direction is widespread. The level of stress is reflected in the large numbers of tranquilizers prescribed by physicians, the excessive use of alcohol and psychoactive drugs, and the irrationality that provokes predictable reaction—either to the simpler life of the country or to the fantasyland provided by motion pictures or to literature that describes starting over on other planets.

Cognitive chaos is quite obviously something to be avoided if possible. What conditions make this most likely? What sort of environment will be most supportive of clarity? The same concepts that provided a basis for a discussion of preference in Chapter 4 speak to this issue as well. An environment that is involving and that makes sense will foster the achievement of clarity, just as the absence of these two factors will incline the balance toward confusion and chaos.

In some way this parallel seems eminently reasonable. Clarity, as we have seen, is of great importance to people. It is certainly appropriate that they prefer environments in which clarity is most readily achieved. On the other hand, clarity and preference are incommensurate concepts. Clarity is a matter of some urgency, a human informational need. The absence of clarity is a source of stress. Preference, by contrast, refers to choice. It is more closely akin to aesthetics than to urgency. Is putting these two concepts together equivalent to saying that what people prefer is what they need? Is it that what people would rather have is what they must have?

The answer to these questions depends upon one's time perspective. In the short run the answer is clearly no. Depriving people of what they would rather have or what they would prefer in any given instance is not going to lead to confusion and stress. It is doubtful that always having what one prefers would be possible—or healthy even if it were possible. In the long run, however, the picture is quite different. Preference points to environments in which clarity is more likely to be achieved. Repeated denial of one's preferences over an extended period of time is likely to result in a situation in which the achievement of clarity will be difficult or impossible. In this sense, preference has a future-oriented function. It increases the chances that the environments people find themselves in will be appropriate not so much in terms of specific and immediate needs but in terms of rather general, long-term requirements. Environments people prefer are those in which they are more likely to function effectively over the long run.

Cognitive chaos is a cumulative concept. Many sorts of issues come together to determine one's mental state on the continuum from clarity to chaos. It is influenced by patterns of attention and fascination. It is influenced by one's purposes and by how well the environment and one's purposes fit together. It is influenced by the degree and kind of uncertainty each individual faces. The concrete present, the abstract, the future all play a role in determining one's place on the continuum. In terms of the metaphor of the straw that broke the camel's back, this amounts to saying that the straws are not necessarily of a kind, but can have many different sources. The positive aspect of such a cumulative concept is that when one attempts to ease the load by unpiling straws, any straw will do.

The pain and stress that result from cognitive chaos are also cumulative concepts. Just as there can be many factors influencing one's state of clarity or confusion, there can be many factors that lead to pain and in turn to stress. Much of the power of these concepts is in fact related to their nonspecificity. As cumulative concepts, they represent a convergence of forces, a focus for many different facets of an individual's life.

NOTES

1. Limited Capacity

The topic of limited capacity illustrates, perhaps as much as any topic in psychology, the time-worn maxim that nothing is simple. There is general agreement that humans can process only a certain amount of information at one time (although Neisser, 1976, has doubts). Miller (1956) has suggested measuring information in "chunks," which are meaningful units of information. (A chunk probably corresponds to a representation in more modern terms.) G. Mandler (1975b, 1975c) has found that people are able to deal with 5 ± 2 such units at one time.

There is also general agreement that the limitation applies to the active processing of information rather than to the vast capacity for information storage, but what constitutes "active processing" is no simple matter. For readable treatments of the various complexities embedded in this issue, see Moates and Schumacher (1980) and Weisberg (1980).

2. The Concept of Compatability

The match between one's purposes and inclinations and what is available in the environment has been a central theme in environmental psychology (see Stokols, 1977). Behavior-environment congruence, a concept developed by the ecological psychologists (e.g., Wicker, 1979), focuses on the constraints provided by the environment that tend to make behavior predictable in a given setting. Further theoretical development of this concept, where both congruence and the salience, or importance, of the situation are included, is incorporated in Stokols's (1979) analysis of environmental demand. The importance of the individual's purposes is also central to S. Kaplan and Talbot's (1983) "compatibility" concept, where the supportiveness of the situation is analyzed in terms of the degree of fit between perceptual and action domains.

part four

FUNCTIONING IN THE ENVIRONMENT

Much of what humans are capable of doing can be described in terms of information processing. As we saw in the previous parts of this book, humans recognize with facility, predict adroitly, and evaluate readily and decisively. They also abhor confusion. Animals, too, show these information-processing tendencies to varying degrees. Surely such a widespread phenomenon cannot be an accident. Information processing must be adaptive, that is, it must play a central role in survival. In the course of evolution, organisms with superior information-processing capacity must have somehow had an advantage over their competitors.

If survival is the name of the game, action is surely the way it is played. Having cognitive maps suitable for every occasion is of little use if one cannot find the right one when it is needed. The basic issue when all is said and done is whether one knows what to do next. Neither comprehending the distant past nor anticipating the remote future is of much use if one is at a loss for what to do in the present.

There are times when knowing what to do is a prompt and straightforward outcome of the way knowledge is stored and processed. As we saw in Chapter 1, smooth and effective action is often the expression of familiarity. Although such relatively routine behavior describes a vast portion of the way we spend our time, there has been little emphasis in the psychological literature on such actions. Chapter 6 deals with such behavior.

We have called Chapter 6 "Coping and Cognition." This may seem misleading at first since the word "coping" is generally used in the context of difficulty or adversity. Many circumstances, however, are both familiar and undesirable. In many of the situations where one must cope, the circumstances are quite familiar and call upon well-organized reactions.

There are two themes that are particularly figural in current discussions on the topic of coping. One is the centrality of the control concept. Striving for and achieving control are seen as defining what coping is all about. The second and related theme concerns what happens when efforts at control fail. The impact of such failure is seen as costly: one starts to feel helpless, and this helplessness in turn has a tendency to spread to other areas of one's life.

The recent discovery of the importance óf control and of helplessness has led to considerable fruitful discussion and research; at the same time, it has tended to create a somewhat lopsided picture. From the perspective of the material covered in the previous chapters, it would seem that there must be more to coping than control. Surely the way people perceive and understand situations must be important in dealing with difficulty. Likewise, helplessness could hardly be the inevitable consequence of the inability to exert control; human cognition is far more flexible and adaptable than such a simple equation would suggest. In this context, action strategies (such as control) are only part of the picture; there can be considerable value in interpretation strategies, too. Such strategies depend on changes in one's conception of things rather than changes in the things themselves.

This emphasis on interpretation, on how one thinks about a problem, can have multiple payoffs. It can help one decide where action is well spent and where it is not. It can also be an essential step in finding the most appropriate action. Finally, it is vital in its own right as a means of keeping one's cognitive map in shape, of updating one's knowledge to incorporate new realities.

While the emphasis in Chapter 6 is on functioning that is based on well-established patterns, whether involving desirable circumstances or not, Chapter 7 focuses on times when what to do next is far from obvious. This process has often been referred to as *problem solving*. Although the two chapters are thus distinct in terms of whether what to do next is already known or not, they share the common theme of the utilization of action and interpretation in the service of more effective functioning.

This part looks at two complementary facets of human functioning. Coping, which in the literature has been associated with undesirable circumstances, is here viewed as a set of mechanisms underlying *all* well-structured, well-practiced decision making. It is what makes possible the majority of our day-to-day functioning. Problem solving is sometimes viewed as a part of coping since it not infrequently occurs in the context of potentially undesirable outcomes. Most of the problem-solving literature, however, does not focus on the issue of undesirability. Rather it covers action that is less immediate, where time is required in order to reach a decision. We continue this tradition, emphasizing circumstances where what to do is not routine but rather the outcome of puzzlement, search, and struggle. Such problem-solving efforts involve discovering or inventing or creating what to do in the absence of suitable, previously learned patterns.

There is little doubt that the material dealt with in this part concerns cognition; it may not be so obvious, however, how it relates to the environment. There are several ways such a link can be made:

☐ People tend to deal with difficulties arising from the physical environment very much as they deal with difficulties in general. Whether it is a matter of the destruction of the immediate, familiar environment (such as by urban renewal or urbanization or, for that matter, suburbanization) or of being relocated to a new and unfamiliar place, the coping and problem-solving issues are not inherently different from those involved in other situations. Even the resistance to seeing the need to adopt less energy-expensive lifestyles and the tendency to deny the damaging effects of pollution have their parallels in human functioning in other domains.

☐ People have only so much capacity to deal with all the difficulties that surround them. Thus a supportive environment is first and foremost an environment that does not add to the burdens that people are already struggling with. An environment that is confusing, that takes total concentration just to keep from getting lost, is in this sense not a supportive environment.

☐ Much of the human impact on the environment is influenced by the processes of design, planning, and management. These are to a large degree instances of expert problem solving. Therefore, to understand what is happening to the environment, it is essential to understand how problem solving works.

chapter six

COPING AND COGNITION

One way to look at knowledge-based functioning is in terms of the question of what to do next. For any circumstance one comes across, ideally there would be an appropriate next action all ready to be carried out. In order for this to happen, there must be some way in which, out of all the information the individual has stored over a lifetime, the information appropriate to the situation is located and turned on. For smooth functioning there must be a rapid and continuous interplay between situation and cognitive structure.

To cast this issue in terms of the concepts we have discussed in previous chapters, "what to do next" crucially depends on the capacity to call up the cognitive map or portion of the cognitive map appropriate to the situation. One must recognize what is going on and locate the appropriate portion of one's associative structure for the situation. Fortunately, the very nature of the associative process will tend to locate the needed information.

When we try to remember something, the more potential associates of what we are searching for that we can bring to bear, the more likely it is that our search will be successful. When we are in the middle of doing something, there are all sorts of potential associates to aid the search. There is the perception of the current situation, the knowledge of what we were just doing, and whatever worries and suspicions, goals and aspirations were accompanying our actions. This network of potential associates underlies the remarkable human ability that Dreyfus refers to in his discussion of "orderly behavior without recourse to rules:"

> Whatever it is that enables human beings to zero in on the relevant facts without definitively excluding others which might become relevant is so hard to describe that it has only recently become a clearly focused problem for philosophers. It has to do with the way man is at home in his world, has it comfortably wrapped around him, so to speak. Human beings are somehow already situated in such a way that what they need in order to cope with things is distributed around them where they need it, not packed away like a trunk full of objects, or even carefully indexed in a filing cabinet. This system of relations which makes it possible to discover objects when they are needed is our home or our world. (1972, p. 172)

121

While the richness of association is a powerful factor in our "being at home in our world," it does raise a potential problem. With each element having so many associates, it might seem that chaos would result. Things would be lighted up all over the place, and confusion would reign. However, each of the "messages," or signals each element is sending out, is rather weak. Alone and unsupported, each message falls on deaf ears; it yields no consequences. For an effect to occur, a number of messages must *converge* on a single element in the system (Figure 6.1). In this way what is retrieved, or located, is that which is an associate of various elements in the current situation. It is, in other words, what is common to the various aspects of the situation. This pattern is called a *simplified broadcast procedure*, a modified version of Holland's (1974) model. Thus the broadcast procedure allows one to retrieve the appropriate por-

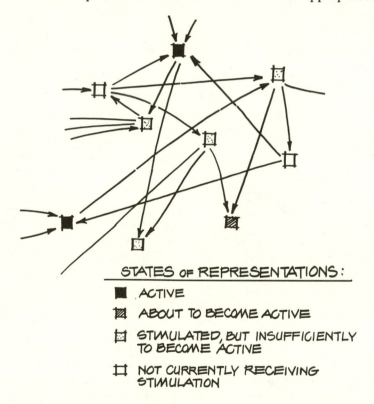

STATES OF REPRESENTATIONS:

■ ACTIVE

▨ ABOUT TO BECOME ACTIVE

▤ STIMULATED, BUT INSUFFICIENTLY TO BECOME ACTIVE

⊓ NOT CURRENTLY RECEIVING STIMULATION

Figure 6.1 Vastly oversimplified diagram of a *simplified broadcast search*. Note that the units here are representations and that their associative structure is directional. Although several units receive signals, only one in this diagram has received a sufficient convergence of stimulation to become active.

tion of the cognitive structure, which in turn can guide subsequent behavior.

This process works very well much of the time, producing a stream of behavior that tends to be smooth and adaptive. The successful operation of this mechanism yields the sort of functioning that is the topic of this chapter. There are times, however, when this mechanism fails. There is insufficient convergence, and no next element turns on. In such cases, of course, one does not know what to do next. Such failures of retrieval place one in a problem-solving situation; the more elaborate search procedures required in such cases are the topic of the next chapter.

Coping With Everyday Difficulty

People are confronted by things they don't like, things that go counter to their preferences. Not only do they face such affronts in the present; they also worry about what happened in the past, and they devote no little time to what might happen in the future. These difficulties are by no means all major; some are, in fact, rather trivial. Nor are these difficulties unique; some are quite familiar and recurring.

The fact that many of these circumstances are familiar and routine can even blind us to the potential difficulties that are inherent in them. Thus, for example, in planning a sequence of events or errands in a highly familiar environment, we can mentally play out the sequence and consider possible constraints well before arriving at the particular locations. It may be necessary to stop at the registrar's office before going to the bank or bookstore. The "logical" place to park may lead to a particular order for making one's stops. In familiar environments the integration of spatial and nonspatial information about the environment with the requirements created by one's own purposes can be remarkably smooth. It is at vulnerable times, however, such as when one finds oneself on crutches or is exceedingly tired, that the potential difficulties of such routines become evident. The seemingly undemanding fine-tuning and projections of one's microroute choice can suddenly demand considerable thought.

Calling on well-learned strategies to deal with familiar difficulties is an important aspect of coping. Such activity may sound too routine to belong in a volume devoted to environmental cognition. It may sound closer to habit than to thought. To hold such a view, however, is to lose track of what cognition is all about. The purpose of cognition is to enhance functioning, and functioning is precisely what such activity makes possible. To cope is to utilize the hard-earned cognitive structures previously laid down in order to maintain effective functioning in the present.

Another possible misconception concerns the use of the term "difficulty" in the context of functioning that is by definition relatively routine. It must be remembered that familiar patterns do not necessarily make doing what one has to do easy—they only make it possible. It must also be remembered that to cope is not necessarily to make difficulty disappear—but only to function. There is no stipulation that one cannot still yearn for what one prefers but cannot have.

The wife of a sea captain does not necessarily like the long separations such a career entails. These separations may never cease to be painful, but she is familiar with this circumstance and has patterns that help in functioning from day to day. A diabetic may not like injecting the insulin necessary to survive. A teacher may hate giving grades. A coach may detest telling aspiring players that they have failed to make the team. A minister may wish it was never necessary to conduct funerals. A parent may find cleaning up after a sick child most unpleasant. The difficulties in these cases are real. Yet despite them, the individuals function. Knowing what to do in these instances does not make life good—only possible. Dealing with the nonpreferred is stressful enough as it is, but it is by no means the whole of it. The uncertainty and complexity that made pattern recognition so demanding intrude here as well. We are hard pressed to prepare for the future since uncertainty and complexity drastically limit our ability to predict. Even if we did know what was going to happen, we could not be confident that what worked last time will work again (Chapter Note 1).

Such difficulties have long been a part of the human environment and the human experience. It is thus hardly surprising that human cultures have been deeply concerned with these issues. In fact, a culture can be viewed as a relatively coherent system of patterns for functioning. Thus, through membership in a culture, the individual falls heir to vast riches in terms of ways of dealing with difficulty.

Let us pause for a moment to review what we have said about coping. First, we are looking at regularized processes, that is, at the handling of familiar difficulties using familiar means. As we saw in previous chapters, familiarity is a shorthand for a tremendous amount of prior cognitive activity. Familiarity does not eliminate difficulties, but it often makes possible ways of dealing with them that are not distracting or upsetting or otherwise disruptive of ongoing functioning. A regularized approach involves cognition in the sense of structure; through experience a compact coding has been achieved so that channel capacity is not usurped.

A second property of coping is that it involves difficulty. Sometimes coping is sufficiently effective to eliminate the difficulty. More often the difficulty is made tolerable. The underlying issue in either case is that it becomes possible to function. Often the difficulty is easy to overlook. The boss who hates to fire people may never admit that such is the case. The dentist who hates to hurt people may not make repeated public apologies. The good loser may cry in private. It is noteworthy that in many instances the associates of a suicide had no idea anything was wrong.

A third property of coping is that it is active. This does not mean the coping individual is jumping up and down or running in circles. Indeed, the individual may not look active or, for that matter, even realize that anything is going on. However, the very fact that the difficulty in question tends not to disappear suggests that it continues to be dealt with. Coping is a continuous process to which some of the individual's resources are devoted.

Perhaps a biological analogy would be helpful here. Scurvy, the disease that results from a vitamin C deficiency, has a number of symptoms, one of which is rather peculiar. Old wounds that healed long ago become unhealed in the individual suffering from scurvy (Pauling, 1970). This phenomenon stands in sharp contrast to the conventional view of healing. Apparently healing cannot be considered to be a process of solving a problem, of restoring the integrity of the body once and for all. Rather, healing must in this light be seen as an active process of maintaining that integrity. Healing represents not a problem solved but a problem under control. The coping process is directly parallel. Coping keeps things under control. It is an active, continuing process, not a once-and-for-all phenomenon. It is ongoing; like healing, it is not irreversible. As with healing, its invisibility is a sign not of inactivity but merely of its continuing effectiveness.

PATTERNS OF COPING

Coping strategies are remarkable in their flexibility and dazzling in their diversity. It would be futile to try to list them all. Despite their number and variety, however, they can be described usefully in terms of a small number of rather general dimensions. One of these is defined by the distinctions between conceptual strategies and action strategies.

Conceptual strategies involve the ways one views things, the interpretations one makes of what is going on. Interpreting the pain in one's arm as an injection of a life-protecting vaccine makes it more tolerable than, say, interpreting it as the injection of some harmful material. Likewise, a mistake that one makes can be thought of as an unforgivable transgression or as another sign of one's personal incompetence or as a natural concomitant of learning a new skill. The "I'm OK, you're OK" formulation reflects a strategy that is explicitly conceptual.

Action strategies require that one do something, that one take overt action. What the action is can vary widely. Chasing an intruder off one's front lawn is an action strategy, but so is knocking on wood or throwing rice at a newly married couple.

Another useful dimension along which these strategies vary involves the directness of connection between the strategy and the physical reality it attempts to deal with. Tromping on worms that are eating the tomatoes in one's garden is a direct strategy. A less direct strategy might involve using plants that have been bred for their worm resistance or planting marigolds with the tomatoes to repel the worms. The distinction here involves feedback: can one test the effectiveness or appropriateness of one's strategy promptly and directly, or is it blurred by time and by other factors? Although there is undoubtedly a preference for the prompt and the direct, there are many matters of importance to humans that cannot be resolved so readily. Philosophies of life and approaches to child-rearing, like many scientific theories, cannot be validated quickly or easily.

Based on these two dimensions, the action/conceptual distinction and the degree of connectedness to physical reality, it is possible to characterize certain basic categories of coping strategies. (It must be emphasized that these distinctions are made for purposes of analysis. In reality, most strategies are undoubtedly mixed rather than pure cases.) The most obvious way people handle difficulties is through *control*. This strategy is so pervasive that it is easy to think that it is the only one available. It tends to be on the action side and generally closely connected to the physical situation prompting it. *Ritual* is also oriented to action, but characteristically lacks prompt and obvious feedback. *Interpretation* involves a class of strategies that are conceptual rather than active and can vary widely in terms of the feedback function.

Control Strategies

A powerful way to prevent a sense of helplessness is to exert control. Knowing what to do, and doing it, are both effective and enjoyable. Individuals routinely exert control over their environment, and over each other as well. They rearrange their furniture, plow their fields, put up fences, and decide who will and who will not enter their dwelling. Control includes securing a desirable environment for oneself and keeping it desirable. Where no desirable alternative is available, it entails taking what is available and changing it to better suit one's requirements. The action orientation of control is quite evident. Control also tends to engender high feedback, although there is quite some variation here. While tromping on marauding worms and planting worm-resistant plants are both control strategies, they differ widely in promptness and directness of feedback.

Control is often exerted in an effort to make an environment more satisfactory for an individual or group. At other times, a major goal of control is to prevent change and to preserve some setting in its current form. The properties for which a given setting was chosen may subsequently be endangered, requiring control to maintain "choice-worthiness." Territorial behavior provides a vivid instance of the use of control to preserve that which was chosen. It expresses itself at the group or community level (potentially contaminating outsiders are repulsed), at the cultural level ("America for Americans"), and at the individual level ("This is *my* room"). Most people are probably territorial at some level, albeit to varying degrees. (Edney, 1976, has a particularly useful discussion of the relationship of territorial behavior to control issues.)

Figure 6.2 Territory at the individual level.
Douglas Kinsey

Territorial attachments are frequently connected with a place, as Fried (1963), Gans (1963), and others have demonstrated so vividly. In other instances, an individual may be involved with an intellectual territory and may be much less concerned with any literal segment of the earth's surface (Greenbie, 1974; S. Kaplan and R. Kaplan, 1978). Although such different expressions of territorial feelings can and do exist side by side without necessary conflict, there are times when difficulties arise. It is apparently difficult for many intellectuals to believe that anyone would be deeply attached to a particular place, a particular neighborhood, a particular configuration of the physical environment (Klein, 1978). Certainly they would not be too attached to want to give up one place for a "better" house somewhere else. When planning for people whose territorial attachments are less cognitive and more physical, this failure of empathy can have tragic consequences. Perhaps the intellectual could understand the strength of attachment more keenly if he or she considered being informed (say, by the government) that there was a need to change professions: "We are a bit overstocked on chemists right now, so we're shifting you to sociology." Or vice versa. The many settings in the modern world where forced relocation has occurred testify to the suffering caused by the failure to acknowledge the literal quality of territoriality for many people (S. Johnson and Burdge, 1974; Scudder, 1973).

Figure 6.3 Behaving as one is expected to.
Douglas Kinsey

Control is sometimes of the environment, sometimes of the behavior of others, and sometimes of the flow of information. Environmental control is exerted every time a change in physical design is carried out. As Newman (1972), Yancey (1971), and others have so forcefully pointed out, control of this kind can either facilitate or impede what happens in the social and informational domains as well. Control of the behavior of others is illustrated by an effective community. While conformity to community norms is in some sense a sacrifice of control on the part of the individual, it is an asset at the same time. Through such behavioral control what the other members of the community do becomes substantially more predictable, thus reducing the uncertainty of that aspect of the environment.

Environmental and behavioral control ultimately lead to informational control as well, but there are times when informational control is undertaken directly. Secrecy, where there is a great concern to limit the access to certain information, is widely practiced. It has engaged the ingenuity of lovers, medicine men, baseball coaches, generals, corporations, and governments, among others.

Ritual as a Strategy

Control strategies are so pervasive that it might seem there are no other strategies for functioning. One might even regard circumstances where there is no possibility of control as inherently debilitating. However, it is a delusion to believe that one could control all the factors influencing one's own life. There are many events and circumstances that do not yield to a direct strategy. Even in cases where one does have some control, exerting it may reduce one's control over subsequent decisions: deciding to run for public office restricts one's privacy; deciding to undertake serious athletic competition may restrict smoking, drinking, staying up late, and how one spends a significant portion of one's time.

The world is full of difficulties that are not manageable in so straightforward a way as control permits. Uncertainty is a particularly powerful factor here. One takes action, but there is no way to ascertain the impact of that action. The consequences may be greatly delayed, or they may be difficult to discern directly. When planting seeds in a particular way, how can one be sure that an increased rate of germination is attributable to the new technique? Many of our activities lack clearcut feedback or confirmation. Educating the young, healing the sick, carrying out foreign policy—in none of these cases do even our most earnest and dedicated efforts have the clear, immediate effect that characterize ideal instances of control.

On the Semantics of Control

Control is at present a popular concept in psychology (Chapter Note 2). Some of its supporters could almost be called imperialistic; concepts only indirectly related to control tend to be brought under what has become a rather diffuse category. The resulting blurring of conceptual lines is not only confusing; it may be harmful for humane and responsive decision-making. It thus seems appropriate to devote some attention to what otherwise might be seen as a merely semantic issue.

Control.   Where an individual has a determining influence on an outcome.

Predictability.   A state of affairs perceived as orderly; functioning is enhanced because one knows what to expect. If one knows what time the mail is picked up every day, one can see to it that one's letter makes it on time. If the time of pickup varies randomly, it is harder to know what to do. In neither case is one likely to believe that one is controlling the time of pickup. (Nonetheless a number of authors use the expression "cognitive control" to refer to such instances of having appropriate prior information, e.g., Averill, 1973; Baum, Singer, and Baum, 1981. Since this usage does not correspond to the usual meaning of the term "control" and could lead to conceptual confusion, it is probably best avoided.)

In control.   A state of affairs that is not only predictable but stable in some larger sense. It includes the belief that those in charge—the powers that be—know what they are doing and can respond to events in such a way that continuity and predictability will be preserved. People are often concerned that the events that happen around them are in control (Cantril, 1966) without wishing to be the ones doing the actual decision-making.

Participation.   An activity that gives one an opportunity for a meaningful role with respect to some valued outcome. Individuals filling out a questionnaire about how they would like water runoff handled in their part of town appreciate the opportunity to be heard (R. Kaplan, 1977a). While they collectively have some impact on the outcome, it is unlikely that any individual considers the activity an exertion of control. The same applies to voters in an election and to participants in a rain dance.

Condition setting.   An individual concerned with solving a difficult problem might utilize various strategies to enhance the process. These might include getting plenty of rest, alternating periods of intense concentration with relaxing and enjoyable breaks, and talking to others about the problem. There are reasons to believe that these might be helpful and appropriate aids to problem-solving. They certainly do not constitute control of the process. It is not unusual in human experience that a desirable state can be courted but not controlled.

As we have seen, control strategies persist despite less than ideal feedback. However, at a certain point the effects of our actions are so obscure, so remote that our behavior is no longer guided in any sense by outcome. In such cases we are forced to rely on lore, on custom, or on expert advice. Patterns of action whose correctness is independent of their outcome are often called *ritual*. Although we tend to think of ritual in terms of patterns dictated by group or culture, ritual strategies operate at the level of the individual as well. This is particularly evident in sports, where uncertainty is perhaps more visible than in other activities. When a winning team suddenly plunges into a losing streak for no apparent reason, the uncertain hand of fate is more forcefully apparent than in some less public, less overtly competitive activity. Perhaps it is for this reason that sports figures cling to their private rituals. The outfielder who always touches second base on the way to the outfield and the pitcher who talks to the ball demonstrate such patterns. Undoubtedly soldiers and surgeons have their share as well.

Although ritual is probably a universal phenomenon among humans, negative feelings toward such practices are not uncommon. Ritual may be seen as inappropriate for members of a modern, advanced, scientifically oriented civilization. But science has nothing to say on many issues. To refuse to act without assurance of effective outcome is to fail to act in many circumstances. Even scientists commit themselves to courses of action that have consequences that are at best in the distant future. In an uncertain world without at least a modicum of faith, one is paralyzed.

It is important to recognize that there are no sharp, clear lines between ritual and control. When one takes aspirin to control a headache, the action is presumably based on cumulative past experience with certain kinds of headaches that respond to aspirin. When one lays out seven kinds of medication to take at breakfast each day—the cumulative advice of various sources—it is no longer clear that these are acts of control as opposed to ritual. Nonliterate cultures have been using various medicinal herbs for eons. Some of them turn out to have no effect. Others are effective and have been adopted in contemporary medical practice. Still others await evaluation. The issue here is not whether or not these are effective strategies, but that there is often no way for the individual carrying out the activity to know whether or not there is a direct relationship to the problem.

There is another benefit of ritual in addition to the possibility that it might be effective. It provides people with a mandate for action in circumstances where what to do is far from obvious. In other words, by providing well-structured actions for difficult situations, ritual prevents people from feeling helpless where helplessness is a real danger.

Seligman (1975) has argued that helplessness readily generalizes, that it often becomes a way to respond to new situations where one could make a difference if one only tried. If this contention is true, then ritual plays a particularly vital role. As Strong (1977) pointed out, by preventing helplessness ritual not only leads people to feel better in that situation; it also precludes their transferring their helplessness to other situations, where passivity could be dangerous.

Interpretation Strategies

Many times situations present themselves where one cannot readily change matters, nor can one know what action would be appropriate. Nonetheless, one feels confused, and finding a way to achieve some comprehension helps substantially. If one has a way of relating what one experiences to some internal model, confusion is reduced. In effect, one must be able to tell oneself a story about it. Sometimes the story or model constitutes a theory about some phenomenon: "It must be something I ate." Even though the discomfort is still there, the explanation helps reduce the uncertainty. Sometimes it involves placing the phenomenon in a familiar context, drawing on associations to other concepts without any effort at explanations: "Don't mind old Uncle Henry. He always acts like that." At other times it may involve representing what is going on as beyond the bounds of one's own competence: When people say, "I never did understand that," they suggest that they do not plan to now either. They cut off. They are not confused by something potentially confusing because they have withdrawn from interacting with it.

These are examples of interpretation strategies. They entail solutions that are essentially conceptual; they reduce one's confusion about circumstances that are difficult to comprehend. As with the other strategies, they are solutions that are fairly regularized and readily repeated. Here again, these are patterns that are applicable at various levels—ranging from explanations imposed by individuals for their own pattern of meaning to those that are the shared understandings of a group or culture. Interpretation involves simplifying and organizing the universe, translating situations into terms that facilitate comprehension or permit ignoring certain situations—at least for the moment.

Both forced relocation and devastating natural hazards such as floods and earthquakes cause major disruption to an individual's physical and conceptual environment. Under such circumstances one would expect considerable damage to the victims' interpretive structure. In other words, one would expect not only feelings of helplessness, but confusion as well. This is consistent with the findings of Birnbaum, Coplon,

"The county must have drained the swamp."

Reprinted by permission of Audubon Magazine and Henry Martin

and Scharff (1973) in their study of crisis intervention. Social workers were able to assist people after a flood by providing them with information about available services and by aiding them to develop appropriate priorities for their new situation. Given the confusion and helplessness following a loss of a familiar and hence supportive environment (Proshansky, Nelson-Shulman, and Kaminoff, 1979), the typical behavior people display in the context of natural hazards seems less bizarre. The denial of the threat, the refusal to leave, the returning to the same site to rebuild (Burton, Kates, and White, 1968), all may be reasonable if the abandoning of the familiar environment is likely to extract an overwhelming cost in terms of the loss of informational and conceptual support.

An interesting perspective on the role of interpretation strategies is provided by an insightful paper on "Coping with undesirable life experiences" (Silver and Wortman, 1980). Dealing as it does with individuals who have faced or are facing personal disasters, the paper provides a rather grim but at the same time reality-based perspective on human cognition. One of the most striking aspects of this material is the urgency such distressed individuals feel to put their concerns and experiences into some sort of interpretive form. They wish to make some sense out of it, to find some way to explain and understand their situation. This sense of urgency apparently has an adaptive payoff. Individuals who ultimately blame themselves for what has happened end up relatively better off as far as recovery is concerned. While help-providers tend to discourage it, self-blame does provide a relatively compact, coherent interpretation and one that need not require a revision of the victim's entire interpretive framework.

Interpretation strategies can involve explanations that are readily confirmed or rejected. We can, for instance, observe the puff adder's ferocious antics and reassure ourselves by remembering that it is just bluffing and will soon turn and slither away. When it does so, we have confirmation of our interpretation. However, the uncertainty that so often undermines control plays havoc with interpretation as well. One can arduously construct a theory about the world, only to see that theory undermined by a blatant exception. One can, of course, promptly abandon one's theory (this is what some scientists like to pretend they would do), but it turns out that any theory, and especially any theory simple enough for humans to find useful, will run into intermittent exceptions. To be constantly abandoning one's theories is to be left without ready interpretations too much of the time. Then things will really be confusing. Thus holders of theories, be they scientists or cave people or theologians, have found themselves forced to weaken the tight connection between their theory and the feedback the world provides. They may speak of being borne out in the long run, or in terms of values that are not immediately obvious.

Thus interpretation is not one strategy but many. As with the action-oriented strategies (control and ritual), these range from ones closely tied to environmental feedback to those that are highly conceptual and far removed from everyday reality. Interpretation is a means of creating boundaries, of identifying where effort is appropriately expended and where it is not. It is a means of reducing disappointment. It is also much more than that. The domains that are beyond human influence, and even beyond human comprehension in any ordinary or direct sense, are not merely walled off and ignored. This would be to leave them strange, alien, disturbing. Through interpretation those domains beyond control, and even those beyond prediction, become recognizable, even familiar. They take their place as part of a larger picture.

Despite the apparent centrality of the interpretation strategy from a cognitive perspective, there is relatively little discussion of this way of functioning in the literature on how people cope with difficulty. Perhaps the most striking exception is Frankl's (1963) treatment of the search for meaning in the lives of survivors of World War II concentration camps. Another perspective on interpretation strategies is provided by the work of a leading researcher in this field who has recently begun to consider a broader range of strategies (Lazarus, 1980). In addition to control (which he calls "direct action"), there are three types of strategies in Lazarus's framework, each of which has ties to an interpretation mode of functioning.

The first of these is "inhibition of action," where an individual decides that not doing something is safer or wiser in the long run. It clearly depends upon some internal model permitting longer-range prediction.

"Information seeking," the second model, nicely parallels R. W. White's (1974) emphasis on the role information must play in any approach that looks at people as active, coping individuals. If successful, such information seeking necessarily leads to information-acquisition. Then, if it is to be useful, such information must be organized into one's pre-existing cognitive framework. It must become a part of one's map, of the story one tells oneself about the world. In this perspective it is easy to see why the philosopher Mary Midgley (1978) has postulated integration ("getting one's head together," in the modern idiom) as a basic human need.

The third type of noncontrol strategy Lazarus refers to as "intrapsychic." As "the things a person says to himself," this is clearly an interpretive strategy. Its role, however, is conceived rather narrowly. "These modes are mostly palliative in that they make the person feel better by reducing or minimizing emotional distress" (p. 38). While this is by no means a trivial function, it makes it seem as if adjustments in one's cognitive maps have no implication (other than emotional) for future functioning. Achieving a new understanding, a new way of relating, is not only an emotional adjustment. When an overly optimistic individual becomes resigned to more realistic goals or when an individual has survived a brush with death and decides on a reordering of priorities, these are adjustments with pervasive implications for future behavior.

Recent research in coping tends to support the functional as well as emotional importance of strategies centering on interpretation. In a discussion of work at the NIMH Laboratory of Socio-Environmental Studies, McNett (1981, p. 43) describes the work of Pearlin on the structure of coping:

> People devise different mechanisms to cope with stress in different areas of life. Mechanisms that succeed in a family situation do not necessarily work very well on the job. Indeed, he found job stress less amenable to coping strategies than other areas of human life. The jobs seem not to bend as much as the people do. He wrote, "In the economic and, to a modest extent, occupational roles, the most effective types of coping involve the manipulation of goals and values."

A pivotal role of strategies of this kind is in redirecting one's energies to where they are likely to be effective. The significance of making such discriminations is forcefully presented in a paper entitled "Expectations and what people learn from failure" (Janoff-Bulman and Brickman, 1980). Learning that some things are beyond one's grasp is not an admission of helplessness but an adaptive advantage. Persistence is not always a virtue. In successful mammalian hunters, for example, persistence is often lacking. The chase is readily abandoned if the outcome seems unlikely to be fruitful (Peters and Mech, 1975). Another benefit of interpretation, as far as behavior is concerned, is that it allows one to stop thinking about a distressing past event. It enables one to put the event in a framework, to treat it as history, and to resume functioning in the present. Behavior benefits from cognitive support and suffers from distraction. Interpretation permits cognition and behavior to become connected once again.

Given that humans are persistently presented with circumstances that defy comprehension, with disasters that know no bounds, with acts by fellow humans that defy understanding, it is not surprising that many kinds of interpretations are shared by groups and cultures. Perhaps nowhere is the human reliance on cognition more evident than in the effort to cope with environmental uncertainty. Here humans look to each other for help; they rely on interpretations that are widely shared. To avoid feelings of confusion and helplessness, humans have found it necessary to rely on mental constructs—on conceptual approaches.

CULTURE AS FUNCTIONAL KNOWLEDGE

There is a deep and ancient need in us to make sense out of important events, and to record the words and deeds of great men, as a part of the process of survival. This goes right back to our tribal hunting past; the story helps us to identify friends and enemies, safety and danger, courage and cowardice. It gives us a wider understanding of the world about us than we can gain from personal experience. (Jay, 1971, p. 280)

Individuals ultimately must struggle to fend off confusion and helplessness on their own, but they receive a good deal of help from their social groups and especially from the larger culture to which they belong. An individual in a culture grows up learning the rituals, the interpretations, and the techniques of control that have become traditional in that culture. However, culture is far more that a collection of successful shared solutions, valuable as that might be. When a member of a culture confronts a problem, the cultural context not only provides directions for solutions; it helps define the problem itself. It provides a way of looking at the problem that shapes its eventual solution. Thus solutions arising in a cultural context tend to have many connections with pre-existing elements of the culture. In part for this reason, a culture tends to be integrated, connected, coherent. Cultures build a critical mass of shared solutions, not as mere collections, but as systems.

Recent research has pointed to the importance of such a coherent framework for healthy human functioning. In a study of the psychological factors that led some people to be less susceptible to illness than others, Antonovsky (1979) identified the "sense of coherence" as the crucial underlying issue. Underlining the critical role of culture in providing this sense of coherence, he quotes Malinowski's description of the sort of challenge the environment provides:

> But however much knowledge and science help man in allowing him to obtain what he wants, they are unable completely to control chance, to eliminate accidents, to foresee the unexpected turn of natural events, or to make human handiwork reliable and adequate to meet all practical requirements. (quoted in Antonovsky, p. 118)

In dealing with these urgent uncertainties, culture provides for its members cognitive maps of all sorts. Some are abstract, some concrete. Some culturally provided maps are extensive and detailed, whereas others are sketchy and fragmentary. Also, different cultures will differ in their emphases and in the ways in which coherence is achieved.

Despite such rampant variability, however, the nature of humans and the nature of the world they live in require that any culture, to be viable, must help people cope with three central issues. These are all issues where cognition unaided by a larger cognitive system tends to fall short. (1) People must have a map that relates them to the environment and particularly to making a living in relation to the ecological constraints characteristic of their particular environment. (2) People must have a map that guides their relations to other people. Being able to anticipate what one's cohorts are likely to do is essential for efficient cooperation, such as that which characterizes human social groups. (3) People must have a map that guides them in that larger world they must contend with. People are highly conceptual and imaginative animals. Their concerns are not solely with the here and now. They worry about where they came from and why they are here. They are concerned not only about the realities of disease and disaster, but also about their origins. They are troubled by indications that the universe might not be fair and that it might not make sense after all. In these and many other perplexing matters, people look to their culture for some larger perspective, for some coherent story that helps them make sense.

Ecological Content

A high priority of any culture must concern ways of making a living, of satisfying physical needs given the resource pattern of a particular environment. This must be dealt with at a cultural level for a variety
of reasons. First, it is difficult for the unaided human to deal with the
time spans involved. Ecological relationships may be discovered only after a great deal of experience. Some important events (e.g., a flood or
drought) may happen only rarely. There thus needs to be some
supraindividual basis for guiding behavior. Witherspoon (1977, p. 180)
describes how effectively such guidance is incorporated in the way the
Navajo views the world:

> A Navajo does not say a prayer to the inner form of a deer explaining his
> need for the deer and asking for the deer's indulgence simply because it is a
> kind and gracious thing to do; he does so also because it reminds him of
> the deer's right to life and the necessity for him not to be excessive or
> overindulgent in his use of the deer, for such excessive behavior could
> throw the whole world out of harmony and balance and that would be
> dangerous to his own survival.

Harris (1974) has described how well suited to the available resources is the pattern in which a poor family in India keeps a cow but
considers eating cow meat taboo. Rappaport (1967) has studied a New
Guinea culture that periodically raises pigs to sacrifice to their ancestors.
He, too, comes to the conclusion that cultural patterns that look strange
indeed to outsiders can be highly effective in relating humans to the
available resources in an enduring, nondestructive fashion. Here, complex and colorful cognitive structures interface humans and the physical
environment in a strikingly harmonious way.

Another reason cultural involvement is essential in the way people
relate to the resources of their environment involves coordination. In
general, a pattern of ecological relationships works only if everyone follows it. Any individual's decision not to kill the goose that lays the gol-
den eggs is effective only if all individuals refrain from killing the goose.
Just as many environmental problems have been created by people behaving without restraint, appropriate ecological behavior characteristically requires restraint. A vital element in coordinated behavior of this kind
is trust. In Hardin's (1968) compelling fable, not adding to one's flock of
sheep grazing on the commons is essential to the long-term viability of
the commons. Such behavior is likely to occur when the culture man-
dates it and when the culture is sufficiently effective that one can trust
others to behave comparably. Without a basis for confidence in the coordinated restraint of others, one is unlikely to accept the restraint one-

self. Lacking a shared pattern of this kind, each individual is likely to maximize short-term gain (i.e., act without restraint), with a disastrous long-term outcome. Hardin has aptly called this result "the tragedy of the commons."

Social Content

A second domain with which cultures must be concerned involves other people. The human pattern of survival has been, throughout human evolution, a social one. Humans have hunted together and tended flocks together. They have defended themselves and challenged other human groups together. Yet there is evidence that humans have the capacity to be dangerous to other humans, especially when frustrated, angry, or confused. They also have a great capacity to be competitive. Thus, to maintain effective cooperation, cultures must be able to deal with these potentially disruptive capabilities.

Douglas Kinsey

One example of such a cultural mechanism is the elaborate status hierarchy that prescribes how people are to behave in all sorts of circumstances and defines who shall have precedence over whom. Another cultural means of dealing with tendencies that are potentially socially disruptive involves heavy emphasis on the correct behavior among fellow humans. It is wrong to lie, to steal, to covet, to murder. Not feeling safe in the presence of other humans is not conducive to cooperation.

There are indications that humans have also evolved certain tendencies toward cooperation. They like to be near other humans, to listen to the stories and songs provided by other humans, and in turn find the attention of others highly rewarding. On the other hand, as D. T. Campbell (1975) has pointed out, humans seem to need additional help from their culture to tip the balance in favor of cooperation. It is certainly striking how common such themes as devotion to others, sharing, and sacrifice are in many otherwise quite different cultures.

Conceptual Content

The third domain requiring cultural involvement concerns the peculiar cognitive nature of humans. As we saw in Chapter 5, humans are inclined to be painfully distressed by confusion and by helplessness. This is a valuable inclination, since it keeps humans struggling to be clear and to be competent. It is also a problematic inclination. It is problematic in part because there is so much in the world that is confusing and so much that one can do nothing about. It is problematic also because humans have the capacity and inclination to explore, to wonder about, and to imagine issues far beyond the immediate time and space. Humans have the capacity to become concerned with such matters as where they come from and what happens to them when they die. They worry about the origin of the universe and the forces that operate in it. These are matters for which direct evidence is difficult to obtain. When humans have difficulty finding out about something, they have a tendency to consult other humans. Given the strain toward coherence that characterizes culture, there will be a tendency for the stories of the various others to agree. In other words, there will be a consistency in the answers to these more conceptual questions.

Such an arrangement is of enormous advantage to the members of a culture since the widespread agreement and support tend to put to rest what otherwise can be disturbing and distracting issues. The more a culture can achieve widespread affirmation of its belief system, the more believable it will be. In turn the culture will receive increasing loyalty from its adherents since it does such a good job of interpreting the world (i.e., being believable). Sharing and affirmation, in other words, lead to conviction, which in turn reduces the suffering brought on by the unexplained and the confusing.

Culture and Perspective

Each of these three central domains constitutes not only an area of cultural concern but an expression of evolutionary influence as well. In the ecological domain, there is indication that humans share certain types of environmental preference. As we have already seen, there are numerous generic influences in the social domain. People are greatly interested in other people, they are greatly concerned to be accepted by their group, and they are strongly disposed to aid at least certain other humans (Midgley, 1978). The evolutionary contribution to the conceptual domain includes the capacity and inclination to build cognitive maps, the capacity to think abstractly, and the powerful motivation to comprehend the patterns of experiences.

Thus culture stands, not in opposition to, but in support of evolutionary themes. Culture has become a necessity for the survival of a cognitive, cooperative, far-ranging animal. As Midgley puts it, people have evolved to require culture.

Culture is, then, a means of extending cognitive power. It functions to share the useful cognitions of individuals across an entire group. It also aids in what is the hallmark of cognition, namely, the weakening of the hold of the immediately present environment on the individual. The development of sensory and response systems through evolution led to animals that could react appropriately to changing circumstances. Viewed another way, however, it led to animals under stimulus control, animals whose behavior was closely tied to fluctuations in the environment. Cognition acts to reduce this tight connection. A cognitive organism can delay. It can wait for a better time or for more information. Cognitive organisms can reflect on the past and plan for the future. Both these capacities reduce the influence of the immediate environment.

With the advent of culture, the link to the immediate environment is further weakened. Culture emphasizes the importance of things that cannot be directly perceived. Comparably it de-emphasizes certain aspects of the here and now. Some cultures focus on a distant place (like Heaven and Hell), some on a distant time (either in the past or in the future), and some on both. Like cognition, culture enhances perspective. It places the present in a larger context.

Culture enhances perspective in another sense as well. Humans have a limited basis for knowing what life will bring them. A child must prepare for a future as yet unexperienced. It is not clear how much it is possible to achieve, how much one can know and do. Indeed, the child's own immediate experience is most misleading in this respect. As a relatively protected, nurtured individual in most societies, a child is likely to have a sense of a rather supportive, friendly world.

Comparably, a child experiences a very rapid development of knowledge and competence. A child could readily come to the expectation of someday being able to know everything. Here, too, the limited experience of the young individual tends to provide a misleading view of the world.

The perspective-enhancing role of culture functions here to offer cognitive structure based on a vast pool of human experience. Culture provides an indication of what is reasonable to hope for and what is reasonable to expect. Relative to the dreams of omnipotence and omniscience harbored by the child, the message of culture is one of human finiteness, of human limitations. It is thus hardly surprising that the young of the species at times view this emphasis as dampening and unwelcome. However, knowing what is and what is not achievable by humans greatly facilitates focusing one's efforts where they might have an effect. Selective resignation frees people from futile striving. There is also encouragement from culture to transfer control, to look to a leader or a higher power to achieve certain things beyond the capacity of the individual. Much interpretive material in culture reflects the message that humans must accept being limited and learn to live within that reality. It is a message of reassurance and comfort to older members of the culture, however defeatist it may seem to the young.

An analysis of the major world religions by Laszlo (1977) suggests how pervasive is the theme of human limitations. Strategies for how to cope with this reality vary, although even here there are striking similarities across religions representing different parts of the world. One recurring strategy involves reducing (or eliminating) one's ties to material things, or even to all things external. The implication is that one can be hurt by what might happen to what one cares about. Hence the less one cares about or is attached to, the more tranquil one can be. Some religions picture humans as too small to see the larger picture. It all fits together, but we cannot comprehend it. A related theme emphasizes the weakness, even the insignificance, of the individual and argues for the necessity of identifying with forces in the universe larger and more powerful than oneself. D. T. Campbell (1975) argues that this strategy essentially commits the individual to the goals of the larger society, here embodied in a higher power.

Thus the perspective provided by culture is that of a smaller human in a larger world. These two themes are often linked together. The content the culture carries from the past (which adds to its legitimacy) both creates a larger world and contributes to the identity of its grateful members. Knowing who our ancestors were expands our cumulative existence and helps compensate for our individual smallness. Culture also provides some idea of what the future might be. In this way, too, the world is expanded, while at the same time the human place in it is made more concrete. A grasp of what the future might hold is a central factor in human purpose; it offers a vision of something worth working for.

SOME CONCLUDING COMMENTS

In this chapter we have dealt with instances of functioning that are based on relatively familiar, well-practiced patterns. The fact that they are familiar is important. As we have seen before, to be familiar is to have internal representations; it is to have the capacity to act in a more decisive, more confident manner. Despite variability and uncertainty in the environment, if one can identify the difficulties in terms of some prior experiences and therefore have some capacity to predict and evaluate possible eventualities or next steps, one can function.

In many recurring situations, especially if they present difficulties, it is well to have relatively ready-made, fairly automatic reactions. Avoiding confusion is worth a great deal. However, to say that coping involves fairly routine, regularized patterns is not to say that these patterns are inflexible, nor that the range of patterns lacks diversity. The richness and complexity of human cognitive capacities apply as much to coping as to other aspects of functioning.

There are several ways in which cognitive structure operates to increase the diversity and enhance the flexibility of this process. The range and variety of reactions available to the individual are vast. Ritual, control, and interpretation are not three possible strategies, but three enormous classes of strategies. What real people in real situations use are not strategies in this sense but complex patterns of strategies, often integrating elements of two or all three categories in a larger whole. Cognitive structure enables people to learn, to remember, and to use all sorts of different rituals, means of control, and interpretations, as well as innumerable combinations of these elements.

Before one can call on some particular alternative embedded in this complex cognitive structure, it is necessary to determine whether the alternative is appropriate to the occasion. In other words, recognizing patterns is prerequisite to selecting a suitable strategy. As we have already seen, human pattern recognition is complex and heavily dependent on pre-existing cognitive structure.

Recognizing a pattern is necessary in determining what one's reaction shall be, but it is not by itself sufficient. It is not the case that people react the same way every time a given pattern shows up. What went before, what other patterns are present, and the larger context all make a difference. The way a given member of our culture reacts to a police officer, for example, depends upon what one was just doing, whether or not one is in need of help, and whether the particular officer is an acquaintance or a stranger. The complexity of potential reactions does not change the fact that the ultimate reaction may be well learned and routine.

The potential richness of cognitive structure makes possible a large repertoire of reactions and the skill to use them subtly and differentially. It makes possible this capability, but it does not guarantee it. Organizing this structure requires experience, and one's own experiences are necessarily limited. One's grasp of the world is enormously extended by incorporating as well the experiences of others, the cumulative lore and experiences of one's culture and group. One is thus both dependent on this knowledge and, in a sense, limited by the way it helps structure one's view of the world.

So individuals cope. They receive help from their culture and help from their group, but they must, in the end, function on their own. They take some things on faith, and they ignore some things. They limit the range of what they consider possible. They put off some things for later. By these and other means, it becomes possible to tackle problems that are within one's scope and capacity.

NOTES

1. Stress

Given the apparent smoothness of so much behavior, the emphasis on difficulty may seem to be exaggerated. An indication that this assumption of smoothness may be mistaken comes from a longitudinal study of a random sample of New Haven residents (Lindenthal and Myers, 1979). An assessment of the degree of psychopathology among over 700 participants in this study yielded the conclusion that 18 percent could be considered "very impaired" and 47 percent "moderately impaired," leaving only 35 percent in the "unimpaired" category. Another indication of the prevalence of serious difficulties in people's lives is provided by the extensive psychological literature on stress. For discussions that are particularly sensitive to the cognitive dimension of human functioning, see McGrath (1970, 1977) and Stokols (1979). Useful overviews of environmental stress are provided by Baum, Singer, and Baum (1981) and Cohen and Weinstein (1981).

2. Control and Perceived Control

The work of Glass and Singer (1972) has been central to the widespread interest in the control concept. Averill (1973) provides some useful cautions concerning the relation of control to experienced stress. More recently, research on control has been carried out in various other contexts as well (see Perlmuter and Monty, 1979).

Although there has been a tendency to consider control as the best means of coping with any and all situations, some recent studies suggest the appropriateness of a more moderate position. Of particular interest is a study by Rodin, Rennert, and Solomon (1980) that directly tests the impact of control on self-esteem when other factors are held constant. Contrary to expectations, self-esteem was *lower* for subjects who had control. After extending and replicating this finding, the authors conclude that having control when one does not understand enough to make a meaningful choice may not be in the least satisfying. Once again, comprehension, prediction, and participation may be the critical variables.

An important caution in terms of interpretation of the concept concerns the expression "perceived control." Various studies have shown that participants who are told that control is available to them tend not to test if this is in fact true and experience less stress (see Sherrod and Cohen, 1978). The suggestion that individuals do not need actual control since they are quite happy with perceived control must not go unchallenged, however. This is a dangerously misleading assumption; in the long run being lied to is destructive of trust and hence of informational exchange. In a moving discourse on this topic, J. Shuttleworth (1979), the founder and editor of *Mother Earth News*, argues that the proportion of false and incorrect information emanating from officialdom has been sufficiently high as to essentially undermine the credibility of this source. While this may seem to be a rather strong statement, citizens attempting to comprehend the Three Mile Island emergency found little to contradict Shuttleworth's contention in their experience with information from official sources (see Baum, Singer, and Baum, 1981). Providing confusing, contradictory, or misleading information is not in the long run an effective means of winning the favor of an astute information-processing system.

chapter seven

PROBLEM SOLVING AND PLANNING

All of us make innumerable decisions all the time. Much of our functioning escapes our notice; we just do it. It is difficult to appreciate that cognitive maps guide our actions when the actions themselves take virtually no time. It feels like we do so many things without thinking; the responses seem automatic and immediate. The lack of hesitation or delay is characteristic of the types of functioning we discussed in the last chapter, on coping.

There are times, however, when decisions are more difficult to make, when the process is halting or even stymied. It is at such times that it becomes believable that the various processes that have been examined throughout this volume are actually requisite to functioning. When one is in a quandary, one might express concern about not being sure that one has properly identified the problem (i.e., recognition) or that one cannot anticipate the likely outcome of a decision (i.e., prediction) or that one cannot judge which is the more appropriate alternative (i.e., evaluation). In groping for an approach, one becomes aware of searching one's knowledge—of using one's cognitive maps—for anything at all that might help.

It is such times, when behavior is not a smooth series of actions, that provide insight into the more usual ways of functioning. The smooth and unhalting approaches we have at our disposal in many instances had their beginnings as groping, hesitant actions. *Problem solving refers to a large class of activities that have in common that they require time, that they involve a break in the ongoing stream of behavior.* This discontinuity occurs because it is not clear what to do next. Problem solving is the process of figuring out what to do. Its "product," the decided-upon action, is what coping is based on.

This is not to say that there is some clear, identifiable distinction between coping and problem solving. Sometimes the time involved in problem solving is so short as to be barely noticeable, and the disruption in behavior may be so slight that one does not realize a delay in functioning. Not only are coping and problem-solving at times similar in appearance; they are actually highly interdependent. It is through problem solving that one discovers the ways of dealing with difficulties that form the basis of coping should those same difficulties occur again. Thus problem solving provides the patterns of action that make coping possible. On the other hand, were it not for coping, the individual would be overwhelmed by difficulty. It is only by treating most difficulties in a fairly efficient, straightforward way that one can afford the often time-consuming problem-solving process for certain difficulties (Chapter Note 1).

PROBLEM SOLVING AS A SEARCH PROCESS

Problem solving is often discussed by alluding to a spatial analogy. There is the current situation, one's current "place," called START, and there is the desired state, where one wishes to be, called GOAL. Between the two there is a gap—a lack of an obvious path. Problem solving can be thought of as the search for that path (Figure 7.1).

In the spatial context, the meaning of "finding a path" is fairly obvious. One is searching for a route from where one is to where one wants to be. Although the emphasis is on a path, what one is usually interested in is the sequence of places, of landmarks, that one must pass to get from here to there. Thus the successful solution of a spatial problem of this kind might be to "go straight until you get to the bank, then left to the corner with the service station with the orange roof, and the store you're looking for is halfway down the hill toward the river." In nonspatial problems, too, the path one is seeking is generally defined by a sequence of things, processes, or entities. *In terms of cognitive maps, the sought-after path is a sequence of associated representations.*

While this is a reasonably intuitive and helpful way to conceptualize the process, one should not be misled by its neatness and simplicity. GOAL, for example, is depicted in Figure 7.1 as a single entity. There is, however, a large set of so-called ill-defined problems, where it is quite unclear what the goal is. Sometimes there are a few criteria for it, but nothing unitary or coherent. At other times, there is only a vague sense of dissatisfaction with the current situation. Like GOAL, START also must be considered to be a convenient fiction. START stands for that portion of the current situation that bears on the problem. Often it particularly concerns the tools and resources one has to work with. As with GOAL, it is often the case that START is quite vague and poorly articulated. These complications need not undermine the usefulness of the conceptualiza-

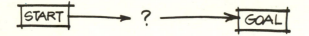

Figure 7.1 The general problem-solving situation.

tion as long as it is kept in mind that START and GOAL are each shorthand for a whole complex of fascinating issues.

A search for a path between the current situation and the desired state is not unique to problem solving. Such a search is involved in every instance in which action is based on information stored in memory. As William James (1892, p. 157) put it:

> In short, we make search in our memory for a forgotten idea, just as we rummage our house for a lost object. In both cases we visit what seems to us the probable neighborhood of that which we miss. We turn over the things which, or within which, or alongside which, it may possibly be; and if it lies near them, it soon comes into view. But these matters, in the case of a mental object sought, are nothing more than its associates. The machinery of recall is thus the same as the machinery of association.

In the case of problem solving, however, the "machinery of association" does not yield a result immediately—the sequence cannot be retrieved without further action.

Let us consider what this means in terms of the scheme of retrieving information described earlier. Certain representations are turned on in the process of pattern recognition. These represent the current situation. Other representations—corresponding to the desired situation—are turned on as one thinks of them. These various representations all send out, or broadcast, signals. In the case of coping, they converge rapidly on the appropriate sequence. This is because the circumstances are familiar and there have developed strong associations that channel the signals along the sequence. In the case of problem solving, these strong associations are missing. A suitable path is not retrieved promptly (Figure 7.2). Thus the smooth, continuous stream of behavior is interrupted. The individual is, at least for the moment, "stuck."

The immediate reaction to such a failure of retrieval is to lower the level of inhibitory control, thus making it easier for representations in the system to be turned on.* This way, a representation that was receiving converging signals but was not strongly enough stimulated to turn on could make its presence known. This lowering of the criterion makes it possible to come up with connections one did not even know one had.

---

*The voluntary attention concept described in Chapter 5 depended upon a global inhibitory mechanism that was postulated to influence the thought process. The purpose of voluntary attention is, of course, to prevent anything from interfering with the currently active representations. When the overall level of inhibition is increased, weak activity is reduced and is less likely to grow stronger. In the initial phase of problem solving, the opposite problem is presented. Here, there is a need to encourage weak activity, which has shown itself to be incapable of becoming strong without help. Rather than increasing inhibition, therefore, enhancing the search process would require that inhibition be decreased, that there be a reduced level of control.

Figure 7.2 Diagram of problem-solving situation where broadcast search has not yielded convergence.

Fresh insights can arise in this fashion. At the same time, by lowering the criterion one is risking coming up with irrelevant material, with "solutions" that do not make sense when examined closely. (One time when the criterion is naturally lower is right when one is falling asleep. It is not uncommon to come up with brilliant insights at such times, insights that, if one can remember them, seem rather foolish in the hard light of day.) To counter such risks, problem solving characteristically includes an evaluation phase, where the adequacy of the possible solution is tested. This will be discussed later in the chapter.

Although the description here is relatively molecular, stated in terms of activity among an individual's representations, it has a close analogy to brainstorming as a way of generating new thoughts or approaches. Here, too, the ground rules are to reduce the controls and permit things to be said that later evaluation might rule unuseful. By generating many ideas, there is a chance of coming up with something worthwhile.

Although lowering the criterion can lead to a blinding flash of insight, such is not necessarily the case. Often the problem is solved gradually rather than all at once. The search for a path between START and GOAL may initially yield only fragments rather than a sequence. In effect, the problem becomes divided into smaller problems, and the GOAL is temporarily considered in terms of subgoals (Figure 7.3). Each such subgoal constitutes a new representation of the scene and hence a new source of broadcasting signals. Thus finding a subgoal can substantially reduce the difficulty of the problem.

Sometimes, however, lowering the criterion does not help. A new convergence still fails to emerge. It may be that the problem is insoluble, or it may be that it is not soluble given the information one currently

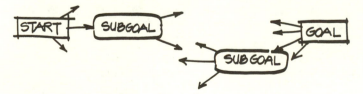

Figure 7.3 Problem-solving situation where search process has generated sub-goals.

has available. Before resigning ourselves to such a dire outcome, however, let us consider a quite different alternative. When one does not find what one is looking for, one may be looking in the wrong place. Let us examine the matter of "where one is looking" in the context of the theoretical framework developed so far.

Cognitive Maps in Problem Solving

One's perception of the current situation and one's conception of the desired state together determine what is sometimes called the "problem space." It is in this space that the path, if there is one, is to be found. However, a space is not a map. For a given space many maps are possible, and, conversely, for many spaces one has no map at all. Efforts to discover a path must depend to a great extent on the individual's associative structure for that particular problem space. It is this structure that we have been referring to as a cognitive map.

Sometimes one already has an extensive, well-developed map of the problem space. When one is asked for directions in one's home neighborhood, one has a substantial map to work with even though the particular path being sought may involve a route one has never traversed before. Many times, however, quite the opposite is the case. One has only a few vague notions of the problem space. One has, in effect, no map at all. A common spatial example of such "maplessness" occurs every time one enters an unfamiliar building and attempts to reach a goal through inspection of the posted floor directory. Unfortunately, what could be an enlightening experience all too often turns into confusion and frustration. Lacking a cognitive map, one can readily experience difficulty even when well-intended efforts are made to correct for such a deficiency (Figure 7.4).

Given the central role that a well-developed map assumes in the problem-solving process, it is perhaps not surprising that the human reaction to important but infrequent events tends to appear strange and even irrational. As we have seen, natural hazards are a class of events that fit this description well. Floods, hurricanes, and the like are so infrequent that people have little experience on which to base their actions. The result is a variety of seemingly inappropriate behaviors. People will build on a flood plain even though they have been warned of the dangers (Burton, Kates, and White, 1968). People who have experienced a flood are likely to rebuild on the same spot. When asked if they are not fearful of a recurrence, such individuals have been known to respond, "Oh, we've had our flood." Kates's (1962) analysis points directly to the critical role of experience, not just for citizens but for managers as well, in forming a basis for appropriate action. He found that it

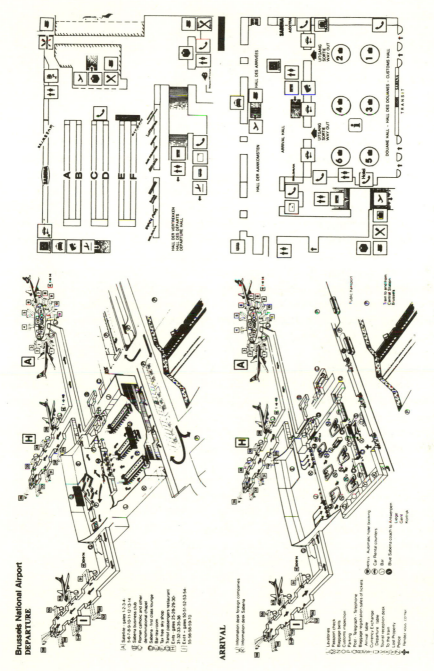

Figure 7.4 Here are two versions of attempts to guide the visitor in an unfamiliar environment. The top row shows the departure area of the Brussels National Airport, while the bottom two maps show the arrival area. Figuring out the correspondence between these pairs provides a useful exercise and no small challenge. (Thanks to Michael Fuller for providing this illustration.)

was necessary for individuals to experience not only the magnitude of floods, but also their frequency. Managers lacking such repeated experience did not prepare the appropriate emergency measures that would enable them to cope with future floods.

Lacking a map can leave one with an uncomfortable feeling. Given a problem and no map to structure it, confusion and helplessness lie just around the corner. It is thus understandable that people tend to be in a great rush to get through with this phase. Short-cut means of establishing a map are widely used. There is a sense of relief when one has a map—any map—that will help structure the problem-solving process. However, if the analogy of looking in the wrong place for a path is a valid one, then the reckless haste to establish a map may cost dearly in the long run.

A cognitive map, as we have seen, is made of object-like units, of coherent patterns for which one has representations. Lacking such meaningful units, one is sorely tempted to create them. One popular means is by definition. Many intellectual efforts, including technical documents, textbooks, and dissertations, are likely to begin with a flurry of definitions. While this often fails to be a map-enhancing experience for the reader, it has the reassuring property of creating what seems to be a structure to organize the problem space.

A related strategy is a spin-off of computer programming. In this case a few key words are extracted from a verbal description and boxes are drawn around them. This quickly establishes an aura of concreteness, of having the necessary entities for building a map. Such procedures can be helpful in capturing a possible rendition of the problem domain, but as a substitute for naturally emerging units, they can actually undermine the mapping process. The units that make up a cognitive map are distinct. Such units tend to be quite separate from one another, thus facilitating recognition and simplifying relationships. Merely stating a definition or drawing a box around a word cannot be assumed to establish separate entities. It is not uncommon to have an essentially similar "entity" referred to by two different names or to include in a long list of items several that are basically the same (Figure 7.5).

These are, then, quick procedures for assembling what might superficially resemble a cognitive map. It is not clear, however, that there is any quick way for acquiring the sort of structure that will facilitate the pathfinding process.

STRATEGIES OF PROBLEM SOLVING

There are times when one faces a problem and is not clear on what map to use, or even whether one has a map that is potentially helpful. What do you do when you don't know what to do? Judging by the

ENVIRONMENTAL PERCEPTION

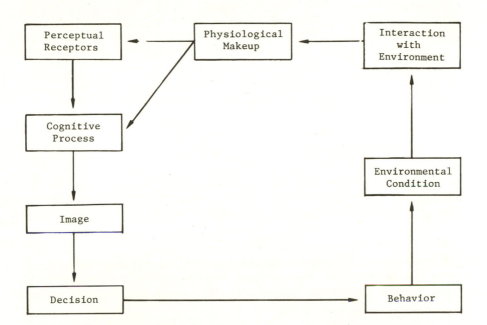

Figure 7.5 A premature flow diagram. There are some problems here with the lack of distinctiveness of elements: how are "image" and "decision" distinct from "cognitive process"? How are "perceptual receptors" distinct from "physiological makeup"? What is the difference between "behavior" and "interaction with the environment"? Furthermore, the elements are on different levels of abstraction and the meaning of the arrows is not consistent. (Note: It is difficult to find a "good" bad example. Reproducing one from a published work would be decidedly unfriendly; making up one seems forced. This is a compromise— a flow diagram based on a reasonable conception by a highly competent graduate student. It has been modified somewhat in the hopes that its author will be spared the embarrassment of recognizing it.)

ready availability of advice on this subject, the situation is not unusual. And judging by the conflicting nature of the advice, either anything will work—or perhaps nothing does. In any event, strategies for problem solving do not lend themselves to a tidy categorization or to a failsafe formula.

When considering the kinds of strategies one utilizes in searching for a path to a desired solution, it is striking that so many of them involve opposite aspects of the same approach. While such a situation is perplexing and confusing, it does not necessarily signify that the approaches are inappropriate.

☐ Leave it alone or keep trying: There are times, as we have all experienced, when problems seem to solve themselves. When considered in terms of the search process requiring convergence, such an event does not seem farfetched. Variations occurring with the passage of time permit one to try out different combinations, some of which can have far stronger convergence than did the original pattern of activity. Yet, at other times, problem-solving is enhanced by persistence. If one is capable of reducing inhibition and permitting increased activity, it is possible to become "unstuck" and to proceed and make progress by staying with the situation.

☐ Relax or pay close attention: This is similar in some respects to the previous contrast. Relaxation involves a reduction in inhibition, and this, as we have seen, can be a useful device. On the other hand, at a different phase of problem solving, close attention may be necessary in order to discover additional properties of the problem space that might be important.

☐ Random trial and error or a concerted and focused approach: Here again, the search for solution can be in different phases where either of these extremes would be appropriate. Solving a jigsaw puzzle can be approached in both these ways. Sometimes, when the components seem hopelessly similar, trial and error may seem the only reasonable "system" to follow. At other times, focusing on the details of the shapes or the pattern of the puzzle may facilitate solution.

☐ Add constraints or reduce constraints: This set of contradictions will be discussed more fully, but for the moment it is useful to point out that both extremes seem to provide useful advice for problem solving.

If nothing else, these examples of scattered and contradictory advice suggest that problem solving requires sensitivity to the state of the problem. Problem solving requires time, and along with the time there seems to be a pace. An attempt to use a persistence strategy when leaving the problem may be called for will do little toward finding the solution and may, in fact, do damage to the process. Ideally one would recognize the nature of the situation and thereby match the strategy to the requirements.

The ability to achieve such a match is necessarily influenced by how well one understands the problem to be solved. If one is thoroughly knowledgeable about the problem domain (or problem space), one can identify the elements to manipulate and carry out this strategy quite intentionally. Such an approach will be called *analytic*. By contrast, when one cannot identify elements, one can deal with the conceptualization of the problem only in an overall fashion. This more groping and less focused approach we shall call *global*.

Global Strategies

Global strategies entail doing something to the entire problem structure. Frequently this involves translating the problem into a different form or manipulating it in an essentially undirected fashion. Some of the misguided strategies that were mentioned in the previous section might fall under this heading, for example, trying to make an abstract problem more concrete by drawing boxes around what seem to be the essential parts. On the other hand, the use of diagrams or charts can also involve helpful translations of one's understanding of the problem to something "out there" in the world, where it is easier to take a look at it. Explaining the problem to someone else may also play a similar role.

When one begins to play with one's diagrams, trying out different arrangements, one has moved from translation to manipulation. If the problem involves physical elements of manageable size, one can sometimes manipulate the actual "places" rather than manipulate a diagram representing the elements. Other manipulations might fall between these extremes. Thus, for example, putting each element of a problem on a separate scrap of paper creates something different from a visual model or diagram, and yet the end result is highly flexible and manipulable for purposes of problem solving. Taking advantage of spatial and visual processing, examples discussed in the next section, may also be useful in this context.

Many of these approaches involve externalizing the problem. One calls on the environment for support to find a way to "see" the problem. Arranging information in such a way that it is readily grasped by eye and brain can facilitate problem solving in a variety of ways:

1. Manipulation of elements of the problem is easier.
2. There is less effort required to "keep the problem in mind."
3. It can encourage a clearer conceptualization of the problem.

Analytic Strategies

In sharp contrast to global strategies are those based on the analysis of START and/or GOAL. Although these analytic strategies also involve translation, and especially manipulation, they do not have the mechanical quality that is characteristic of global situations. Instead of dealing with the problem space as a whole, analytic strategies are sensitive to the parts.

In general, analytic strategies focus on *constraints*, on the factors that limit or restrict the possibilities. For a designer planning a project, for example, the constraints would include the purposes the project is to serve, the terrain, soil conditions, and other properties of the physical environment, and so on (Chapter Note 2). Although constraints often seem obvious, they can be difficult to nail down. The financial constraint, for example, is often rather obvious. Consider, however, designing a housing project that is to be attractive, inexpensive, and a satisfying place to live. "A satisfying place to live" is a rather vague specification; it would probably be necessary to consider such matters as legibility, identity, and privacy before one could spell out the constraints involved.

Knowledge of constraints is used in different ways in different circumstances. Sometimes one's map is greatly enhanced by the addition of constraints. This is particularly true when one has only a limited grasp of the problem and has trouble coming up with a map in the first place. Just as it is easier to think of a word when there are constraints (what is the name of a flower?) than when there are none (just think of any word), it is easiest to structure a problem space given constraints. The task of designing a house that can be of any size and for any site and without cost limitation is rather difficult to tackle. Many people would structure such a problem by adding their own constraints. Without that it is hard to know where to start.

More commonly, one is surrounded by too many constraints. Given enough constraints it is always possible to preclude all paths. There is simply no way to get there from here. Eliminating constraints is a rather different process depending upon whether one's focus is on the START side of the problem or on GOAL. On the START side one is dealing with reality constraints. One is dealing with things about the situation (such as site characteristics or available resources) or about the world (such as gravity or Parkinson's Law) that one assumes to be true. Reducing the constraints in this portion of the problem space often requires a playful stance. One pretends that some identified aspect of the situation is not pertinent. For example, one chooses to ignore for the moment the fact that the site is covered with 20 feet of solid rock or that the people who will use the facility are elderly. Taking such an "as if" stance is hard for some people; on the other hand, the problem-solving literature suggests that it can be an important way to proceed.

The other domain where reduction of constraints can make a map more amenable to pathfinding is, of course, the GOAL region. There one is dealing with evaluative constraints. Reducing constraints here is equivalent to lowering one's aspiration in some respect. One might consider "what if we didn't have to complete the project in a year" or "what if the individual units didn't have to look like Swiss chalets." Sometimes by weakening a single evaluative constraint one can not only solve the problem, but solve it in a way that involves strengthening some of the other constraints at the same time. At other times an overall lessening of evaluative constraints is called for. In such cases one considers one's previous goals to have been "unrealistic expectations."

If one is stuck, then something about the way one is going about the problem must be wrong. If one is not successful in generating possible paths between START and GOAL, then alternative ways of viewing the

Figure 7.6 Redefining the present situation changes the character of the search process.

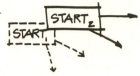

problem must be sought (Figure 7.6). Anything that changes how one defines some aspect of the problem has a chance of ending the impasse. When the search process fails to yield a new path, finding some way to modify the basis of one's search is essential. As William James (1892, p. 359) has so eloquently pointed out, even so common a substance as water has no single, correct characterization. There are multiple ways of viewing things, and hence there is room for considerable variety in the way one thinks of any given problem:

> Readers brought up on Popular Science may think that the molecular structure of things is their real essence in an absolute sense, and that water is H–O–H more deeply and truly than it is a solvent of sugar or a slaker of thirst. Not a whit! It is *all* of these things with equal reality, and the only reason why *for the chemist* it is H–O–H primarily, and only secondarily the other things, is that *for his purposes* of laboratory analysis and synthesis, and inclusion in the science which treats of compositions and decompositions, the H–O–H aspect of it is the more important one to bear in mind.

A central theme in our discussion of the perception of objects (Chapter 3) was the absence of critical features in the way things in the world are recognized. It is a consequence of this variability that there is likely to be more than one way in which any given thing can be thought of. By seeking some of these alternative "essences," a solution may be reached. The inflexible insistence that the problem is as stated is likely to generate no new insights. Through variability then, through the variety of ways of playing with the parts, one might reach a different conceptualization of START, of GOAL, or of both.

EVALUATION AND PLANNING

Problem solving involves a complex set of processes for dealing with circumstances where one does not know what to do—or what to think—next. Up to this point our primary concern has been how to produce possible next thoughts or next actions. This production phase of problem solving generates not solutions, but *possible* solutions. Since the production of alternative thoughts or actions occurs in the absence of any obviously correct alternatives, it is an inherently risky process. For this reason evaluation is an intrinsic part of problem solving. Any alternative that is produced must be evaluated to determine if it is satisfactory or if the search process must be continued.

We have already considered how the organism evaluates what is going on in the environment (Chapters 4 and 5). The evaluation of possible solutions to a problem is essentially similar. The common evaluative coin of the system is the same. The primary axes of evaluation are, as before, pleasure/pain and clarity/confusion. Sometimes one or the other of these dimensions is particularly salient, and sometimes both operate. A "good" solution, for example, may make "everything fall into place." It produces a feeling of clarity that is often the hallmark of successful problem solving. On the other hand, a solution may "feel good" or "feel right" without being accompanied by any sense of clarity. It may, for example, be favorably evaluated because it "has all the advantages." In such cases the connection to pleasure elements is presumably dominant.

Lookahead and Problem Solving

For the type of problem studied in the laboratory, the production phase is usually by far the most difficult part. Consider some typical examples: one is asked to complete a puzzle or to construct a hatrack out of what seem to be inadequate materials or to tie together two strings that apparently are out of reach of each other. In each of these cases generating a solution absorbs most of the time and effort. Evaluating the solution is trivial; it either works or it does not.

In the problems dealt with by environmental professionals, by contrast, the *evaluation* is often the most difficult part. For the environmental designer or manager, alternative solutions can be produced in large numbers. The trick is to evaluate their implications, to choose among them. A major factor underlying this difficulty is the necessity of involving the future in one's considerations. Using one's capacity for lookahead (a concept introduced in Chapter 3) becomes central in evaluating solutions to problems of this kind.

All problem-solving requires a lookahead phase, at least to some degree. This is the case because all potential solutions are, literally speaking, for the future. For practical purposes, however, there is a great range. Some problems are concerned with a future so close that it can be considered to be essentially in the present. For other problems, the future plays such a pervasive role that it permeates the entire process, not just the evaluative phase. In a rough-and-ready fashion we can categorize problems in terms of their degree of future involvement:

START	GOAL
1. Present	Present
2. Present	Future
3. Present/future	Future
4. Future	Future

The Type 1 problem is well represented by the typical task used in laboratory experiments. The GOAL is so immediate that it is for all practical purposes in the present. Problems in real life often take the Type 2 form. Small-scale land use decisions—buying a house, planting a field, drilling for oil—begin in the present but have their implications in the future. Type 3 problems violate the orderliness of the table. This hybrid type is included because it is characteristic of so many planning decisions. The action is to be taken in the present, but the present may be taken to include a substantial period of time, such as the "present decade." In other words, much of the START condition has not yet happened but is assumed to be continuous with what already has. In this way the planner is often dealing with an "extended present."

Such assumptions about the continuity of present trends into the future have an air of unquestionable reasonableness about them. It is, after all, essential to establish some sort of baseline if any sort of planning is to occur. How could one object to so straightforward a way of anticipating the future as to assume that whatever is the case today will probably be the same or more so tomorrow? Such projections can, however, be self-fulfilling. If many people want houses in the suburbs, one can assume that there will be more such demand in the future. *Assuming* the demand and planning for it will certainly permit, and may even encourage, the trend. However, such a convenient and narrow view of the future ignores issues of energy consumption, the need to preserve agricultural land, and even the advantages of preserving some of the qualities that people went to the suburbs to find in the first place. As with other activities that require extensive lookahead, the quality of planning is heavily dependent upon the way that the conception of the future is constructed.

It would appear from the table that Type 4 problems are among the most difficult, and this is indeed the case. Unfortunately, many of the most important environmental problems fall in this category. Running out of oil, for example, is not something that has happened yet, but unless strong measures are taken now, it will. Hence we have a problem which has not yet happened but which may be orders of magnitude more difficult to deal with by the time it does. It goes without saying that people do not have a good record on this sort of problem (Chapter Note 3). Envisioning the future, a crucial missing link in both this and the Type 3 problem, is discussed in the final section of the book.

Decision Making and Rationality

Decision theory in psychology and the "rational man" theory prevalent in economics and related disciplines address themselves to how people make choices given alternatives whose payoffs may be uncertain (Chapter Note 4). These theories tend to characterize humans as attempting to optimize their expected gain; it is taken for granted that humans in such situations have all the information they need. From the perspective of theories of this kind, actual human choice behavior is, to say the least, disappointing. People fall far short of this conception of rationality, as seen in laboratory studies (e.g., Nisbett and Ross, 1980; Tversky and Kahneman, 1981), in the behavior of victims of natural hazards (see Kates, 1962; G. F. White, 1974), and in many other contexts.

As a matter of fact, from the perspective of the rationality theories, people often appear downright stupid. While human behavior can, in many situations, leave much to be desired, there is as much problem here with the theory as with the fact. *Implicit in these theories are three assumptions, all of which are demonstrably false.* Fortunately, they are false in interesting ways. Thus by examining these assumptions we can gain some insight into what does go on in the decision-making process—with both the strengths and the weaknesses that are involved.

☐   *People have perfect knowledge.* Given the difficulty of acquiring cognitive maps and given their potential for incompleteness and even distortion, it is hard to take the perfect-knowledge assumption seriously. On the other hand, the very existence of this assumption points to the importance of the cognitive map in the decision-making process.

☐   The assumption that people are motivated to maximize their gain hides within it two implicit assertions. It is assumed not only that people wish to maximize but also that *there is some unitary gain dimension to which all valued events can be compared.* Since all things can be related to this ultimate good, then things can be substituted for each other according to this metric. In other words, if one's feelings about a view of green things rates a 5 on this universal scale and if one rates having a friend as a 2.5, then two additional friends should compensate for a loss of a green view. Foa and Foa (1974) have demonstrated that there is a minimum of six basic areas of concern (love, status, money, goods, services, information) that are not fully substitutable for each other. Based on our prior discussion of needs and preferences, there are likely to be even more.

Another problem with this emphasis on gain is that it assumes people are making their decisions based on the expectation of some particular outcome. Midgley (1978) appropriately raises the question of when that outcome is to be calculated. One is in process most of the time; for so many decisions it is hard to know when to stop and decide if it was the right one.

☐ *People's choices represent attempts to optimize, that is, to select the best alternative out of all possible alternatives.* Here again the assumption is instructive because it provides such a sharp contrast to so much human behavior. While there are certainly times when this assertion is true, there are at least four reasons, or groups of reasons, for the frequently observed departure from optimality. Each of these reasons constitutes not an area of human perversity or stupidity, but an adaptive reaction to a world of enormous complexity and uncertainty.

Choosing what is "Good Enough." Simon (1957) speaks of the human tendency to "satisfice." While this has been criticized as an overly broad and imprecise concept (Tversky and Kahneman, 1981), as a part of the larger issue of nonoptimization it is a meaningful, useful, and even insightful concept. The basic principle here is the human inclination to choose what is *good enough* rather than to hold out for the best. People are characteristically impatient and intolerant of ambiguity. They find indecision uncomfortable. If a choice is adequate, that is, good enough, why not take it and get on with things? Having evolved in a world where indecision would often have been more dangerous even than wrong decisions, such a bias is not unreasonable.

Problems of Information-Gathering. The issue of the high cost of additional information is typically included in the concept of satisficing. There is, however, an important distinction here. Satisficing as used here refers to the disinclination to seek beyond that which is good enough. Even when one is inclined to seek the best, however, there are formidable difficulties in one's path. One may not know that pertinent information exists, or one may simply find the costs in time and energy prohibitive. Choosing a college (or other significant environment) might be a more optimal decision if one first visited all colleges. For practical reasons this is not common practice. The disinclination to persevere in such situations is quite obviously adaptive.

The Management of Uncertainty. Human decision making based on probabilities exhibits a number of peculiar characteristics (see Slovic, Fischhoff, and Lichtenstein, 1976; Tversky and Kahneman, 1981). A typical study in this area involves describing situations to people in terms of a mixture of probabilities ("30 percent of the cabs in the city are yellow") and concrete instances ("three cabs have just gone by, of which two were green"). Given descriptions of this kind, people reliably take the concrete information far more seriously. Such behavior is considered to be irrational by researchers in this area. On the other hand, in the environment—as opposed to the laboratory—the probabilities of events tend to fluctuate over time. It may thus be that people's caution at accepting probabilities at face value makes good sense.

The Familiarity Bias. Familiarity is so powerful a factor in human cognition that it is hardly surprising that it makes a difference in how people make decisions. One factor here is what Tversky and Kahneman (1973) have called *availability*. The examples one can most readily think of, those that are most available, are a powerful determinant of how likely people consider a certain outcome. Thus recent experience, direct as opposed to indirect knowledge, and frequency of contact all play a role here. There is a bias toward a reality that is concrete, current, and frequent.

Many times, however, several potential solutions can be equally available. A further bias that operates in these situations is in the direction of the alternatives that are not very different from the current situation. Such a bias toward *incrementalism*, toward making only small changes whenever possible, ensures that one stays reasonably close to one's knowledge base. By leaving the familiar only slowly and cautiously, one is more likely to be able to comprehend and guide what is happening, and there is always the possibility of returning to the starting point. Lindblom (1964) has argued that, contrary to traditional decision-theory formulations, this is actually the way people in management situations make their decisions. He calls this cautious, feedback-sensitive pattern of behavior "muddling through." W. Johnson (1978) has utilized this model of decision making as a tool to look at how the growing scarcity of fuel and other resources is likely to be responded to. In his perceptive book *Muddling toward frugality*, he suggests that if the resource picture changes gradually enough, the characteristic muddling mode is likely to keep us on track as we stumble down that arduous road toward a sustainable existence in a finite world.

Together these biases suggest how pervasive is the human commitment to the status quo. The pull of the familiar, reflected both in availability and in incrementalism, is understandable as an expression of the functioning of a knowledge-dependent species. In this light the widespread resistance to adjusting to a world of scarcity is hardly surprising. On the other hand, the analysis suggests the potential power of *prefamiliarization*. If people were to become thoroughly familiar with alternative futures and their implications, then the terror of the unknown would play less of a role in the process of making necessary adjustments. In this regard it is particularly fortunate that the futures we face are not totally without precedent. The high utilization of fossil fuels is a very recent phenomenon. The pattern of life in this country a mere 50 years ago would be regarded from our current perspective as a highly conserving one. As Johnson points out, far from being unthinkable, living on a low-energy budget may even have quality of life advantages that were more characteristic of former times than of today.

Thus the familiarity bias need not express itself as a status quo bias. Rather it is a cognitive map bias; it mirrors the strengths and weaknesses of our current conceptions and of our imagination. Information and the sharing of information are thus central to defining the space within which we can solve problems and make decisions.

The failure of the rationality or decision-theory model to characterize the ways alternatives are evaluated does not mean that humans are inherently irrational. Human behavior is not unreasonable given the nature of the environment and the pressures of human evolution. Repeatedly we have seen that the departures from "rationality" are reflections of the dependence on cognitive maps, on the knowledge that people have incorporated about themselves and their world. There is little point in becoming obsessed with the issue of whether, according to some preconceived set of standards, humans are rational or irrational; rather the focus must be on conditions under which human behavior is reasonable in terms of the limits inherent in the environment and the requirements of our—and other—species. Our concern here must include humans in their various roles—as planners, as public officials, as citizens—since the same decisional biases apply. The pattern of evidence appears to be quite clear; reasonable behavior at any level of influence and responsibility depends upon an adequate grasp, upon a comfortable comprehension of the constraints and possibilities that define the available choices.

EXPERTS AND UNCERTAINTY

The more the future plays a role in problem solving, the more complex the process becomes. With increasing uncertainty it becomes difficult even to comprehend the problem, let alone solve it. In our society, as in many others, problems so laden with uncertainty are often delegated to experts, to people who function as professional problem solvers. Through education and experience such people come to approach problems in their area of specialty quite differently from the way a novice would approach the same problem. In fact, some problems are managed in such a smooth, essentially routine fashion that one might be tempted to say that the expert is no longer going through the struggle of problem solving but merely relying on well-learned, and by now rather routine, patterns of behavior. While this is undoubtedly true to some degree, in part it is a misunderstanding based on the image the expert often likes to project. The "leave it to me, I have everything under control" stance often found in experts tends to obscure the struggling and fumbling that often do take place (more on that in Chapter 10). Problem solving in expert hands may be better organized and more confidently undertaken, but much of it is still problem solving.

There are a number of reasons one might want to take a closer look at expert problem solving. From a practical point of view, it is the basis for a great deal of decision-making concerning environmental and other public policy issues. It is also of particular theoretical interest because of its very facility. Watching an expert solve a problem with skill and efficiency, one cannot help but wonder about the special tricks that exist to help bridge the gap between START and GOAL. Thus there are reasons to study expert problem solving in terms of what it might be able to tell us both about experts and about problem solving.

In terms of the framework we have developed so far, perhaps the most striking factor that sets experts apart from the rest of us is their familiarity with the content in question. Experts are more familiar with the pertinent material for many reasons. To begin with, their education involves reading about case studies, struggling with projects, perhaps even dissecting the results of other experts' failures. Beyond the formal education stage there are often apprenticeships, internships, clerkships, and the like to further extend the experts' familiarization. In some professions fledgling experts are then expected to work in the back room, to be a part of a larger office, to acquire even more of that priceless experience. Other professions permit their fledgling experts out on their own at that point, to acquire further experience on someone else's problems.

This emphasis on broad familiarity with a particular class of problems is certainly understandable. Experts are asked to take on areas of enormous uncertainty. They are asked to determine what will make a sick person well, what will make a bridge cheap but safe, what will enable a school system to teach all its charges to read. These are problems where failures are rather visible and where causation is frequently obscure. There is much unavoidable uncertainty in these problems. At the same time, there is a component of the uncertainty that can be reduced. Beyond that, there is much benefit to be gained from creating a familiar structure around the unpredictable. Being able to recognize areas of uncertainty, and to label them, to place them in a larger framework, helps one to keep such areas within bounds.

Familiarity and Representation

As we have already seen, internal representations are the consequence of experience. They provide the benefits of simplicity, of essence, of discreteness, and of unity. These are powerful assets to call on in a problem-solving situation. Their effect is so pervasive that it is hardly surprising that familiarity constitutes an enormous advantage in the way an expert approaches problem solving. Let us consider some of the ways this facility affects various aspects of problem solving.

What will be represented? When one first confronts a problem—whether it be a sick tree or a faltering transportation system or a house plan that does not fit the budget—there is a potentially infinite number of things one could look at. It is easy to be overwhelmed right there, without ever taking the problem any further. Having experience with a class of problems leads to possession of a set of representations that gets one over this initial hurdle. Being familiar with a type of problem means that one knows where to start, that one knows what to pay attention to. Here the property of *simplicity* is particularly crucial since so much potential noise is eliminated. One is also depending on *essence* in that one is able to look beyond first appearances to the aspects of the situation that are likely to be critical. Thus START is less likely to be ill defined since recognition of the salient features of the problem is greatly facilitated.

How much can one grasp at once? There are, as we have noted, a staggering number of different things going on in any given situation that might be pertinent to problem solving. So much is going on that it is unlikely that an individual can represent the situation in its entirety. The notion of "limited channel capacity" refers to the fact that only a small portion of all the knowledge that is stored in long-term memory can be active or in "working memory" at any particular moment (Chapter 5, Note 1). Figure 7.7 provides a graphic rendition of this state of affairs.

The limitation here is on how much of the system can be active at one time. This in itself does not determine how many different conceptual units—different representations—can fit within that limitation. In order to answer that question, it is necessary to consider not only the

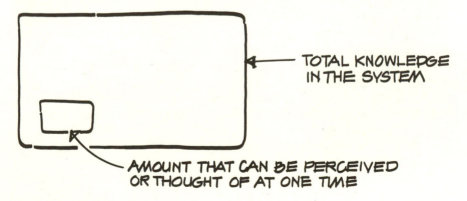

TOTAL KNOWLEDGE IN THE SYSTEM

AMOUNT THAT CAN BE PERCEIVED OR THOUGHT OF AT ONE TIME

Figure 7.7 Diagram of the limited capacity of working memory.

number of representations one has for a given situation but also how *compact* they are.

A recently acquired representation is likely to be comparatively large. It would be diffuse and relatively disorganized since the experiences on which it depends have not benefited from repetition. Clearly, not many such representations would fit within the limited capacity of the system. A well-learned representation, by contrast, will tend to be well organized and compact. As we have seen, increasing familiarity leads to the loss of less closely connected features and to the strengthening of connections among those features that turned out to be more salient. The resulting representation, having benefited from familiarity, is more general and more economical of neural units at the same time. Thus more of these well-learned representations would be expected to fit within the limited capacity of the system. In fact, for well-learned representations, the rule of thumb that some $5 + 2$ units can be held in working memory at one time probably applies (Mandler 1975b, 1975c). Thus how extensively one can represent a given situation depends upon compactness, and compactness in turn depends upon familiarity.

Here again the experts have a substantial advantage. They can represent the situation fully because well-learned representations are less demanding of limited capacity. The use of technical jargon is an example of such compactness, where the labels stand for well-learned representations. Thus, for example, the ability to recognize a seemingly arbitrary set of features as aspects of "good conservation practices" (a label) achieves great cognitive economy, leaving room in working memory to examine additional aspects of the problem needing solution (Figure 7.8).

Manipulation. In discussing some strategies available to the problem solver, it was clear that there were advantages to being able to isolate and deal with the parts of the problem. Analytic strategies, in other words, are often more powerful than are global strategies. Once again it pays to be an expert. Having well-formed representations, the expert views the problem in terms of components that are *discrete* and possess a *unity* of their own. They are, hence, far more manipulable than is an inexperienced conception of the same situation. In this way the expert can handle more representations at once and at the same time be far more flexible in dealing with them.

A simple thought experiment may make these points more vivid. Imagine a hammer. Presumably you are imagining it with the head above and the handle below. Can you now imagine it upside down? Can you imagine it rightside up with its handle tied in a knot? How about with a small head and a very long handle?

Now consider a snork. This tool has a wooden handle like that of a hammer but a head like that of a pipewrench, except that instead of be-

Figure 7.8 These scenes appear to be quite varied in terms of the nature of the land cover, the condition of the soil, etc. Nonetheless, all of the photographs have been taken with the explicit intention of demonstrating "good conservation practices."
USDA Soil Conservation Service

ing made for gripping, it has sharp edges. Now try manipulating your image of the snork as you did the hammer. If, like most people, you are considerably more familiar with hammers than with snorks, you probably find substantial differences in your capacity to manipulate your images of these two tools. Familiarity not only fosters compactness; it also leads to a coherence, almost a concreteness, that greatly increases the capacity for manipulation.

Familiarity thus provides ways for facilitating the basic process of searching for a solution, a way to connect START and GOAL. Still the dream remains of finding some methods that are really powerful, that can make a problem dissolve before one's eyes. One argument for examining the way experts solve problems was to see if these special maneuvers could be discovered in that context. Experts seem to depend, however, more upon facile representation and associative structures than upon any special methods.

Some empirical progress has recently been made on this intriguing topic. DeGroot (1965) has studied expert chess players in an attempt to determine what they do that distinguishes their play from that of ordinary, though thoroughly competent, chess players. His conclusion was surprising. Master chess players used no special tricks or operations. Their patterns were in no way exceptional—except for their initial representation of the problem. It was, in other words, the way they saw the problem that gave them their advantage, not what they did with the information subsequently.

DeGroot performed an ingenious experiment to demonstrate that master players were literally seeing the board differently. He asked his chess players to reconstruct a pattern on a chessboard that they were allowed to view for five seconds. The master players were much better at this than were their less expert counterparts. This was true, however, only when the pattern viewed was a meaningful one, a pattern that could actually have occurred in a game. When the pattern was random, the master players completely lost their advantage. They were no better at seeing in general, but only at seeing the patterns that matter in chess.

The key to solving a problem thus seems to lie in the way it is represented. *One of the greatest assets of the expert is a more facile initial representation of the problem.* This conclusion brings our analysis of the cognitive process full cycle. The formation of economical representations out of a diversity of overlapping experiences is a basic means of handling environmental uncertainty. This turns out to have its payoff not only in perception but in problem solving as well.

Costs and Benefits

There are thus many advantages to being familiar with a problem domain. Experts can more quickly feel comfortable in an unfamiliar situation. They possess generic maps that allow them to see more readily aspects of a situation that are common to many other similar situations. They know what to look for and can grasp the problem more readily. Through more compact coding, more of the pertinent information can be represented at once. Finally, should manipulation of the parts of the problem be necessary, the experts' familiarity provides greater facility in doing so.

There is a price to be paid for all this facility. The efficiency of expert problem solving depends heavily upon highly practiced perception, and such perception gains its efficiency through an astute ignoring of much that goes on in the environment. Although in some sense experts see more than the rest of us see, in another important sense they see less. This can be most effective much of the time, but it can nevertheless create difficulties.

Sometimes solving a problem requires a new way of representing it, which in turn requires that one take in new information. At such times the differential sensitivity of the highly experienced observer may become a serious handicap. Decision makers and other experts have been found to be highly selective in the new information they are willing to consider, to say nothing of the new information they would be able to comprehend (Ingram, 1973; Ingram and Ullery, 1977; Jervis, 1973).

Another difficulty may arise out of the very efficiency afforded by the compactness of representations. This can lead to a case of "hardening of the categories." It is not unusual for an expert to diagnose a problem too decisively. Having been acquired across numerous specific instances, a label may be applied too hastily, leading to the decision to proceed with the "right" solution—namely, the one that has been applied numerous times in the past. Perhaps it is for this reason that planners have a tendency to bring the status quo to places that had been functioning well but differently up to that time. Perhaps, too, this is the reason so many parts of the country have lost their local distinctiveness.

A police chief who had grown up in the city he served commented to a friend on the number of special places in the city that had been destroyed in recent years because of redevelopment projects. He pointed out that none of the city's planners were city natives; they seemed not to be aware of these special places. Whether this analysis was correct or not, one would certainly expect this sort of outcome to result from the hasty reliance on one's past experiences, on an overly confident labeling of a set of circumstances in accordance with well-established categories.

The difficulties created by the expert's greater facility with problem solving can be particularly disturbing in circumstances involving change. The impressive structures the expert has built up in the course of considerable experience work best when the present problem resembles past experiences. Being highly effective at picking out the crucial elements of a problem can become a handicap when what was once crucial is crucial no longer. In other words, when the nature of the problem itself changes, the expert may not be aware that all is not as it was. Another sort of change is even harder to detect and is hence potentially more damaging. This involves a change in the larger framework. Thus, for example, much expertise about major economic activities was acquired during a time when materials and energy were cheap and labor was the factor to be minimized at all costs. Today that entire framework has changed. Materials and energy are increasingly costly, and unemployment is a persistent and growing problem. Thus problem solving about, say, farming and manufacturing is at an entirely different level from what it was in past times. Yet many experts behave as if the implicit framework they grew up with still holds. There is little as frustrating as watching experts conduct business as usual while the world undergoes radical changes. It is perhaps because of this capacity to be oblivious to what is so obvious to others that an expert has been described as "someone who makes only big mistakes." Thus, for some problems—such as many of the Type 4 problems discussed earlier in this chapter—the nonexpert may be at least as likely to ask the right questions and find novel solutions.

While few treatises on cognition deal with the costs and benefits of expertise, concern for this issue is not new. Writing over 50 years ago, Laski (1930) considered what he called "the limitations of the expert." His context was foreign policy, and his message included an emphasis on the necessity of consultation with experts. Nonetheless, he was vividly aware of their limitations and articulate in his reservations:

> But it is one thing to urge the need for expert consultation at every stage in making policy; it is another thing, and a very different thing, to insist that the expert's judgment must be final. For special knowledge and the highly trained mind produce their own limitations which, in the realm of statemanship, are of decisive importance. *Expertise*, it may be argued, sacrifices the insight of common sense to intensity of experience. It breeds an inability to accept new views from the very depth of its preoccupation with its own conclusions. It too often fails to see round its subjects. . . . Too often, also, it lacks humility; and this breeds in its possessors a failure in proportion which makes them fail to see the obvious which is before their noses. It has, also, a certain caste-spirit about it, so that experts tend to neglect all evidence which does not come from those who belong to their own ranks. Above all, perhaps, and this most urgently where human problems are concerned, the expert fails to see that every judgment he makes not purely factual in nature brings with it a scheme of values which has no special validity about it. He tends to confuse the importance of his facts with the importance of what he proposes to do about them.

SOME CONCLUDING COMMENTS

In the foregoing discussion the term "expert" was used rather loosely. When one realizes that familiarity is at the heart of expertise, then there are many experts in the world. Most of us, in fact, are expert in one area or another.

Consider for a moment a not unusual scene consisting of two little children, perhaps a doll or two, and possibly some doll-related paraphernalia. Their dialogue is likely to have a "let's pretend that" opening line, followed by a description of the key characters and essential places that will form the arena for their world of the next half hour or so. They clearly have some of the ingredients of expertise in their formulation of family composition, roles, routine activities of the day, and so on. The essential representations are, of course, highly familiar components of their young lives.

When one imagines the decision-making process about the feasibility of locating a major shopping center at an expressway interchange, the dialogue has many parallels. It entails identifying the key elements of that situation and trying out a series of hunches relating to likely markets, accessibility, and so on. The essential representations are highly familiar to the professionals who have undertaken such plans many times in the past.

Not surprisingly, many of the characteristics of the expert accrue quite readily to the older members of the population. They have, after all, experienced similar situations many times over and have a personal sense of the past that must take time to acquire. In some cultures, the elderly are, in fact, regarded as the experts; they are revered for their perspective and wisdom. In many organizations, seniority is an important basis for status. However, one also associates the expertise of the senior members with some of the costs mentioned earlier. There can be a tendency to pigeon-hole a new situation in terms of the categories that have served so well many times in the past. There can be an adamant insistence on the "right way" to approach any given problem.

William James has referred to this disposition to know more and more about the past with increasing experience as "old fogyism." One of the striking features of such knowledge is the difficulty of anticipating when it will be of great value and when it will be dismissed out of hand. The perspective of the past seems to go through cycles of welcome. As economic circumstances trigger periods of "back to the land," the interest in low-technology know-how rises. At such times, young people seem quite receptive to tales of "how we used to do it when I was a child." The vision of a person like Ralph Borsodi, social philosopher and self-reliance advocate, might today be considered far ahead of its time, whereas to many in the 1920s his message might well have seemed to be a case of "old fogyism."

In considering what he calls "reasoning," James emphasizes the many ways there are of thinking about any particular thing. None of these alternative abstractions, he argues, should be considered to be "correct." Any one of them might be the most appropriate given the nature of the problem at hand. This suggests, once again, that representing a problem is far from obvious, and at the same time it is crucial to a solution. In James's terms the issue is finding the right abstraction. This is where novices may be perplexed, experts facile, and old fogies inflexible. Depending upon the nature of the particular problem, any one of these groups might be the most effective in finding an appropriate path between START and GOAL.

Regardless of one's level of experience, problem solving draws upon all aspects of cognitive processing. It depends heavily on recognition, on the identification of the elements of the problem domain. It is necessarily predictive—though the future can vary from the immediate to the long distant. Problem solving must furthermore incorporate evaluation; the process is inherently risky. Any path one comes up with is necessarily tentative until it has been evaluated in terms of its payoffs and the sense of clarity that it creates.

NOTES

1. Problem Solving

A brief and insightful discussion of problem solving can be found in Posner (1973); for an analysis of various problem-solving strategies, see B. F. Anderson (1975). Mayer (1977) is useful for a brief and readable treatment that includes traditional and modern approaches to problem solving. In addition, many texts on cognition and thinking concern themselves with this topic. Much of the difficulty in solving problems centers around the same issues of uncertainty and complexity that were central constraints in our discussion of pattern recognition. MacCrimmon and Taylor (1975), writing in an industrial and organizational context, provide a thorough treatment of the management of uncertainty and complexity in the problem-solving and decision-making processes. Interest in problem solving has also been high among those interested in environmental design. Both Lang and Burnette (1974) and Chermayeff and Alexander (1963) consider problem solving in the context of the design process.

2. Constraint Manipulation by Overlay Maps

A fascinating example of the flexible manipulation of constraints is provided by the use of overlay maps by landscape architects and planners. By placing each constraint (which can be physical features, natural features, cultural features, etc.) on a different map, various combinations can be created and their implications examined. This is a powerful spatial analytic technique that arrays constraints in such a way as to be readily grasped by eye and brain. For an excellent review of this technique, along with proposals for transforming it into an even more flexible computer-based procedure, see Steinitz, Parker, and Jordan (1976). For some interesting applications of a related procedure, see McHarg (1969).

3. Social Traps

There is a growing body of literature that is concerned with what are called *social traps*. These involve instances in which people attempt to maximize short-range payoffs while causing great long-range harm to themselves and others. The paradigm social trap is, of course, the "tragedy of the commons," discussed in Chapters 6 and 10. These instances (essentially Type 4 problems), where future considerations are both crucial and ignored, are of growing urgency in an overpopulated, resource-depleted world. Discussions of research in this area include Shippee, Roitman, and Gregory (1980) and Dawes (1980), who emphasizes the three factors of knowledge, morality, and trust as central to counteracting the social trap. Cross and Guyer (1980) deal with the same issues, but from a more reinforcement-oriented and less information-centered perspective. A thoughtful analysis from the perspective of environmental psychology is offered by Edney (1980), who points to the potential interaction of trust and territory in dealing with this urgent class of problems.

4. Decision Making

This is an active and fascinating area of research. Since there is considerable overlap between work on decision making and work on problem solving, some useful discussions fit both categories. A good example of this is the chapter by MacCrimmon and Taylor (1975), which was also mentioned in Chapter Note 1 on problem solving. Intended to be of practical use to the decision maker, these authors use their central themes of complexity and uncertainty as a context for the analysis of alternative decision criteria. Janis and Mann (1977), whose work also covers both problem solving and decision making, provide a useful treatment of the complexity of the decision process, the pervasiveness of biases, and the continued sampling of pertinent information even after a decision has been made. An excellent discussion of decision making in the context of natural hazards is provided by Slovic, Kunreuther and White (1974), who are concerned not only with the interfacing of theory and data but with the improvement of policy making as well.

Much of the current emphasis on the "irrationality" of decision making stems from the stimulating work of Tversky and Kahneman (1981; Kahneman and Tversky, 1973). For a discussion that questions whether such tendencies are in fact irrational from an evolutionary perspective, see Thomas (1977). For another analysis of the rationality issue, see S. Kaplan and R. Kaplan (1978, Chapter 5).

part five

SHARING ENVIRONMENTAL KNOWLEDGE

Humans depend upon information. It is central not only to their survival, but to their everyday functioning as well. It would be difficult indeed to understand the relationship between humans and their environment without paying close attention to the informational exchanges that occur. At the same time, humans not only need information; they crave it. They explore, they solve puzzles, and at every opportunity they seek to make sense of what goes on around them.

Since humans have different experiences and explore different topics, it stands to reason that different humans will possess different information. By sharing this information with each other, each individual's knowledge can be vastly extended. Fortunately, people seem to enjoy sharing what they know, and much of the information we have has been acquired by this means.

Yet despite all these positive indicators, sharing knowledge turns out to be astonishingly difficult. Well-intended communications frequently miss the mark, to the mutual frustration of speaker and listener alike. It is a paradox of human functioning that something so valuable and willingly offered is so often rejected or ignored or overlooked. This last part of the book explores some of the many domains in which attempts to share information go awry. Further, based on the perspective of human information-handling developed thus far, some alternative and more hopeful approaches to information-sharing are explored.

The first of the three chapters in this part looks at knowledge, the stuff that has proved to be so central to the way people deal with their problems and relate to the environment in general. In emphasizing both the importance and the difficulty of sharing knowledge, Chapter 8 brings together many of the themes introduced earlier in this volume. The discussion of ways to make the information-transfer process more likely to succeed is crucial to the subsequent chapters since both research and participation depend for their effectiveness on the quality of the information transfer that has taken place.

Chapter 9 looks at the research process. Its focus is on ways to gain knowledge about human/environment relations. Research is presented as a highly cognitive activity, inseparable from the way people think, what they comprehend, and what they find convincing. Research combining people and environments forces one to confront conceptual problems that are easier to ignore in other contexts. The environment in question must be sampled adequately and

175

must be communicated successfully. Given thàt one must often deal with not-yet-existent environments and with environmental configurations that are not necessarily available to be viewed, surrogate ways of presenting the environment must be considered.

Chapter 10 is about public particpation. Since public participation is mandated by law for many environmental decisions, this process is an important element of the human/environment interface. Despite sincere and at times heroic efforts, this process has in general produced more disappointment and frustration than enlightenment. Since participation in the world around one is important not only in terms of influence on policy but also in terms of psychological impact, better ways must be found. The role of successful transfer of information in this context is particularly vital. People cannot participate effectively—and are unlikely to try—if they cannot comprehend what the possibilities are.

There are a number of ways of looking at the relationships between research and participation. The trend in the field, unfortunately, seems to be to consider them antithetical. From that perspective there are two opposing ways of obtaining "people information." One is to study people, to observe them, and in that way to come up with principles or guidelines that speak to what is appropriate to people. This is the "research" approach. Alternatively, one "goes to the people," seeks their reactions, their suggestions, perhaps even to the extent of training them to serve as fellow planners or designers. This opposition is neither necessary nor constructive. There need be no conflict between research and participation; rather these two processes can be not only mutually supportive, but at times so similar as to be indistinguishable.

Research might be a substitute for participation if it provided an exhaustive set of specifications of human reactions under all circumstances. Obviously it cannot do this. Thus in any specific situation participation is necessary to connect any general principles we may have found in the particulars of history, site, and context.

On the other hand, participation might seem to be an adequate substitute for research. This is not the case for a number of reasons. First, people rarely know what they want in the sense that just asking them is likely to be fruitful. It is necessary to formulate the issues, to provide means of communicating them, and to provide an appropriate medium for human reaction. It is necessary, in other words, to create much of the structure that is characteristic of any research. The relationship, however, goes even further than this. The process of participation is greatly facilitated if people are provided with alternative versions of possible futures to respond to. Such alternatives should be devised so that they are understandable to people and so that they speak to the needs and requirements that people have. All this calls for some prior understanding of human behavior, which ultimately depends on prior research.

Those who look to research as necessary and sufficient for guiding decisions tend to emphasize experts and expertise while de-emphasizing the role of people. Conversely, those who view participation as the be-all and end-all tend to disfavor experts and expertise. However, neither people nor experts are in short supply. Both can play constructive roles in decisions that affect the public. The critical question is how those roles can be structured to enhance the contribution of both.

chapter eight

THE TRANSFER OF INFORMATION

Unlike so many topics psychologists deal with, the environment is tangible; it is physical; it is immediately present. It is here and now. Yet, in order to deal constructively with problems of the environment, it is essential to see beyond the tangible and the present. The here and now is not enough.

Through a vast majority of the time that there have been humans on the earth, many potential problems were solved by shipping them somewhere else. Wastes of all kinds, noisy activities, polluting factories could all be put somewhere else. Unfortunately, we are fast running out of "somewhere else." There are no longer vast spaces of no interest to anyone. When one takes a larger view of the distribution of human activities in space, it becomes clear that the traditional policies of waste disposal make little sense in a crowded world.

A frequent expression of spatial myopia is a conception of human existence that might appropriately be called the *city model*. According to this model, the presence of cities proves that the world is not overpopulated. Since entities of high density can function, the rest of the country (or globe) could be of high density, too. Implicit in this model is an illusion of self-sufficiency. Cities in fact are totally non–self-sufficient. They are dependent upon the less populated rest of the environment for food, for energy, for waste disposal. It is interesting to find the city held up as an environmental model given the data on employment patterns. For a job at a given level of skill, the larger the city, the more one has to pay to find someone suitable (Hoch, 1976).

Just as the space beyond what we can immediately perceive is vital to our comprehension of environmental problems, so, too, is the time beyond the present. There is an irony in the way time influences our capacity to deal with environmental problems. On the one hand, things are happening too fast. We are subject to what Toffler (1970) called "future shock." We do not have the time to develop genetic or cultural adaptations that were available for many previous problems. The global population growth rate is vastly greater than it was in previous eras; to compound the urgency, these growing numbers of people are entering a world already seriously resource-depleted. The importance of coming to terms with the future has never been greater. On the other hand, these changes are slow relative to our capacity to perceive. The changes are gradual enough that we become habituated. We fail to notice the hazards that are creeping up on us. As Ehrlich (1968) once pointed out, if the smog in Los Angeles had begun suddenly, people would have run yelling and screaming into the hills.

Thus if people are to react appropriately to environmental urgencies, they must be able to think about circumstances distant in time and space. It is necessary to deal with calamities that have not yet happened. Planning requires compehension of what might be, of alternative uses and arrangements of space that are necessarily in the future. Given human cognitive capacities, this will be no simple matter.

It is hardly news that people learn from past experience. Since lookahead is based on previous learning, people's conception of the future must be based on the past. This works well enough for recurring events. Thus, based on past experiences (and a good deal of cultural support), people living in northerly climates come to expect winter and at the same time realize that it is not permanent. However, many environmental problems are not recurring. Instead they tend to grow progressively worse. Somehow people have to be able to grasp the implications of these problems without experiencing them innumerable times.

The necessity of conceptualizing what has never been experienced may seem to be an overwhelming challenge, but it is not unprecedented. Medieval humans were greatly influenced by a possible future that none of them had ever experienced. They had a vivid conception of Hell, and it apparently played an important role in their behavior. Hence, there is no reason to believe that people could not conceptualize and relate to a not-yet-experienced future. The issue for us here is to identify the principles whereby this conception can be achieved.

ON THE DIFFICULTY OF TRANSFERRING KNOWLEDGE

Given the urgency of environmental problems, the simple solution would seem to be to give people the information they need. The dependency of cognitive processes on past experiences, however, makes such approaches of simply "giving" people a conception of the future unlikely to be useful. Even if such a direct transfer were possible, the connection between the information and the corresponding change in behavior is not a simple one. To get a sense of how attempts to transmit information go awry, let us consider a number of examples of efforts at knowledge transfer.

☐ Scores of well-intentioned, dedicated individuals have attempted to meet this challenge head-on by educating people about the issues. Both programs with the school system and efforts to reach the public at large have been undertaken. Despite the effort and enthusiasm invested in these activities, the results have, by and large, been disappointing. The national "environmental literacy" level has remained low, and people who have been the recipients of this information have not, in general, shown the hoped-for changes in behavior. People have not even shown great enthusiasm for receiving the information, despite the fact that it is directed to their very own well-being and possibly to their survival. What seemed so urgent and obvious has turned out to be difficult and ineffective. Some observers have gone so far as to conclude that information does not matter to people after all. Could it be that the way people behave has nothing to do with information? Is it possible that people do not care whether they comprehend their environment? What has happened to the information-based, information-seeking creature we discussed in the previous seven chapters?

King Features Syndicate, Inc.

Part of the problem here is the outgrowth of an apparent paradox. It is not that people are disinterested in information, but rather that they may feel they already have the information they need. When an individual already has information in some area, the definiteness of representations and the connectedness of maps tend to inspire confidence. While this is vital to functioning in many circumstances, it can also lead an individual to the conclusion that no new information is needed. Comparably, since new information tends to be mapped into old categories whenever possible, an individual may readily conclude that a message that bears at least some old content is "just the same old stuff." It hardly seems necessary to add that people do not enjoy being told what they already know.

☐ Geographers in particular have studied how humans react to natural hazards such as floods and earthquakes. In many cases it is possible to predict where such events are likely to take place. As we have seen, a large proportion of people ignore such warnings. Here, information that is directly related to survival is spurned. Even after such events have occurred, when their reality has been amply demonstrated, people persevere in ignoring such salient information. People who have been flooded out characteristically rebuild on the flood plain right where they were before.

Although such behavior is frustrating to experts and seemingly highly irrational, from a motivational perspective it does not appear particularly strange. Being asked to think of a disaster when to do so would leave one terrified and not knowing what to do is not an attractive option to most people. It is a circumstance likely to render an individual helpless, and this is a state people tend to avoid. It is perhaps for this reason that threatening messages are avoided. Likewise, information that confuses, that muddles one's conception of the world can undermine one's effectiveness. To some extent this may be the plight of people advised to leave their home on a flood plain. Their way of life, their way of relating to the environment may be completely tied to their territory, which they have been told is in danger. The unknowns of starting over elsewhere may be far harder to bear than the rather specific hazard entailed by staying put.

The reaction to natural hazards would be more bizarre than frightening were it not for its parallel to the reaction to many environmental problems. Watt (1974) has referred to the human tendency to find enormous disasters unthinkable as "the Titanic effect." The Titanic was regarded as unsinkable; not only did the crew never take warnings of nearby icebergs seriously, but even after the collision there was a refusal to believe that anything serious had happened. Watt sees the possibility of running out of the earth's resources as comparably unthinkable for most people.

A slightly different version of the cognition of disaster is put forth by Catton (1975). He suggests that the recent boom of unprecedented affluence was the result of exploitation of nonrenewable energy resources. Many people believe, however, that it was technology that brought these many gifts. Hence they look to technology to restore their luxurious circumstances. Catton considers this pattern of belief a form of "cargo cult." The original cargo cults arose in the South Sea Islands, which experienced boom times when they became American air force bases during World War II. The cargo cultists believe that some day a big bird will come again from the sky, bringing great riches as it did in the past.

☐ Environmental professionals, particularly those in the area of environmental design, are coming to recognize the importance of information about people. At the same time there has been no lack of research in this area, resulting in a growing body of literature on the behavioral effects of design. A widely held feeling among the researchers is that this newly generated information is routinely ignored. This feeling is often expressed in terms of the "gap" between the researcher and the practitioner. It is a source of considerable frustration that this information, which seems to be needed and perhaps even wanted, is not being used.

As is all too clear from the preceding examples, cognitive maps cannot be transplanted directly. The hard-earned knowledge in one head cannot become the easily acquired knowledge in another head through some simple telling process. Certainly years of experience can be expressed as a written summary, and that summary can be read and even memorized, but it is unlikely that comprehension will be transmitted in this way. It is even more unlikely that such an approach will produce the desired change in behavior.

The Portable Model

Although this direct attack on the problem is unlikely to be effective, there is an indirect route that has great potential. As we have seen, people's perception, their thought patterns, and ultimately their behavior are greatly influenced by their model of the world—or their model of the particular aspect of the world they are trying to cope with at any particular moment. People are indeed resistant to attempts to tell them what to do or even to facts that they have no idea what to do with. However, they are eager for information that helps them understand and relate to the world more effectively. Thus information that aids in model-building is likely to have far more impact than information that may seem more directly related but fails to speak to that agenda of implicit questions people have about the world.

The third example of unsatisfactory information transfer that was just described provides a good example of this indirect approach. The researcher produces data that, it is hoped, the environmental designer will use in the design process. As it turns out, such data are rarely used, for a host of reasons. The designer has trouble locating the data when they are needed, the data fail to speak to the particular problem at issue, and, anyway, projects are always put together under considerable pressure with little time for finding and reading and relating.

Much of the information in question here arises from environment and behavior research. Even though the designer does not read it, designing requires that one have some notion of what people are like. This notion may be vague; it may be distorted; it may be downright misleading. When the pressures are on, however, one uses the model one has. If the environment and behavior research were to offer a model instead of a collection of data, it might get used in time of need. It cannot be just any model, however; it must be a *portable model, that is, a model that is simple enough and intuitive enough to be carried around in the designer's head.* If the model is part of the designer's way of thinking, it will be used. Data are impor-

From *Human Information Processing by P. H. Lindsay and D. A. Norman © 1977 Academic Press, Inc., reprinted by permission of the publisher.*

tant in constructing such a model and in providing evidence for it, but data alone rarely influence behavior.

Too often have information-providers set out with inflated expectations. Talk of behavior change is intoxicating stuff. Since unconfirmed expectations can be painful, it might be wise to adopt a realistic stance at the onset.

A portable model, even if intuitive and cogent, is unlikely to be adopted by people who have not yet recognized the need for one in a given area. Nonetheless, being intuitive and cogent, it has a good chance of being remembered. Then, when that aspect of an individual's world begins to fall apart, an alternative interpretation may be available. As far as environmental deterioration is concerned, we can count on more and more human impact as time passes and hence on more and more people suddenly open to new models.

It is also the case that behavior does not change merely because a model changes. Many people now share the model that casts public transportation in a far more reasonable role than the private automobile. Yet as long as public transportation tends to be noisy, dirty, inconvenient, slow, and not notably less expensive than automobile travel, the holders of these models are unlikely to change their behavior. Behavior is a function not only of models but of the environment as well. Environmental support for environmentally sound behavior is at least as important as appropriate cognitive structures. In the long run, after all, the environment is the source of our cognitive structures.

SOME PRINCIPLES OF KNOWLEDGE TRANSFER

Identifying Units

If the transfer of knowledge depends upon the recipient's capacity to build a model of the material, then our first concern must be with units, since any model must ultimately function as an interconnected set of cognitive units. Without the basic units, there is nothing to interconnect. Education often fails because the learner lacks the basic units. The teacher presumably does not realize this because (a) the student has been *told* what the units are and (b) not only does the teacher have the units, but they are evoked by the words that refer to them. The result is that the student acquires a "model" of interconnected words rather than concepts. Based on experiences of this kind, some people decide that "what you learn in school" has little applicability in the real world.

Flow diagrams, as we have seen, often lead to a similar situation. People have become facile at drawing boxes around words and drawing arrows between the boxes. A box around a word certainly makes it look much more like a thing, a basic unit, but if careful thought has not preceded the drawing of the box, the result is still just a word, although now a word with considerable pretensions.

The first step in working with the units involved in a body of material must be to identify them. They must be distinct from each other; they must cover all the central concerns of the material. They must, in other words, provide the basic vocabulary that, along with the relations among them, is sufficient to provide a structure for the material. These are difficult requirements calling for a careful analysis of the issues in question.

The Meaningfulness Principle

Knowing what the key units are does not in itself guarantee effective information transmission. It is a necessary condition but not a sufficient one. The fact that the key units have been identified does not guarantee that the information receiver has appropriate corresponding units. Even having them does not mean that they will turn on at the right time. For a body of information to be useful to someone (and for it to have a chance of influencing behavior), it must be connected both within itself and to pre-existing knowledge. It must, in other words, form a coherent pattern.

To form a coherent pattern, a body of material must, in effect, tell a story. It must have connections leading from one part to the next. In this way sequence is established and a structure created. And structure is, as we have seen, a powerful factor in the comprehension of information. A study of visitors' reactions to informational displays in interpretive centers supports this principle. Structured presentations were of substantially greater interest to visitors than were fragmented presentations (Wagar, 1974; Washburne and Wagar, 1972). Although not originally stated as a facet of cognitive functioning, this principle has been a part of the lore in nature interpretation instruction for many years (see Hammitt, 1981).

Another aspect of forming a coherent pattern is providing the information in such a way that it is relatable to the individual's prior knowledge. This is what might be called the "starting where they're at" principle. In order to make connections to pre-existing structures, one must know what structures are there. There is rarely a time when one does not benefit by exploring with one's intended recipients the pattern of understanding that they start with.

At other times it is beneficial to use an approach that takes advantage of the amazing cognitive power of questions. Perhaps more than anything else, the sort of information people will be most eager to get and most attentive to is the information that answers their questions. Answering questions greatly increases the likelihood that one is relating material to pre-existing cognitive structure. In addition, the very asking of a question seems to be enormously effective at activating the relevant portions of this pre-existing cognitive structure. Even with relatively simple-minded questions, information seems to be more salient when in answer to a question. In a memory study, for example, some participants were given questions to ask. They remembered the answers better than did the control group, which received only the answers (Berlyne, 1954, 1966). At a higher level, a major component of the Socratic method of teaching involves getting the learner into a questioning mode; it is then that the learner begins to wonder about the very issues the teacher is trying to communicate.

Questions depend on an individual's cognitive structure. As such, a question not only provides for a clear place to put the new information, but also is a sign of recognition that it is needed. Being in a questioning mode thus constitutes a striking contrast to those times when the individual, through definiteness and connectedness, is disinclined toward information.

Some questions are explicit. When one suddenly stumbles upon a gap or discrepancy, when one has difficulty recognizing, or predicting, or evaluating, or acting, one is quite aware of having questions. In addition, though, people carry with them a large agenda of implicit questions. Certain things whose workings one never really understood, things that never quite fit in, that failed to make sense in terms of some larger picture, constitute the sort of unfinished business implicit questions are made of. They involve the extension, clarification, and general improvement of one's model of the world. They are appropriately considered questions in that people are eager for such information and readily bring up the cognitive structure it pertains to.

Capacity Limitations

All these possibilities would be far less demanding if they could be handled quickly and simply. But, alas, they take time. A human can absorb only so much information at once. Beyond that, increasing input produces rapidly decreasing returns—and might even undo what has already been accomplished. The capacity to hold in active memory only some 5 ± 2 units (or "chunks") of information at one time (Chapter 5, Note 1) is indeed a severe limitation. In fact, from the point of view of trying to transfer information, it is hardly safe to assume that one can therefore aim for seven or even five units. If an explanation requires five concepts and the recipient is not functioning after the third one, the difference between what is delivered and what is received will be great. For practical purposes the "magic number" is three. Surely a speaker who promises to deliver "only three main points" is more reassuring than one who threatens to offer "only seven main points."

The dislike of being overwhelmed with information is unlikely to be a recent development. What has changed in the relatively recent past is the availability of information. As Simon (1978, p. 13) has pointed out, we now have far more information than we have attention to deal with it:

> In a world where information is relatively scarce, and where problems for decision are few and simple, information is almost always a positive good. In a world where attention is a major resource, information may be an expensive luxury, for it may turn our attention from what is important to what is unimportant. We cannot afford to attend to information simply because it is there.

Having some feeling for capacity limitations is vital because it is otherwise all too easy to overload the intended recipient. Clearly there are compelling reasons for wishing to avoid overload. First, it leads to a certain amount of information being ignored or otherwise lost—and one never knows which part that will be. Second, it is a painful experience for the recipient. There is often enough pain in absorbing strange and unfamiliar ideas without adding to it unnecessarily. Third, it is implicitly coercive. Since overload produces pain, the recipient will be motivated to leave. If the recipient has not left, there must be something in the situation preventing departure. Coercion in education is sometimes unavoidable. Since cognition is intimately related to feelings, and since what use of the information occurs later will depend to a large degree on these feelings, coercion is not the method of choice.

On the other hand, the capacity limitation need not present insuperable difficulties, thanks in part to the hierarchical nature of the system. Although one may be able to handle only three main ideas at once, one may be able to handle several examples for each as well as a higher level representation that ties the three ideas together. Further, what constitutes a unit depends to a large degree on the recipient's prior knowledge—on the pre-existing units and structures. As we saw in Chapter 7, experts, by virtue of great familiarity with an area of knowledge, can handle much more information at one time in their area of expertise.

A powerful argument for self-pacing, for allowing the recipient to control the rate of information flow, follows from these considerations of capacity limitations. While one can very likely squeeze the information in at a faster rate when the recipient is not the one controlling the rate, there may be little gain in terms of what ultimately happens to the information. New information can interfere with the mental activities relating to the comprehension and storage of the prior information.

It is instructive to look at the operation of these general guidelines in terms of what happens when they are not followed. A classic experiment on memory for meaningful material provides a useful example. Bartlett (1932) asked participants to reproduce from memory stories that they had read. The stories were Native American folktales, quite unfamiliar in structure and content to the British college students participating in the study. Further, only the first of a series of participants read the original story. The first participant wrote the story down from memory and passed it on to the next reader. In this way each "chain" produced ten successive stories based on the same original, each a little further removed from that original.

The transformations in the retelling of these stories were remarkable. Bartlett identified three different trends:

- Leveling: details tended to drop out. The stories became simpler.

- Sharpening: some details were not only retained, but sometimes even exaggerated. In other words, landmarks were created.

- Rationalization: the story came to be more coherent. It came to make better sense in terms of the experiences and expectations of the readers.

One way to look at these transformations is that the readers, finding the raw material they were presented with difficult to comprehend, made whatever modifications they found necessary to make the material manageable. *They created landmarks, which they placed in a simplified structure that had connections to their prior experience.* In other words, they forged cognitive maps for themselves. Such maps may be extracted even from rather unpromising material—but at a cost. In this case the information underwent considerable distortion in the process. There are many times when people simply ignore material that is hard to map. If they must deal with it, however, they seem to be quite capable of making the adjustments necessary to meet their cognitive requirements. Being unwilling to accommodate to human cognitive patterns in the information one provides may not prevent transmission. It may simply render the resulting "understanding" unrecognizable.

SOME WAYS OF PRESENTING INFORMATION

Even if one is working with clearly identified units, a good sense of the knowledge of the intended recipient, and an appreciation for how little material one can deal with at one time, one still has to make decisions about how the material is to be presented. Certainly whether one is trying to build new concepts or reawaken old ones will make a difference. Nonetheless, it is possible to identify two properties that are vital to any material that is intended to mediate successful knowledge transfer.

☐ What one presents should be *vivid*, calling on material that people care about (see Nisbett and Ross, 1980, Chapter 3). For a variety of reasons certain material is unusually effective at holding people's attention (see Chapter 5). Attention is, of course, essential; without it all else is lost. On the other hand, using material just because it is vivid, although it is otherwise irrelevant, can be a serious error. In such cases the material becomes a distraction, calling attention to itself and away from the intended content. How often, despite all the ingenious tricks, do commercials fail in accomplishing their basic mission: that one remember the brand! There is the story of a former student meeting up with a teacher from some years back. They reminisce together, and the student tells the teacher how she will never forget the day when the teacher startled his class by standing on the desk and telling the students, "This is the most important point to remember about the English language." "I don't remember what you said," the former student continues, "but I'll never forget your standing there."

☐ What one presents should be *concrete* so that it can be imagined, visualized, related to. As Rosch (1978) has demonstrated, people have a preferred level of thinking that involves concrete objects. Thus most people deal more effectively with the concept of "hammer" than with the concept of "tool." At the same time they do better with "hammer" than with some specific kind of hammer (unless their experience has inclined them to have highly differentiated hammer concepts). Concreteness is often introduced into domains whose very abstractness may make them hard to think about otherwise. Religions and cultures often clothe abstraction in rituals, where concrete sensory patterns and concrete actions make otherwise remote ideas tangible. Nisbett et al. (1976) have pointed out how little influence abstract information can have. They contrast this with the huge impact often carried by even casual and unreliable information when experienced in concrete form. (They are so impressed with this phenomenon that they call the conclusion of their paper "communicating with creatures of concreteness.") Fund-raisers have long taken this advice to heart.

On Gaming and Role-Taking

One method of presenting information that tends to be vivid and concrete, and that has received considerable attention in recent years, is gaming (Chapter Note 1). Certain facts about games are immediately evident. Gaming is an activity characterized by great involvement on the part of the participants. It is also a procedure that automatically communicates that there is a need to build a model without actually having to come out and say so. Striving to acquire a model (usually described in gaming contexts as "learning the rules") is a great asset, and any procedure that achieves this deserves our careful scrutiny.

Environmental games often call for the adoption of highly structured roles. Game participants might, for example, be asked to play from the perspective of central government or the perspective of the general interests of the community, of a land speculator, a planner, or a police officer. Playing a structured role is supposed to put one in someone else's shoes. In this way one is supposed to understand how the other person feels, what pressures control the other person's activities. This may give one the feeling of deep insight, but it is almost certainly an illusion. Having the feelings of another requires having the experiences that created the cognitive structure that resides in the other's head. This does not happen merely by taking on the other's part in a game.

The inclination to regard oneself as capable of putting oneself in the shoes of another is widespread and occurs outside the context of gaming as well. Environmental designers are sometimes encouraged to do this (Jensen, 1974). Canter (1977) describes one architect who reaped considerable publicity by living for several weeks in a housing project he had designed. As Canter rightly points out, however, all the architect found out was what it was like for an *architect* to live in that project! There is, alas, no magic that can transport one to the shoes of another. An alternative strategy is to provide the people whose shoes are in question with some basis for understanding possible alternatives. Simulation, which can be so helpful in achieving this goal, is discussed in the next two chapters.

The involvement of games is hard to resist. While this is one of their assets, it is also a potential liability. It is a liability in part because one can become so motivated by the game aspect that the content issues become overshadowed (see R. Kaplan, 1976). Involvement can be distracting, particularly when it is external to the content, as is readily the case in gaming. At the same time, games readily become coercive. One is under great pressure to participate fully, that is, to play the role one is assigned and to follow the rule structure imposed on the situation.

Some of the greatest assets of games do not necessitate a gaming context. Involvement can be achieved in other ways as well. Physical models of the environment are often sufficiently engaging that they can be used directly as modes of information transfer without the artificial aspects that a game brings with it. Comparably, many environmental problems have built-in requirements and constraints (e.g., see Steinitz, 1981) that make an imposed rule structure unnecessary.

On Analogies

One of the strengths of the gaming approach is the use of a concrete pattern to stand for something more complex and initially unfamiliar. An approach that is in some respects similar involves the use of analogies. There are times when a familiar or easy to understand pattern can convey a great deal of information about something that might otherwise be quite obscure. The description of mountain-climbing tech-

High Adventure On Cupboard Rock

How Mickey and Minnie Mouse Sew Up A Climb

Our scene opens with this mouse, Mickey, carefully scurrying up a kitchen cabinet after some goodies—as mice are inclined to do on occasion. He is hauling the end of a thread with him (actually, it's tied around his waist). Below him is another mouse, played by Minnie, and she's holding the same thread at a point between Mickey and the spool. As Mickey climbs, Minnie pays out the thread so that it is always slightly slack. Minnie has also tied herself to the cabinet so as not to fall or be pulled off.

Now if Mickey went 30" above Minnie, stumbled and fell, he would fall 30" to Minnie. This would cause 30" of slack thread to build up, and Mickey would have to fall another 30" below Minnie before the slack

paid out; a total fall of 60". That long a fall is pretty hard on the ole gut. Well, it's really not the fall that hurts, but the sudden stop at the end.

Let's go back and watch Mickey start again—the correct way. Instead of climbing the full 30" at once, he only climbs 5", stops, drives an upholstery tack into the cabinet with his little mouse hammer, and attaches a jeweler's clasp to a hole he has drilled through the tack's head. He then clips the thread into the clasp. Now, if he slipped, he would be held by the tack, clasp, and thread which Minnie is holding the other end of, and would hardly fall any distance at all. If, as he continues to climb, he attaches his thread to the cabinet every 5" in this manner, he will not be able to fall more than 10" no matter how high he goes. Much safer this way.

When Mickey gets to the top shelf, he scoops up the Camembert cheese and rye thins, sets up his thread for the descent, and slides down with the goods. Whereupon

Minnie says, "Gee, that was great, Mickey, but wouldn't it have been easier to walk up the other side without all this hoorah?"

"I guess so," replies our hero, "but I dig it." And together they polish off the succulent morsels, washing them down with a thimbleful of white wine (Liebfraumilch, Blue Nun, vintage 1968).

Afterword. *Substitute rock, snow, or ice for cabinet; leader for Mickey; belayer for Minnie; rope for thread; piton, chock, or bolt (nah—we don't like bolts!) for tack (point of protection—anchor); carabiner for clasp; and rappel for "slides down." If we've done this right, you'll have a pretty good idea of what free climbing is.*

From Explorers Ltd. Source Book, *story by Chris Patterson, art by Bill Mack, reprinted by permission of Explorers (ETM) Ltd.* © *1973.*

niques (see box) shows an ingenious application of this approach. Note, however, that both the analogy and the information to be conveyed are concrete. By contrast, the description of how paging systems work in digital computers (see box) illustrates how helpful an analogy can be for giving concreteness to a description that otherwise might seem hopelessly abstract.

Another popular use of analogies is in their use as vehicles for understanding natural processes. There has, for example, been something of a tradition in psychology of using physical models in exploring mental processes. Freud used the analogy of a hydraulic model, calling upon a knowledge structure presumably familiar to readers of that time. Since then the telephone switchboard has served as a model of the mind, followed by the digital computer, and, most recently, the hologram. Despite the great advantage of being able to call on pre-existing structure, such analogies have an inherent difficulty. They apply to an unknown degree. At some point they break down, and precisely where that point is located is rarely clear. Not infrequently one hears that the mind is like a filing cabinet. It undoubtedly is in certain respects. It does hold information, and it is organized. As we have seen, however, there are a great many ways in which the mind is not like a filing cabinet. Such borrowed structures lack built-in markers telling us which respects are the salient ones and to what extent the analogy holds.

On The Usefulness of Graphic Material

In our consideration of material that is both vivid and concrete, graphic material would have to be considered a strong candidate. In earlier chapters we saw that the cognitive process itself seems to be built on

Paging

Below are two descriptions of the paging process, an arrangement used to increase the effective memory capacity of a computer. The description on the left uses traditional computer terminology; the description on the right is parallel, item by item, but replaces the jargon with concrete and familiar terms.

The Paging System—Rules

1. Any computer job can have up to 16,777,216 **bytes** of memory at once.
2. Memory is divided into **pages** of 4096 bytes each.
3. Pages are stored either in the **real memory** or on a **paging device**. The real memory is almost always too small to hold all the pages.
4. There is only one real memory (eight million bytes of storage) and four principal paging devices (IBM 2305 fixed-head file storage units). All the jobs share them.
5. Each byte has an **address**.
6. What you do to bytes is to **reference** (i.e., store data in or fetch data from) them. Jobs take turns referencing.
7. Jobs can reference only their own bytes, not anybody else's.
8. Bytes can be referenced only when they're in real memory.
9. Only the **operating system** (i.e., MTS, the supervisor, and paging-device program) knows whether a byte is in real memory or on the paging device.
10. The longer a byte (or a page) goes without being referenced, the **less recently used** it is said to become.
11. The way a job gets bytes is to request them from the system. Memory is allocated in groups of eight bytes (doublewords) to make the system's recordkeeping process easier.

The Crafting Game—Rules

1. You can have up to sixteen million **things**. So can everybody else.
2. Things are kept in **crates** that hold 4,096 things each. Things in the same crate are called cratemates.
3. Crates are stored either in the **workshop** or a **warehouse**. The workshop is almost always too small to hold all the crates.
4. There is only one workshop and four warehouses. Everybody shares them.
5. Each thing has its own **thing number**.
6. What you do with a thing is to **zark** it. Everybody takes turns zarking.
7. You can zark only your things, not anybody else's.
8. Things can be zarked only when they're in the workshop.
9. Only the **Thing King** knows whether a thing is in the workshop or in one of the warehouses.
10. The longer a thing goes without being zarked, the **grubbier** it is said to become.
11. The way you get your things is to ask the Thing King. The Thing King gives out things only in bunches of eight. This is to keep the royal overhead down.

Reprinted by permission of the author, J. Berryman. Excerpted from University of Michigan Computer Center Newsletter, October 24, 1979, vol. 9, no. 16, p. 203.

the demands of a visual/spatial environment at least as much as on the demands of a verbal one. People readily understand visual material; they often use visual and spatial expressions to try to understand abstract concepts.

The emphasis on the visual/spatial presentation mode has not, however, gone unchallenged. The argument has been made that this constitutes far too much concern for "visual information," for the "appearance of things." This is an understandable misconception, but a misconception nonetheless. Information received in the visual mode is not "visual information"; it is information. If one determines by way of vision that a lion is stealthily approaching, then the appropriate conclusion is that a lion is approaching, not a "visual lion" or the "visual image of a lion." Vision, like the other modes of attention (Gibson, 1966), provides information about the world. It provides information that is the domain of other senses as well as vision. In humans, of course, the visual mode is particularly rich in the number of dimensions it is sensitive to and in the discrimination it can make. It is also a mode that people tend to trust (Posner, 1978; see also Chapter 2).

Since vision is oriented to things and spaces in the world, and into what the things and spaces afford for the viewer, what one achieves through vision is not "mere appearances" but a complex assessment of what one's possibilities are, of what one could do. It is this functional world that one experiences; vision is one of the most effective means humans have for finding out about it.

Photographs are a particularly useful mode of presentation in many cases. They provide an easy means of showing various examples of possible approaches or solutions to a problem. They seem to be understandable by people across different cultures (Collier, 1967; Kennedy, 1974). In practical terms (and for research purposes, too), this means that the capacity to deal with photographs is close to universal; there is no concern about literacy levels, as might be the case with verbal material.

There is also a growing body of literature pointing to the validity of a photograph as an environmental surrogate. This issue has been particularly carefully studied in the area of landscape assessment, where it has been repeatedly demonstrated that people's ratings of an environment are very highly correlated with their ratings of pictures of that environment (Chapter 4, Note 2). On the other hand, there is some evidence that ratings of a photograph of some aspect of a setting are not necessarily similar to ratings of a corresponding brief verbal description. The verbal description seems to encourage a highly stereotyped reaction (R. Kaplan, 1977a).

It is not only the case that people understand photographs; they also enjoy looking at them. This bias toward the visual and spatial was turned to great advantage by an anthropologist. Finding that his informants soon tired of answering questions, he requested permission to take pictures. When the pictures were printed, he asked if his informants wished to look at them and comment on them. They were delighted to do so, providing extensive interpretation and analysis. In one case an expert weaver who had resisted the picture-taking process reacted to the resulting photographs in an unexpected fashion. He indicated that the photographs were unsatisfactory; they did not show the important steps, and they must be taken again. During the retakes he told the anthropologist exactly when the picture should be taken; he also rounded up some weavers who had trained with him to have pictures taken of slight variants in the process (Collier, 1967).

The positive reaction people tend to have toward photographs points to the feasibility of using such a procedure for knowledge transfer. Photographs are effective for many environmental issues since one's experience of the environment so frequently comes from visual and spatial information.

There are times when photographs of how environments are structured in other places give one a good idea of what the possibilities are. There are many times, however, when the unique properties of a particular setting limit the usefulness of photographs from elsewhere. In such cases the cognitive principles we have discussed strongly suggest environmental simulation as a promising means of information transfer. Essentially the goal is to present information in a form that facilitates forming a cognitive map. A simulation does this very well or, rather, is capable of doing it very well. Here, too, it is possible to function in many different modes, some far more supportive than others of human cognitive functioning. A number of these issues are discussed in the next chapter.

SOME CONCLUDING COMMENTS

People prefer environments in which they can make sense of what they perceive and in which they can learn more. When a person becomes an information recipient, those preferences remain pertinent. Some communications expand a person's comprehension; these tend to be valued and even to be sought. Some communications either are hard to understand in themselves or make the world harder to understand. These are, not surprisingly, ignored or avoided. People are motivated to achieve clarity; they tend to evaluate information in terms of its contribution to this process.

If people's reactions to information can appropriately be cast in a larger preference framework, then the same factors that predict preference in other contexts should apply to the messages people perceive.

Here the parallels to Chapter 4 are quite straightforward. *Complexity* is important in that a message must be about something to be worth attending to. It must have substance; it cannot be trivial. *Coherence* refers to the unity necessary for a message to fit together, to form a whole. *Legibility* is a particularly important aspect. It involves the feeling that one is gaining in comprehension, that one has a sense of increasing grasp. *Mystery* functions as a sense of open-endedness. It involves the feeling that there will be more to learn, that the communication points to new possibilities still to be explored.

Just as the sharing of knowledge can be related to the prior discussions of preference, it can also be tied directly to the cognitive map material. Sharing knowledge, after all, can be viewed as a process of attempting to assist someone in building a cognitive map. A cognitive map cannot be transplanted; that much is clear. It must be built by its new owner-to-be, but this by no means rules out the possibility of assistance. To begin with, a cognitive map is easier to learn if the units are coherent within themselves and separable from each other. Secondly, there is the matter of respecting what the learner already knows and providing new information in a way that is both coherent and relatable to that prior knowledge. Such an approach has both cognitive advantages in terms of connectedness and the motivational advantages that go with the satisfaction of extending one's knowledge. In one's eagerness to be helpful, however, there is a danger of providing too much information. Here, too, violation of the principle can be costly on both cognitive and motivational grounds.

The attempt to communicate knowlege thus presents a study in contrasts. The communicator is clear, organized, eager. The intended recipient of the information is readily susceptible to diffusion, confusion, and overload. One can sympathize with both perspectives, but if the communication is to be effective and the experience is to be a positive one, it is the perspective of the recipient that is paramount. Understanding and respecting the cognitive requirements of the intended recipient constitute probably the single most effective step one can take in improving the process of sharing knowlege.

NOTES

1. Gaming

The literature on gaming is diverse and growing. Horn's (1977) volume provides detailed description and information on hundreds of games. The title of their chapter notwithstanding, Fromkin and Steufert (1975) present a great deal of material on this topic. Duke and Greenblat (1979), Sanoff (1979), and Tester (1974) present a variety of environmental and design-oriented games. Despite the emphasis on user participation and on the educational aspects of games, however, much of the material is low on imagery. Nonetheless, these sources are useful in showing how readily games can be adapted to a wide range of settings.

chapter nine

RESEARCH AS INTERMEDIATE TECHNOLOGY

There are many things we do not know. For some, we must be resigned to this state of affairs. For others, we accept one or more of the interpretations that are offered. However, as cognitive, information-processing beings we do not rest easily. Our desire to comprehend, to extend our maps, seems boundless. We seek solutions, explore new directions, challenge yesterday's explanations. There are many people in our culture who devote their lives to this quest. Research is a process of seeking answers. It is an important activity if we are to find ways to cope with ever-changing conditions.

Research also has its adversaries. The point is not that we know all we need to know, but that the consequence of this expensive, massive search for answers often has been short of successful; it has perhaps even been damaging at times. It has generated information that is so complex that it is seen as having little or no use. It has raised hopes to no avail. It has permitted a sense of false confidence on the part of the users of the information. Furthermore, it has brought no answers for so many of the most pressing problems.

There are many approaches to research that, although vastly different from each other, have in common that they characteristically lead to unfortunate consequences. For example, there are the well-intended studies that are overly sloppy, leading to false faith in the results. There are also many research efforts that are more enamored with methodological subtleties than with a concern for the generalizability of the results. It is to such work that Hebb (1974) applied the maxim "What's not worth doing is not worth doing well."

The purpose of this chapter is to provide an alternative perspective of the research process. We are concerned particularly with those areas of research that are related to issues of environmental cognition—research that is concerned with environments and with people, that examines the questions of how people comprehend, evaluate, and function in the environment. In a sense, the chapter constitutes a special application of the framework developed throughout the volume to a set of activities

197

that are dominant in our culture. Research constitutes a particular form of expertise, one that can be of vital significance, but all too often is not.

As we have seen, experts often have difficulty sharing information. This is doubly a problem for researchers, since they face the necessity of sharing information at two critical junctures in the process. Participants in research often must comprehend the task and the setting if they are to respond meaningfully. At the other end of the process, the results must be shared with potential users if the purpose of the research is to be realized.

Viewing both of these requirements from a cognitive perspective may be helpful. If research involves people, then it must be remembered what people are like. Further, if people are to cooperate, they must be dealt with as people, not as objects obligated to the researcher. If the results are to be used, the nature of the recipient of the information must also be addressed. In other words, the likelihood of application, of the use of knowledge, is in large part a cognitive problem. It is ultimately dependent on how readily what is discovered can be incorporated into the way people think, the way they conceptualize and solve practical problems. It is inseparable from the problem of sharing knowledge.

At this point a cautionary comment is probably in order, a warning on the label, so to speak, in big, red letters. Research is clearly many different activities accomplished in a great variety of ways. The view of research portrayed here must be considered out of the mainstream of contemporary academic research—a distant drum perhaps, but hopefully one worth hearing.

AN ALTERNATIVE VIEW OF RESEARCH

Technology has received widespread acclaim for bringing us where we are today. At the same time, an increasing number of people are less than pleased by where we are today. It is becoming popular to wonder whether science and its applications are more part of the problem than part of the solution. Is science a cornucopia, or is it a sleek, highly polished Pandora's box? In the midst of a debate that readily becomes polarized, surely one of the most thoughtful voices to be heard in recent years is that of Schumacher (1973). His concept of "intermediate technology" points to the importance of the *kind* of science (and application of science) that is to meet human needs and help solve human problems. Intermediate technology is within people's means and comprehension; it extends what people can do rather than replacing them.

Schumacher's thesis was developed in the context of aid to the less-developed countries, but foreign aid has no monopoly on technology-gone-beserk. We seem to have progressed from knowledge for its own sake to science for its own sake to methodology for its own sake. Perhaps the intricate technology of sophisticated research methodology has advantages in allowing experts to remain beyond criticism (especially from other experts), but in the process it clearly has acquired the handicaps that Schumacher associates with advanced technology. It is expensive. It is too complex for ordinary people to use, or even to understand. It makes the already challenging problem of sharing knowledge orders of magnitude more difficult. It we have any hopes of involving people in the decision-making process, we have to concern ourselves with making the research process accessible to a wider audience.

The approach we are trying to convey here views research as an intermediate technology. Such an approach can be adapted to the needs of a citizen group, it can be comprehended by researcher and participant alike, and it need not be expensive. Perhaps it should be called "research for the left hand." It recognizes the limitations imposed by reality and the unavoidability of imperfection. This should not, however, be confused with research that is sloppy or ill-conceived. Certain imperfections can be tolerated; others are inexcusable. One cannot always (in the real world) count on a stratified random sample (or even on a random sample, for that matter), but to use material that the participant cannot understand as the basis for the participant's reactions is inexcusable. Research that is meaningless or uninterpretable is not worth doing.

It cannot be emphasized too much that meaningless research is never a contribution. At the same time, imperfection in research must not become a hangup. All research is imperfect. The critical issues are (1) careful selection of the dimensions on which imperfections are acceptable and (2) careful thought as to the expense that greater perfection would involve. Often the practical choice boils down to doing it approximately or doing it not at all.

Doing it, if it is not fundamentally flawed, has two advantages. First, theory rarely rises or falls on the basis of a single study. Every study is incomplete and provides only a partial view. Multiple studies across different groups of people and different settings will be necessary no matter how elaborate each individual study:

> In a way, the scientific method might be considered as a tool for constructing telescopes for viewing nature. A particular telescope may be turned in one direction or another, and different telescopes will have different magnifications and different kinds of distortions built into their optical systems. It is unlikely that any single view will provide an even remotely adequate picture of the complex territory that we want to understand. Perhaps by piecing a large number of partial views together and making allowances for

certain probable distortions, a rough "map" of the totality can be constructed. Even such an inexact representation may offer better understanding of the territory than no map at all. (Scott and Wertheimer, 1962, p. 12)

The second argument in favor of an intermediate technology approach to research is highly pragmatic. Decisions about the environment are being made every day. Designers, planners, and managers continue to ply their trade, with or without adequate information. Often guidance from research can be enormously helpful, but the decision will be made without if the data are not available. People continue, as they have for centuries, to fumble along, doing the best they can. This is no different now than it ever was. The difference is how widespread an impact such decisions can now have. As it is possible to make bigger changes in the environment and to implement them more rapidly than ever before, the scale of possible mistakes, even disasters, has risen proportionately. Thus there is disproportionate payoff for even a few data—if the data are available in time and in comprehendible form.

To guide decision-making, then, the emphasis must be placed on the usefulness of the information. Scientists, however, have long been trained to emphasize precision. Their inclination toward exactitude, and the associated yearning for the definitive and the certain, may in quieter times have seemed a harmless idiosyncracy. Such luxuries may, however, no longer be affordable. McHarg (1969, p. 125), who holds the scientist in high regard, raises a similar concern:

> One of the most serious criticisms is that they are thoroughly irresolute in the absence of impeccable evidence, and this is a profound weakness in a world which is finally unknowable.

Such concerns for exactitude and definiteness are by no means unheard of among scientists studying problems in environment and behavior. One sometimes runs into the disclaimer that the results of a study may not apply to any other group or setting. While this might be considered "truth-in-packaging," it can also be viewed as utter irresponsibility. If the study yields no information that can be used beyond its own confines, it is a doubtful contribution.

Another area where precision may be overemphasized is environmental simulation. Since design and planning necessarily deal with environments that do not exist, models of future environments are an important tool. Such models could also be a valuable aid for enhancing human comprehension of possible futures. A major obstacle to greater use of this potentially powerful tool is the generally unexamined assumption that the more exact a copy an environmental simulation is, the better. Since this is an issue that very well demonstrates the costs of inappropriate exactitude and since it has some thoroughly practical implications both for research and for application, it is worth looking at in somewhat greater detail.

Simulation and Purpose

Of the several misconceptions that limit the effectiveness and usefulness of a simulation, one of the most pervasive is the idea that a simulation is a copy of the environment it depicts. This notion leads to an emphasis on detail, on exactness, in the simulation. It leads to packing in too much information, thus encouraging overload and ignoring the need for simplicity. It also fails to take advantage of cognitive structures. Since the mental representations the simulation hopes to call up are highly simplified and schematic, the use of simple, prototypic forms in the simulation would be far more appropriate. Ironically, failing to recognize the merits of simplicity leads to simulations that are extremely expensive. Although cost per se may not seem to be particularly vital issue, it has consequences that are practical and critical. Environmental simulation as it is now practiced in a number of leading centers (e.g., highway planning) is too expensive and technologically too complex to be available to many groups who might otherwise find this procedure enormously informative and helpful (Chapter Note 1).

A further consequence of the "copy of the environment" orientation is that environmental simulations are often evaluated to see if human reaction to the actual environment is identical to the reaction to the simulated environment (e.g., Danford and Willems, 1975; McKechnie, 1977). To create an identical reaction, people have to be convinced that they are seeing the real environment when in fact they are not; in other words, people have to be deceived. Perhaps for this reason, Appleyard (1977, p. 46) comes to the conclusion that:

> The credibility of these simulations is now in question. The products do not always live up to the simulations. Materials have a different color; wind, rain, and snow radically affect character; trees take time to grow; maintenance is costly; cars park everywhere; and unforeseen side effects materialize.

Knowing that something is a scale model need not destroy its effectiveness. When one examines a scale model of the heart or of an internal combustion engine, how much one comprehends has little to do with the confusion of model and reality. *Presumably a simulation is constructed for a purpose.* The issue is whether people respond the same way to the model as they would to reality with respect to that purpose. The model is intended as an aid to thought, not as a full-fledged substitute for reality.

Ironically, these two stances with respect to simulation are at opposite poles when it comes to their way of relating to human cognition. To attempt to fool people into thinking that a model is a reality is to work against the human capacity. Under such circumstances people take great joy in discovering discrepancies between model and reality. The alternative approach, by contrast, calls upon human cognition to aid the process. People are told, "Look at this model and try to figure out how you would feel about x and y if you were in the real environment that this model represents." People have a considerable capacity for the subjunctive, to operate in the "as if" mode.

Simplification as an Asset

It is not hard to argue for simplification as an economic necessity as far as simulation is concerned. Simplification, however, is not merely a necessary evil. It is a positive asset. A simplified model of the environment is more likely to parallel people's cognitive structure. Hence the very simplicity of the model may encourage its use. A simplified model also encourages generality; details make things particular, thus narrowing their range of appropriateness. Finally, simplification reduces the total load on one's processing system.

Despite all these virtues, the question of validity remains. Can people effectively relate to an obviously simplified model? Can they make the same judgments, the same inferences that would be possible if extensive detail were included? This is a rather basic issue (Chapter Note 2). An enormous amount of money and skill has been lavished on detailed models. Is one justified in questioning this widespread practice on theoretical grounds alone?

Fortunately this issue has been the subject of an empirical test. R. Kaplan, S. Kaplan, and Deardorff (1974) contrasted people's reactions to two different levels of models, one highly detailed and one extremely simple. The same two housing developments were depicted at both levels of detail. Since the high-detail models were quite obviously more attractive than the simple ones, it was clear that if the same people saw both they would greatly favor the "prettier" material. Thus each participant saw only one level of detail, but for both housing developments (Figure 9.1).

The participants were not asked how much they liked the models, nor, for that matter, were they asked how much they liked each of the housing developments the models represented. Rather, to make the task more realistic, they were asked to rate the projects in terms of a series of characteristics salient to such situations—how satisfactory each would be for privacy, for raising children, for meeting people, for getting where one wanted to go, and so on. The results were most informative. While participants found the settings more adequate in some respects than in

Figure 9.1 Sample views from Kaplan, Kaplan, and Deardorff (1974): the top row depicts high-detail models, while the scenes in the bottom row show low-detail versions of the same sites. The views at left and right represent two different housing developments.

others, these reactions were not affected by the level of detail that was provided. There was one exception to this: participants who saw the simple models did not feel they could evaluate the architecture—hardly surprising since the simple models provided little architectural information.

The study essentially confirms the appropriateness of using simple environmental simulations as a means of knowledge transfer. There was, however, a pattern of findings that makes it incorrect to say that the level of detail makes little difference. One of the groups participating consisted of architecture students. For this group the general findings did not hold. They found the arrangements depicted by the simple models unsatisfactory; in other words, they felt the sites were not adequate with respect to any of the characteristics mentioned. They also felt that the housing development with poorer architecture was unsatisfactory even when they saw it in the high-detail version. The site with superior architecture, when presented in its high-detail version, was the only one they found acceptable, and it was considered to be highly satisfactory with respect to all the items. This tendency to react in a global fashion, demonstrating what is sometimes called a "halo effect," was not characteristic of the other participants in the study. Given these results, the possibility of an architect's standing in the shoes of another, of experiencing the world from the view point of someone else, seems even more problematic.

While it is reassuring to know that most participants can make meaningful judgments based on simple models and that their responses are no different from those made by viewers of more articulated models, these findings do not speak to the critical issue of "reality." In other words, do the responses to the models provide any useful indication of people's reactions to the actual environment? After all, the use of models is most appropriate in helping people to image environments that are not yet existent. Based on the simulations that are often provided, the response to the final structures is often one of surprise.

Participants in this study were presented with eight views of the actual housing developments after they had expressed their reactions to the photographs of the models. For these they were not asked to make the same judgments, but rather to indicate how well the actual arrangements coincide with their expectations based on the prior visual information. The participants who had viewed the more detailed models were no different in their indicated "surprises" than those whose initial input was based on simple models. Across virtually all the comparisons, viewers of both the simple and the detailed models expressed virtually the same pattern with respect to the adequacy of the models in communicating information about the sites.

Figure 9.2 Top row: Models using children's building blocks on chalk-shaded ground plane. Bottom row: Urban setting with buildings made of Lego blocks.

Simple models are feasible at a variety of scales. Not only can one use them to depict housing developments; they are equally effective at smaller and larger scales (Figure 9.2). In fact their usefulness as a research tool, as a means of "bringing the environment into the laboratory," is just beginning to be explored. They create a much more interesting and realistic laboratory setting than one usually finds; at the same time they offer far more experimental control than is characteristic of a field study.

RESEARCH AS PARTICIPATION

The themes of intermediate technology in the research context lead to a variety of issues that modify the way one does research. Many of these focus on the human element implicit in the process. A pervasive misreading of science links the legitimate concern with objectivity to the conception of researchers as nonhuman (so as not to be biased by their own feelings) and subjects as nonhumans (lest they, too, become biased). Viewed as an intermediate technology, however, research must become participatory. It cannot afford to ignore the nature of the humans touched by the research activities.

Research necessarily involves various groups—those who conduct the studies, those who might benefit from the results (directly or indirectly), and, in the case of behavioral research, those who are the source of the data. They all share some human qualities: a concern to understand, to make a difference, and an irksome irritability when this concern is stifled.

Collaboration

Research is done for many reasons. Despite this variability of motivation, however, it is safe to say that research is being done on the assumption that someone somewhere will care about and make use of the results obtained. Often this someone is a rather abstract, hypothetical being. Unfortunately research oriented to such a vague and generalized individual frequently turns out to be of little interest or use to real, concrete people.

To be useful, the results of research must be comprehendible and they must in some sense "fit" with the needs of the potential user. One way to increase the probability that this will happen is to ascertain these needs beforehand. In other words, if the researcher has some contact with the potential user of the research, it is more likely that the research will be responsive to the requirements of the user.

There is nothing new in these statements. The studies that have shown that "in-house" research has a much greater likelihood of being needed (than research carried out by researchers in academe) are in part illustrative of these issues (Caplan, 1976). Such in-house research is more likely to ask the questions that require answers, is more likely to be reported in a form that others will find usable, and is more likely to become known to the potential users of the information.

Having information about the requirements of the potential users of research is a big step toward research that makes a difference. An even bigger step in this direction involves not merely knowing about potential users but actively collaborating with them in formulating and carrying out the research. The idea of research as intermediate technology is particularly appropriate to a collaborative approach. Maintaining the research process at the level of extreme specialization, where only a very few can exchange insights, effectively puts a damper on collaboration. Conversely, by avoiding obscurity and complex research technology, it is easier to bring together the complementary expertises of the various pertinent parties. Ideally the researcher is knowledgeable about where imperfections are tolerable in the research process and about how to create the instruments that will lead to meaningful responses. Other expertises are also essential to the project, however. Intermediate technology makes a contribution not merely by resisting the most complex and most expensive choices, but by fitting the local and the human requirements of the situation. Collaboration makes it possible to deal with these requirements not as tag-on or afterthought but as a basic constraint in the way research is designed. The very fact that the different groups who have a stake in the results may have different requirements and approaches (see Ostrander, 1975) suggests the need for collaboration early in the process.

A brief word of warning. Effective collaboration is no simpler to achieve than effective research! For different people to work together, for different disciplines to work together, it is important not to expect too much (see Bechtel, 1977). All too often such efforts do not work. It is hardly surprising that experts might have trouble working together. As we shall see in Chapter 10, they are often easily threatened. Furthermore, their cognitive maps are different. Once again the process of sharing information is crucial, and once again the different views of the world characteristic of the way the expert thinks play a central role. As we have seen, such difficulties are not resolved easily. Coming to a mutual understanding takes time, patience, and skill. For optimal effectiveness the collaborators have to do more than just understand each other's contributions. A higher-level map must be constructed so that what each party has to offer comes to be counted on and appreciated. *Thus collaboration is most effective when the areas of expertise complement each other, when the people involved have a desire to learn from each other, and, finally, when they have respect for each other's potential contributions to the process.*

The Scientist as Human

When research is seen as a participatory activity, the scientist abandons the proverbial white coat. For some, this comes with much relief. The view of the scientist as superhuman—devoid of emotion and quite neutral with respect to outcome—must be an outsider's view. Many scientists care deeply about how their research comes out—this is not what sets them apart from other people. Indeed, it would seem strange to go through all that work if one did not care deeply. The special character of science is an outcome of having all those other scientists always figuratively looking over one's shoulder. The objectivity of science comes not from the scientist's disinterest, but from the nature of the procedures. The procedures must be so explicitly described and repeatable that someone else could obtain the same results.

Despite the sacrifice of the white coat, working in a collaborative setting often augments the researcher's satisfaction with the process. It becomes much easier for the researcher to see that the answers are, in fact, of interest to others.

The Participants

We have used the word "collaborators" to describe the various groups who are involved in developing a study and who are likely to use the results to formulate decisions. The people who respond to the research material are also in a sense collaborators, but we have chosen to refer to them as "participants." They are also sometimes referred to as "respondents," "actors," and "subjects," depending on the circumstances and the training of the researcher. By calling these people participants, we make evident several implications of doing research. If someone is "party" to your project, it is (hopefully) more difficult to deceive, to raise unwarranted expectations, or to treat the person as a thing. As a human being, a participant has the characteristics the rest of this book is devoted to portraying. Humans are capable, cognitive organisms with an almost insatiable desire to comprehend and an annoying inclination to become angry and destructive when frustrated. On the other hand, under certain circumstances, they actually enjoy being helpful.

Is that consistent with the researcher's purposes, though? Does that not lead to the participant's saying what the researcher wants to hear? How can one maintain objectivity when the subject is party to the goals of the research?

These are important questions, and, not surprisingly, they have rather complex answers. In part the issues seem to depend on the interaction between the structure of an experiment and the way people think. Perhaps because of the fear of contaminating the results, there is an inclination for researchers to keep their "subjects" in ignorance as to the significance and intent of what they are doing. While there are obviously times when too much information could in fact bias the results, this inclination toward secrecy is often well beyond what is necessary. At the same time the consequences of this ignorance-ensuring attitude can ultimately undermine the researcher's purposes. Not knowing what is going on inclines the "subjects" to have little stake in what they are doing. They are particularly likely to please the experimenter when they care little about the content of the experiment and want to take an easy way out (see Argyris, 1968). As Sarason (1973) has pointed out, the attitudes that are easiest to change are the ones that people have little invested in.

The human concern to comprehend, to make sense of what is going on, operates even in a research setting. People want to know what they are doing, what the point of it is, what the intended use is to be. If they are not given sufficient information to place what they are asked to do in context, they may devote a substantial portion of their processing capacity to trying to figure it out, to creating a sensible story that relates the aspects that are accessible to them. Since human processing capacity is limited, the quality of effort devoted to the researcher's task is likely to suffer. It is rare in the environmental domain that hiding the intent of the research is called for, but many researchers have a way of being secretive—as if the "best subject is an ignorant subject." When it is realized that people who are given insufficient information are likely to invent their own, the shortsightedness of this point of view becomes evident.

The implication here is that a participatory research style requires that information be given to the participants in order to make the process useful. Some simple examples involve determining what people might wish a park to be like, or a shopping mall, or where they would like transfer points on a new transportation line. The straightforward approach of simply asking the question is very likely to lead to a stereotyped response, and the questioner has little idea of the person's potentially knowledgeable reply.

Essentially these situations cast the participant in the role of problem solver. Problem solving, in turn, is totally dependent upon the way the problem is presented. In most instances it cannot be assumed that the participant can call up an appropriate representation of the problem at the mention of a few words. *Providing information in such contexts may require informing the participant of some of the existing constraints or, better yet, providing a few feasible alternative solutions to the problem to set the effort in motion.* By seeing even two possible solutions, the participant has a much better idea of the range to be considered, and the input might lead to new combinations or modifications.

By keeping research manageable, within the reach of ordinary people, and by permitting the process to be understandable and meaningful to those whose lives are affected by the results, researchers may find some new answers to the basic questions of environmental cognition. What appears to be emerging bit by bit is a tool that makes it possible to share widely both the process of finding out and the results.

RESEARCH AS COGNITIVE ACTIVITY

Research involves an attempt to find things out, to seek answers. As such, it is not an activity restricted to a particular subgroup; rather, it is a basic human effort. In fact, all of us are likely to have done some research within the area of environmental cognition: checking to see which route works out best, arranging a room to everyone's satisfaction, trying out ways of achieving a little peace and quiet in an otherwise demanding environment. The procedures may not have been explicit, and there may not have been any effort to share the outcomes, but the activities were nonetheless an informal kind of research.

When one wants the outcome of the research activities to be shareable, or at least to be convincing to others, it is necessary to make explicit what may have previously been purely intuitive. In order to convince the planning commission that a proposed zoning change would be harmful to the sense of community, it is necessary to come to terms with what one means by "sense of community." Perhaps it is unfortunate that such important concepts are not defined in the dictionary, but it is unlikely that a dictionary definition would be of much help anyway. Dictionaries tend to provide defining, or critical, features. As we have seen, however, such definitions are likely to misrepresent the way one actually knows or thinks of things. Further, the implicit question in many applied situations is not "what are the defining features?" but "how would you know if it were there?" and "how would you know if it changed?" In other words, when one attempts to "go public" with one's intuitions and informal research, the problem of how one would define something readily turns into the issue of how one would measure it.

Constructs

It turns out that many of the important and interesting topics that concern environmental psychologists are based on amorphous, hard-to-define, rather abstract concepts. (In the context of research such concepts are often called *constructs*.) While this poses a certain handicap for general discourse, it becomes a major obstacle when one attempts to do research. Simple, little representations, such as "neighborhood," "scale," "nature," and "knowledge" to name a few, involve a great deal of shared imagery among people who use the words in discourse. Therefore it is not too difficult to talk about these concepts; nor is it difficult to have hunches about what affects them or how they affect people. What is difficult is to come up with convincing empirical support for these hunches; part of the reason for this involves the difficulty of measuring these nebulous ideas.

Science has always involved abstract concepts and their measurement. Scientists are accustomed to talking about "things" that have no direct, visible reality, and in time others, too, talk about these "things" as if they had seen them. Therefore, rods and cones, genes, and subatomic particles are just as much inventions as are the notions of design and territory (Chapter Note 3). With any hypothetical entity we feel reassured if there is some basis for believing that there exist real, physical indicators. For example, knowing that "it" can be seen in an electron microscope is reassuring, even if most of us never have. Comparably, the idea of stress seems more reassuring if we believe there to be a physiological measure of it.

These are, relatively speaking, delusions. The reality of the constructs that are essential to our making sense of the world is rarely available in the form of a direct physical entity. The more we know about a construct, the more evident this becomes. Perhaps for this reason, the constructs about which we know quite a bit—and this includes much that is the concern of environmental psychology—seem particularly elusive when it comes to measurement.

How can one go about finding measures for such amorphous concepts? One approach is relatively straightforward. It involves the assertion that, at least for purposes of the present study, a particular construct will be defined in terms of a particular measure. For example, one could measure subjective distance (the sense of how far something is, as opposed to its physical distance) in terms of participants' estimates of how long it would take to traverse the distance. Whatever results the study might yield would be stated in terms of subjective distance, but the basis would be time estimates.

Another example might involve measurement of the kinds of environments in which the subjective distance is being studied. Thus, a study might conclude that distances seem longer when one is new to a place. "Place," too, is a construct, and its measurement is also problematic. The direct specification of place might involve a particular setting, perhaps interpretive trails at a particular nature center. Of course, "new" is simple enough to measure. One simply asks people if they have ever been to that place before.

These, then, constitute examples in which the construct is "defined" through one particular aspect of the various interrelated components underlying it. When one incorporates more of these components—other aspects of subjective distance, for example—the research becomes more involved and the possibility of discovering contradictions increases. One is asking for trouble! Let us examine this matter more closely.

Construct Validation

Imagine a newspaper headline that reads, "Learning facilitated by noise from low-flying planes." It may well be that the researcher who is cited would be less than pleased by the headline. The headline is blunt about the underlying constructs, as opposed to the particular ways they were measured. The researcher, in all likelihood, would prefer to describe the study in terms closer to the particular measures that were used. The issue here is not whether the study has adequate controls (i.e., the research design), but the translation between the constructs and the ways they were measured. This is an important distinction. Inadequate controls, for example, might lead one to question whether the results are a function of the plane noise per se or of the novelty of the situation. The issue of translation, on the other hand, leads one to question whether it is reasonable to use each of the words in the headline, given the particular assessments that were made (Figure 9.3).

It may turn out in this hypothetical example that the study involved a group of children in a first-grade class who were supposed to work on their penmanship exercises. As they did their work, different sound patterns were played on records, with noise level held constant. On one day the record was of low-flying planes, and on another day it was train sounds. The teacher took note of how much the students completed in their exercise book during each of these ten-minute sessions. The *measure* of noise consisted of the various sound patterns, and the *measure* of learning consisted of how many lines in the exercise book were completed. Before we ask whether the results of the study are justified (valid), we can ask whether these measures are justifiable for the constructs they represent.

We are using the term "construct validation" to refer to the justification of particular measures to represent particular constructs. This involves an extension of the original use of the construct validation notion, making the ideas underlying this powerful concept applicable to any and all research. Any

ENVIRONMENTAL PERCEPTION

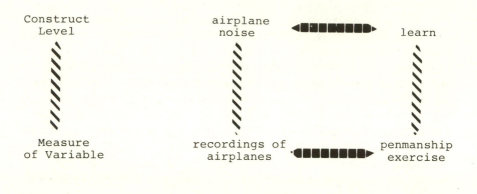

Figure 9.3 Diagram showing relationship between constructs and measures in research design.

study, after all, involves variables that are measured in some way. These variables are selected as more or less close approximations to the constructs under study.

Construct validation was originally proposed in the context of psychological tests (Cronbach and Meehl, 1955), where the problem of the reasonableness of the test (measurement instrument) had to be defended in terms of the construct that it purported to assess. If someone invents a measure of creativity, one wants to know how its inventor knows it is actually creativity that is being measured. Might it not be a measure of how fanciful a story is being told, or is it perhaps just a measure of alertness? When such tests are being relied upon as selection criteria (for jobs, schools, or whatever), the issue of their validity becomes of great concern. Notice that it is the validity of the test itself that is of concern here, not of the use of the test in a particular context. Once again, it is the vertical arrow—the relation between construct (creativity) and a measure of test (particular instrument)—that is being questioned.

The relevance of the idea of construct validation is perhaps greater the more amorphous the construct, the more difficult it is to measure, or the more the results of the study "matter." However, the idea pertains in all cases; the recognition of this fact might make the researcher more concerned about being able to justify how each of the constructs in the study will be specified. After all, if the construct is "scenic quality," the justification of the measure is no less important, nor less difficult, than if it is "creativity." Hopefully the researcher will be haunted by how the anticipated result might look in headlines. The measurement of the constructs will necessarily be less straightforward, less singular, if the "headline version" of the hoped-for outcome is confronted squarely as the study is being planned.

There is an interesting parallel between the idea of construct validation and the way in which a representation is constituted. In both cases there are multiple aspects, and in both cases no one of these aspects is critical or defining. In both cases the aggregate of the various aspects or measures brings one closer to a satisfactory specification. Let us return for a moment to the example of the citizen group concerned with the impact of a proposed zoning change on the sense of community. (Let us say the proposed zoning change is related to a plan to build a large apartment and office complex in a formerly low-rise, single- and multiple-family residential area.) Perhaps the citizens' concern is related to a projected increase in traffic if the zoning change were to be approved and the project carried out. How would one recognize the sense of community? How would one know if the sense of community was harmed by an increase of traffic?

A landmark study by Appleyard and Lintell (1972) shows the power of multiple measures, each insufficient in itself, to define a construct in a way that is intuitively as well as methodologically satisfactory. They studied the impact of traffic on three streets that were relatively similar except for the differences in the characteristic level of traffic flow. They found that people living on the heavy-traffic street experienced more stress, felt the street was more hazardous, interacted less with their neighbors, had a more constricted sense of territory, and noticed less of their surrounding environment. One hardly requires a critical-feature-based definition of community to understand from these results that high traffic density is likely to be damaging to a community.

Sampling

When measurement involves "people" or "adults" or even "wilderness purists," it is clear that the measurement will involve more than a single instance. So familiar are we with this idea that it is simply ludicrous to think that any one of us can serve as an adequate instance. Realizing that individuals vary, social science researchers have expended great effort to be sure that enough different individuals are sampled in any study to make the study meaningful. In fact, so great has this emphasis been that in many social sciences the "sample" refers exclusively to the individuals involved.

Individuals are not the only source of variability, however. Particularly in the environmental context—where it is assumed that environments make a difference—sampling must apply to environments as well. *In fact, one of the most important implications of a construct validation stance is that any contsruct at all, if it is important enough to be measured, is the better for having been measured in more than one way.* In other words, it is always sounder practice to sample from the amorphous, interrelated set of ideas that constitute the construct. In any situation, if the sampling procedure is dependent on a single instance (one person, one item, one setting, one case), the generalizability of the results is undermined (Chapter Note 4).

Thus it is discomforting to think that subjective distance would be measured simply in terms of time estimates, that place referred to a single and particular location, that plane noise was measured by comparing recordings of plane and train sounds, and so on. Even if the participants had been adequately sampled in any of these situations, the other aspects were not. Whatever the results, they are that much less convincing because it is impossible to know if they would be similar given different circumstances.

The *more-than-one* principle is particularly important in many studies that focus specifically on environments. Here one must sample not just two but many different settings. The importance of this lies in the multidimensional quality of many environments of interest as well as in our lack of knowledge of what these dimensions are. Consider, for example, the concepts of "natural environment" and "urban environment." Say we wanted to look at psychological measures of stress for people recovering from the rigors of an exam period. Some would recover in a natural environment, some in an urban environment. But what is a "natural environment"? Must it be untrampled wilderness? Or can it be a landscaped park? Does evidence of human habitation detract from its naturalness? To clarify such a concept in a nonarbitrary fashion, it is necessary to sample widely.

Consider for a moment a landscape architect who wishes to have a sense of the citizens' feelings about impending development in their little community. She realizes that they may feel quite differently about different kinds of development and approaches this issue with a questionnaire by asking the participants to indicate the desirability of more "housing," "commercial development," "institutions," and "recreational facilities." Whatever the results, the landscape architect will have a very poor basis for decisions. It is true that the construct "development" was sampled more broadly than with a single item, such as "how do you feel about development?" The subconstructs were not, however. To some, "recreational facilities" might entail a regional park which they do not wish in their own community, whereas to others it may mean something entirely different, and so on with each of the four subconstructs. In the minds of the citizens, the important issue may be not whether a particular development falls under the heading of "institutions" but whether it entails jobs, whether it is in keeping with the kind of community they have, and so on. It would thus be far more useful to drop the headings and include in their stead a few examples of each: single-family housing, townhouses, mobile home park. Separate reactions to each of these take very little additional time and provide much more information than the answer to "housing."

The pattern of responses, even without extensive statistical tools, can then inform the landscape architect in what ways the citizens view development. The tool provides the citizens with information about possible directions of growth, and it provides the designer with information that the citizens view their community in terms of an entirely different set of assumptions.

To come up with appropriate measures of a construct, then, requires coming to terms with what is to be meant by the construct—and with what is not to be included, as well. Such a process often leads one to realize that what seemed like *a* construct, like some discrete entity, comprises several subconstructs, or separable facets. Perhaps the focus of the study shifts to one or two of these subconstructs, which now become *the* construct under study. In any event, sampling the content of these facets is often not as difficult as is their initial formulation. It is this conceptualization process that is central to the meaningfulness of the study.

The recognition that a construct is multifaceted and therefore requires multiple measurements is nullified, however, if one then ignores these subconstructs in making sense of the data. If, for example, one developed a questionnaire dealing with "neighborliness" that was based on the separate measurement of several facets of this complex construct (e.g., exchanging favors, friendship, shared values), it would violate these insights to aggregate over all the items and give participants a single neighborliness score. It may well be that some of the subconstructs that are part of the larger construct lead to very different insights. Perhaps it was misleading to include "friendship" as part of "neighborliness." It is by examination of the relationships among the subconstructs that one gains an understanding of the meaning of the construct itself. Including a diversity of such facets in a study makes possible insights that might otherwise have been obscured. Coming to terms with these insights also provides a basis for reassuring oneself that the measurement used did indeed have a relation to the intended construct.

Although adequate environmental sampling may be good in principle, it raises the serious problem of generating too much information. Researchers have learned to handle the "people-sampling" problems. Many statistical procedures are based on sample sizes and sample variability. What about environmental sampling? There is the very real problem that the more instances one chooses, the greater the possibility that the results will reveal contradictions. It might well be more comforting to think that one has substantial results even if those results are based on inadequate measurements than to be forced to realize that the results apply only to certain situations based on what one might learn from broader sampling. It is because of such apparently reassuring results, however, that many have become disillusioned with the benefits of research. *Meticulous research that makes no claims to generalizability can hardly be considered a contribution.*

In other words, the practical problems of becoming overwhelmed by too many data require separate attention. The goal of producing results understandable to potential users of the information is obviously threatened by a procedure that could lead to data that are incomprehendible even to the person who collected them.

Discovery

The procedure we have advocated involves careful conceptualization of each construct under study and conscientious sampling of instances that are part of the construct. A construct that turns out to encompass five or six subconstructs, each of which needs to be sampled adequately, might then lead to quite a few items about which information is gathered. Thus, "natural environment," for example, might lead to a series of photographs depicting a range of natural settings, including parks and backcountry, some untrampled and some with sign of human intervention. Some other construct might lead to the development of a questionnaire having verbal items to sample the domain of that construct.

Once participants have responded to this material, the question arises of what to do with it. How does one proceed from perhaps 30 or 40 responses from each of, let us say, 200 citizens to a manageable understanding? To determine what percentage of the pariticipants responded positively to each of the separate items (or photographs or whatever) leaves one with a great deal of undigested information. To average across all these items gives one a meaningless summary. What is needed, then, is a procedure to reduce the 30 or 40 responses to a smaller set that does not exceed one's comprehension span but is nonetheless meaningful.

The most common way to accomplish this reduction is to return to the facets of the constructs that were initially formulated to help in selecting the items. Thus, for example, scenes of "parks," of "backcountry," of "little human intervention," and of "considerable intervention" may have been included in a study involving "natural environments."

These then can provide the categories for analyzing the data. Instead of responses to 40 items or scenes being examined, each one is allocated to its predetermined category and the average response for each category is computed.

As considerable thought went into the selection of the facets of the construct, approaching the data in this way certainly has merit, but it also has some disadvantages. Such an approach makes it difficult to determine whether one's intuition was correct. Perhaps the scenes that had been designated as reflecting little intervention and those showing considerable intervention were not perceived in those terms by the participants in the study. If, for example, the salient feature for the citizens is the degree to which trees are evident in the scene, this would never be determined by analyzing the data in terms of the a priori categories.

An alternative approach to the data-reduction problem involves examination of the *pattern* of responses that was obtained in order to determine what categories are embedded within it. Such examination could be frustrating and futile if left to trial and error. Fortunately, there exist a large variety of computational procedures that accomplish this task at remarkable speed. What these approaches have in common is that they extract from the data a series of categories or groupings of items that is coherent. Rather than relying on one's a priori categories, they yield categories generated from the data. In this way, one is afforded a check on one's intuition; discovery can take place (Chapter Note 5).

This alternative approach, then, makes it possible to sample broadly and still reduce the large quantities of data to a relatively small number of themes or categories. These still represent facets of the construct under study, but the facets may be somewhat reformulated. By seeing the pattern of the participants' responses, one can better understand their perception of the problem. If the environmental sampling was not quite adequate, this, too, becomes evident.

It is important to build such discovery into one's research, and not just because it makes the research more exciting. Many insights into what participants are trying to tell decision-makers can come from these discoveries. They provide a direct test of the hunches the expert or decision-maker has about what is important. The content of these groupings reflects the different ways different groups of people see the world.

Perhaps some examples would help. These are taken from studies that used either slides or black-and-white "photoquestionnaires" as the means of sampling the respective environments. In each case, participants were asked to indicate for each scene how much they liked it, using a five-point rating scale (Chapter Note 6).

☐ To explore the way unfamiliar urban environments are experienced, 70 slides were presented to undergraduate students. The resulting groupings indicate that the likely function of the buildings shown is far less salient than are such issues as their age and distinctiveness and the surrounding vegetation (Herzog, Kaplan, and Kaplan, 1982).

☐   The interaction between vegetation and the built component of nearby ordinary settings was also the subject of a study by S. Kaplan, R. Kaplan, and Wendt (1972). In this case, the a priori categories of "nature with no visible human influence" and "nature with some human intervention" proved to be unrepresentative of the participants' pattern of responses. To them this distinction was immaterial. The presence of an unpaved road, even with a parked car visible, did not affect the perception of the scene as a natural environment. While the *preference* for particular scenes may be affected by intrusive elements, the *categorization* did not reflect it.

☐   The kinds of settings that are visible from various multiple-family neighborhoods were the subject of a study reported by R. Kaplan (1983). Here the resulting categories exemplify the salience of the relationship between structures and open space. Areas that were equally appropriate from an activity point of view (e.g., playing ball) were perceived as distinctly different. Barren, anonymous areas, where the buildings dominate the grass, emerged in a distinct grouping. Other

Figure 9.4 Although having large mowed areas in common, these scenes represent different categories based on an analysis of residents' ratings.

Figure 9.5 These scenes also represent different categories, although they show much content in common.

scenes, reflecting equally open areas but where buildings and natural areas were in a more balanced relation, formed a separate grouping (Figure 9.4). Scenes with no visible structures, showing only the "natural," emerged in two distinct categories also. Here the smoothness of the ground texture and the sense of spaciousness seem particularly salient as distinguishing characteristics—as discussed in Chapter 4 (Figure 9.5).

These examples involve visual displays, but the procedure is, of course, equally applicable to verbal items. The Environmental Preference Questionnaire (R. Kaplan, 1977b), for example, was originally intended to reflect a range of natural settings that people may respond to differently. Given the items that were included, however, the results repeatedly reflected a single, large "nature" grouping. Nonetheless, a few of the nature items appear in other categories, such as "suburban" and "romantic escape."

The examples also reflect our interest in the natural environment, but there is nothing in the procedure that limits it to such settings. What is required is the identification of facets, or components, of the construct. In a sense, this involves some sort of theory, either explicit or implicit, that points to what is important to sample. By then sampling these facets adequately and obtaining responses from citizens, one determines the extent to which that theory (explicit or otherwise) is confirmed. We have repeatedly found our hunches improved by this process.

SOME CONCLUDING COMMENTS

It is essential that research be kept manageable. If the researcher is not clear on the purposes and uses of the research, it is quite unlikely that the participants will be in a position to participate effectively in the project. Also, it is hard to imagine that the consequence of such research will lead to any implementation. Perhaps the most important step in keeping research manageable involves some thinking and conceptualization; some measures can all too easily be useless without such forethought.

This is true whether a study is oriented to the solution of specific problems in specified situations or to the quest for more general knowledge. The real-world setting and the consideration of people as participants do not preclude a systematic investigation of either the constructs or their relevance to theory. Conversely, the impetus for a study stemming from a theoretical formulation does not prevent the outcome of the study from being useful, nor does it preclude treating the participants as competent, cognizant human beings.

Rather than including a raft of constructs (or potentially pertinent areas) in a study "while one is doing it anyway," we are suggesting that any construct that is pertinent to the study must be measured adequately; otherwise it is better deleted. The likelihood of drawing false inferences from poorly constructed measures is not farfetched. False inferences in important areas are damaging.

This does not mean that research need be dull. Quite to the contrary, the more thought one gives to the key constructs in a study, the more cognizant one becomes of their multidimensionality, their amorphous nature. To measure adequately such a complex entity is likely to lead to many insights. Rather than relying on a single approach, one must have multiple measures. These in turn are likely to lead one to see the underlying relationships as complex and intertwined. Dullness is no problem; coming to terms with conflicting "truths" may at times be an even greater challenge than one is willing to encompass.

The construct, with its attendant multiplicity of possible measurements, is the correlate in research of what the representation is in thought. Indeed, the problem of measurement in research is the reverse of the process of acquiring representations. A representation requires the convergence of many environmental inputs over a period of time. Measurement starts with the construct—a higher-level representation—and attempts to identify the environmental inputs that are a part of it. Measurement is in this sense an externalization of the thought process. To the extent that experience with the environment results in the building of representations, the instances upon which they are based tend to become lost. We are left with ideas that, as researchers, we wish to measure. So we find ourselves back to instances, to specifics again. Just as a representation constitutes a convergence of many instances and has no simple definition, a singular approach to measurement is unlikely to do justice to the richness and power of our ideas.

NOTES

1. Environmental Simulation

There is by now an extensive literature on environmental simulation. A number of books (e.g., Burden, 1970; Hohauser, 1970; Janke, 1968) deal with creating architectural models. While mention is made in such books of the use of simple models, these are characteristically created only for "back room" use by the designers and not for use with the public. Hohauser does acknowledge the general usefulness of such low-detail, inexpensive renditions; nonetheless the primary emphasis in such books is on creating models in which realism is paramount. By contrast, in the context of creating games of human settlement, F. Wilson (1975) illustrates the production of quick and simple environmental simulations.

The Berkeley Environmental Simulation Laboratory stands as a landmark in the history of simulating environments for both research and practical application. It is discussed in Appleyard and Craik (1974), and K. H. Craik (1975) and McKechnie (1977) present information about extensive attempts at validating the simulator. As McKechnie (p. 185) indicates:

> Indeed the present writer can think of no other instance in the history of psychology as an experimental science in which such considerable amounts of time, energy, and research funds have been invested to evaluate systematically the validity of a laboratory technique.

Despite this monumental effort, however, McKechnie acknowledges that work to date is only a "first step in the full validation process." The adequacy of the procedure for environments other than mixed land-use suburban settings has not been addressed, and generalizability to other land-uses, vegetation types, and regional characteristics is uncertain.

Appleyard (1977) casts the issues of environmental simulation in a broader context, examining both a variety of presentation media and criteria for their evaluation. Zube (1980), in a chapter on "evaluating alternative futures," provides a range of examples of the use of simulation models in applied settings. The *Proceedings of Our National Landscape Conference* (1979) constitutes perhaps the most impressive collection of information on environmental simulations using a vast array of technologies.

2. Simplicity and Visual Presentation

Several studies have compared the effect of degree of detail in reactions to graphic material. Using a task involving matching of animal pictures with names, Franzwa (1973) found no significant effect of different levels of detail. Looking at concept learning, Gorman (1973) presented simple and detailed line drawings of architectural concepts to different groups. Again no significant differences were found.

3. On Constructs and Reality

There is a widespread misunderstanding concerning the nature of such constructs. The idea of a gene, for example, was used as an aid in understanding a body of results long before there was any means of identifying a physical correlate. One might have thought that the advent of the electronmicroscope and the rapid advances in molecular biology had transformed this construct into a directly observable thing. A recent review (Lewin, 1982) of this area of research, however, indicates that what we thought of as a gene, a basic genetic unit, actually has a complex and changing substructure. The instability of this substructure and the variety of alternative states it can take, suggest that this "thing" is more likely to be a useful way to think of a complex process than a direct observation from nature. In fact, this review explicitly states that "genes and alleles can no longer be thought of as simple entities" (p. 1092). Nonetheless, we can be confident that the construct will continue to be used—and found useful—for many years to come.

Rods and cones constitute a similar example. While we may find it comforting to think of them as physical realities, the neat and well-organized constructs we think of contrast sharply with the observed anatomical evidence (Morgan, 1951).

4. Environmental Sampling

Brunswik (1956) is closely identified with the concept of environmental sampling, which he considered as essential for valid research as the sampling of individuals. He emphasized the importance of sampling events not in an arbitrary fashion but so that they are representative of the events in which the organism in question functions. Petrinovich (1979) offers a thoughtful discussion of the importance of adequate situational sampling to the generalizability of the results (external validity). He also discusses the construct validation perspective in this context.

The notion of multiple instances to reflect settings or occasions or measurement instruments is referred to as "multiple indicators." Sullivan and Feldman (1979) examine these with respect to validity and reliability. The recognition of the importance of environmental sampling has grown slowly (Hammond, 1966). It is surprising that this subject receives little mention in treatises on environment/behavior research.

Rather, much of the research in this area can be characterized as sampling adjectives as opposed to environments (R. Kaplan, 1975). By asking participants to rate a particular instance in terms of long lists of attributes (e.g., using adjective checklists or semantic differentials), the research suffers in two respects. Environments are not sampled because the task would become too lengthy, and the resulting insight from the research often yields little more than what a thesaurus already offers. Many are the studies that have found that affective words go together, that participants who rate an environment as "pretty," also indicate it is "pleasant" and find it "beautiful," etc. This situation led Appleyard (1973, p. 87) to assert that "research methods do not provide professionals with usable environmental variables. . . . [They] describe poorly the environment which is the professionals' primary variable."

5. Approaches to Extracting Categories

The description here perhaps sounds like magic. It is certainly not the case that all computational procedures are equivalent in generating meaningful results. Nevertheless, many people who approach data in this way do, in fact, have a feeling of magic. To submit a huge matrix of numbers to a computer and have output that translates to intuitively meaningful thematic groupings is a process that never fails to be instructive and exciting. (Here is a striking example of an appropriate and humane use of high technology.) After attempting several kinds of factor analyses and related procedures, we have relied on two approaches to this problem. The relationship between the two sets of solutions has turned out to be in itself a useful form of check. For descriptions of these procedures see R. Kaplan (1972, 1974, 1979a). Samples of the kinds of information these procedures generate can be found in studies by Frey (1981) on residential neighborhoods; Hammitt (1979) on bogs; Herzog, Kaplan, and Kaplan (1976) on familiar urban places; C. J. Smith (1977) on supportive communities; and Ulrich (1974) on roadside environments. S. Kaplan (1979a) provides a comparison of results generated by a series of studies using this technique.

6. Response Format

The task that is given the participant quickly communicates the researcher's attitude toward this person. To be asked to answer an involved question with a "yes" or "no" answer can be most frustrating if one finds neither alternative appropriate. Similarly, to be asked to provide one's reasons for favoring or opposing a decision can also lead to frustration and a sense of incompetence. People easily get the impression that they are viewed as incompetent and ignorant. In fact, as we have seen throughout the book, this is hardly the case. The researcher's job is to find a response format that is compatible with the participant's considerable knowledge and ability. We have found that the use of a preference rating has numerous advantages. As we have seen, there is considerable theoretical basis for using such a procedure; not surprisingly this is something people do readily and happily (R. Kaplan, 1979a, 1979b).

chapter ten

PARTICIPATION IN ENVIRONMENTAL DESIGN AND DECISION

In dealing with environmental issues, we are repeatedly confronted by the paradox that the biggest obstacle to a more humane world for people is—people. Again and again designers, planners, citizen groups, policy makers, and managers set out to solve "real" problems and end up mired in "people" problems. Partly because of the failure of solutions to anticipate such people problems, a popular view of decision making is as a power struggle, a conflict between good guys and bad guys or at least between the poor and the establishment.

While there is some truth to this view, the reality is considerably more complex. One of the flaws of the position is not merely factual, but strategic. It creates a "zero-sum" conflict, a situation where, for someone to win, someone else must lose. When viewed more closely, however, the "bad guys" (the experts) do not necessarily have evil intentions. A win/lose framework casts them as fully knowledgeable about the repercussions of their decisions. In the final analysis, however, many of the failures of the decisions can be attributed to the experts' ignorance or noncomprehension rather than to a power struggle or to ill intention.

The "tragedy of the commons" (Hardin, 1968) provides another instance where factors other than evil or power operate in decision making, though in this case not by acknowledged experts. This by now widely known paradigm, which was discussed in Chapter 6, involves the grazing of sheep on a common ground (Figure 10.1). Individuals are motivated to add sheep to their flocks to increase personal wealth. On the other hand, every sheep added to the total degrades the commons a little bit. Although the degradation for each additional sheep is small relative to the gain in wealth for the flock owner, if all flock owners follow this pattern the commons will ultimately be destroyed. As we have seen, this parable applies to a great many environmental problems. It involves no simple power struggle, no simple operation of evil forces. Rather it de-

Figure 10.1 The tragedy of the commons.
Douglas Kinsey

pends upon (a) understanding the long-range implications of one's actions and (b) having knowledge of what the long-range actions of others
will be. If one knows that such knowledge is shared by all *and* trusts
others to behave in terms of the long-run issues, then the dilemma could
be solved (see Chapter 7, Note 3).

How one conceptualizes environmental decision making has considerable influence on how one might go about improving it. If there is
more to it than a power struggle, if matters of information and cognition
are involved, then there might be new angles to explore. If the people
problems that so characteristically contribute to the failure of environmental solutions could be anticipated, perhaps a more effective approach
could be found.

GAINING INFORMATION ABOUT PEOPLE

There are a number of ways of increasing the likelihood that people
factors will be incorporated in decision making. One could gain hind-
sight from prior failures. One could include a "people expert" along
with the other experts on the decision-making team. One could train
people in traditional areas of expertise to be more sensitive to people's
concerns. However, to get specific, focused information pertinent to a

specific problem within a specific situation, the participation of potentially concerned individuals is needed as well. This is not to say that public participation is fail-safe. Working properly, however, as part of an interactive cognitive process, participation can yield results that are highly satisfying (Chapter Note 1).

Impediments to Participation

Probably the single most striking aspect of participation as it is now practiced is how badly it works. It is no accident that a book describing a federal program that was to have "maximally possible participation" was entitled *Maximum feasible misunderstanding* (Moynihan, 1969). Gatherings nominally convened for purposes of participation have often been the setting for befuddling people, for confrontation, or for various mixtures of these (Figure 10.2). Experts who have experienced such events would greatly prefer to schedule them at times and places that make it practically impossible for people to come. The public, having "participated" in this way, may come to feel that its worst fears have been realized. While there are exceptions to this dismal picture, they constitute a small minority. There must be some basis for this widely unsatisfactory pattern. Surely it is not by chance that what could be such a useful procedure creates so little in the way of positive results.

Figure 10.2 Maximum feasible misunderstanding.
Douglas Kinsey

There is probably no single reason for all the frustration and bad feeling. Rather, a number of factors come together to have this effect. No small portion of the difficulty lies with the role and training of the professional. What experts are asked to do is inherently difficult. Society has cast experts in the role of absorbing many of the uncertainties that people unavoidably face. Experts are asked to deal with disease and death, with the fertility of farm and field, with the potential impact of storm and flood and other possible future events. At the same time experts—at least some of the time—are expected to deal with these uncertainties as if they were not uncertainties, as if they were matters that are thoroughly understood, if not under perfect control.

These are glorious expectations the public holds, expectations the experts come to share. In being asked to control what cannot be controlled and to face confidently life's irreducible uncertainties, the experts are being called upon to play the role of witch doctor. The inner world of the experts, however, contrasts sharply with these inflated expectations. The uncertainties remain despite any pretense to the contrary, and the uncontrollable is no easier to control than it ever was.

A further impediment to participation stems from the expert's different perception of the situation (discussed in Chapter 7). In acquiring information, one's view gradually changes. New information replaces old as experience "corrects" the map. One's representations grow more compact. What was once obscure becomes obvious. What was once complicated becomes simple. Much of this process of cognitive growth takes place unconsciously. We readily lose track of how it all looked at the beginning. First one's facility increases, then one becomes accustomed to the greater facility. The familiarity with this new way of seeing leads one to believe that it is the only way to see. It is so comfortable, so natural. It is easy to believe that one has always thought this way, that, in fact, everyone thinks this way. Thus the special way of perceiving makes the world *look* different, but it does not make the expert *feel* different. And the way the world looks is, of course, the way one assumes it is. Therefore the expert, faced with extraordinary expectations, often feels very ordinary indeed. It is perhaps for this reason that experts are readily threatened (S. Kaplan, 1977a; see also Langer and Imber, 1979).

Given this discrepancy between expectation and inner feeling, some of the traditional stances about professionalism are perhaps more understandable. They help keep people at a distance while at the same time providing an explanation for any lack of appreciation on the part of the populace. In terms of the expert's sense of vulnerability, they may be helpful; in the context of participation, however, they are clearly part of the problem.

One such model of the professional involves the "bringing gems to the masses" point of view. It is assumed that the masses may not immediately appreciate the gifts being bestowed upon them, but this is understandable since they are, after all, "the masses." At the same time, one is reassured in what one is doing; "gems" are, by definition, good.

Some professions that must contend with people's problems fairly directly have a supplementary model which argues that the good professional must be able to imagine the needs and requirements of the individuals who will be affected. One must be able to "put oneself in their shoes," as the saying goes. The slightly different Native American admonition that one not "judge another until one has walked a mile in his moccasins" suggests that it takes more than imagination to determine the likely feeling of other people.

The witch-doctorly stance of the expert might be acceptable to people if they consistently preferred to have their problems dealt with by apparently omniscient and omnipotent others, but these are relatively rare, albeit dramatic, instances. In times of emergency, when people know neither what to think nor what to do, having superhuman experts is reassuring. However, the cost is high. When people are faced with a potential loss of both control and clarity, they will sacrifice control for the promise of clarity, but under more ordinary circumstances, they greatly prefer both control and clarity. The paternalistic stance of the professional, besides offering little if any control, offers only a limited degree of clarity as well. Granted, in an emergency, being told by the expert that the situation is in good hands, that everything that is necessary will be done, provides more clarity than one might otherwise have. However, this is not the same as comprehension, an understanding of the larger picture and how one fits into it.

These various stances and expectations come together when participation is to occur. Not surprisingly the expert often prefers to cultivate the appearance rather than the fact of participation. By overwhelming the "participants" with information, the expert achieves two goals. First, it is reassuring to remind oneself that one really did one's homework, that one does have something to say after all. Second, the public is likely to be "snowed" by the performance. They will hopefully be impressed. They will certainly be rendered incapable of formulating an intelligent reply.

In this way the downhill drama blunders on. People feel confused and put upon in such situations. Their suspicions that the wool is being pulled over their eyes and that their input is not really wanted seem to be confirmed. They react, if they react at all, with anger and frustration. Confrontation results. Now the worst fears of all parties have been confirmed.

Participation need not work this way. There are possibilities far healthier than this, and they are not impossible to achieve. At the same time it is important to keep one's expectations under control. Perfection is not characteristic of human experiences; it will not be characteristic here either. There is an antiestablishment stance among some young environmental designers that contains a strong dose of romanticism. There is the belief that in "true" participation some sort of ultimate will be reached. Here as in so many other practical matters, the adage Simon (1957) cites in his discussion of satisficing applies. "The best is the enemy of the good" is an excellent description of the likely outcome of such romanticism. A great deal of improvement can be achieved if our hopes and expectations can be kept in bounds.

Participation as Research

The designer/planner/manager eager to avoid people problems has available two traditional courses of action. There is the public hearing, and there are the studies reported in the literature of how people behave under various circumstances. The former is called *participation*, the latter is called *research*. In general neither has been found to be fully satisfactory. From a cognitive perspective it would seem that a more appropriate solution should be possible. Indeed, from a cognitive perspective it is not even clear why the split between participation and research is either necessary or helpful. There are many times when the requirements of these two activities are quite similar. In both cases things tend to go better when the participant comprehends what the issues are. In both cases the likelihood of success is greater when the participant and what is supposed to happen are not at odds.

A good example of research that might benefit from greater interest and cooperation on the part of the participant is the traditional survey. This approach is based on a sequence of questions asked by an interviewer. The participant usually has only a vague and general idea of the purpose of the survey and no opportunity to get a sense of the whole before answering the individual questions. The material tends to be entirely verbal; the choice of answers is often frustratingly narrow. The process is under the close control of the interviewer; the participant comes close to playing the role of research object.

This pattern of conducting surveys is by now so traditional that it is almost ritualized, but it is not clear that this standardized pattern is necessary. Is it necessary to treat people this way to obtain valid data? One might learn more from a procedure that called on an individual's cognitive ability rather than one that tried to skirt it.

What is inadequate in the traditional survey is surprisingly parallel to what is wrong with the typical public hearing. There is insufficient attention to (or interest in) helping people comprehend the issues. The opportunity for people to respond is too limited, and the control is totally on the side of the expert. There is, in both cases, little respect for the individual's competence and little comprehension of how to capture it.

Imagine, by contrast, a participatory procedure based on a mode of presenting the issues that was cognitively comfortable. Imagine that provision was made for examining possible alternative solutions and that the timing was such that the major decisions with respect to the alternatives had not yet been made. Finally, assume that the reactions available to the participants are not unduly frustrating. There is every reason to believe that this would be an effective and satisfying participatory procedure. At the same time it constitutes a way of doing research, a way of studying the human reaction to certain kinds of environments. It could even be expressed as a survey, although a kind of survey very different from the traditional version.

As this hypothetical example suggests, there is no necessary incompatibility between participation and research. Indeed, much of what could be done to strengthen one of these enterprises would benefit the other as well. While research of this kind could tell us a great deal about human concerns and preferences, it is neither likely nor desirable that the knowledge gained from such research will ultimately eliminate the need for participation. Research will hopefully contribute to a more adequate conception of human functioning. It should be possible, with increasing understanding, to do a better job of incorporating human concerns into the development of the alternatives. Each new situation, however, is too complex and too particular for a decision to be based on research results alone. Reliance on research findings alone would lead to decreased diversity, as the "one right answer" is applied over and over. Since diversity is a factor in preference, in way-finding, and in the functioning of the human enterprise, the relative advantages of combining the two procedures are evident.

Some Examples

It may be useful to examine a few examples of participation that was neither futile nor particularly frustrating. Each was a "real-world" venture carried out in response to a practical problem. The participants in each case included people directly affected by the decision under study. These are all cases of participation related to environmental design decisions, and they occurred early in the process.

Basement resettlement project.   This project grew out of the possible relocation of a group of teaching assistants to a new space in the basement of a large classroom and office building. Although the move represented a considerable increase in square footage, it also meant leaving the old three-story frame dwelling in which the group was now housed. In part because of the fire hazard involved at this location and in part because of the cost of renting the house, the university was eager to move the present occupants when space became available. It was not surprising, however, that the teaching assistants were solidly opposed to the move as they were familiar with their current quarters and had developed effective patterns of functioning.

Nonetheless an attempt to achieve a participatory design solution was undertaken. The rationale was that, if the move was deemed necessary, it was better to move to space that one had helped design than to move to space that bore no relation to one's needs and requirements.

A straightforward approach to this situation would have involved taking the affected group to view the proposed new space. This was ruled out for two reasons. First of all, the "new" space was in terrible condition, uninhabitable in its present state. In addition, however, it would be difficult to comprehend the space just by taking a tour. Thus, in order to provide a concrete and understandable basis for discussion, a simple but sturdy cardboard model of the basement area was constructed (Figure 10.3). Some of the walls were made moveable so that modified arrangements could be tried out.

Working in small groups, the teaching assistants played with the model, exploring alternative arrangements until a satisfactory solution was reached. Each group was asked to propose an arrangement that would not only meet their own needs but would also accommodate each of the other groups that were to share the basement space. (The space was to house teaching assistants from several courses as well as a seminar room, library, and lounge.) The various solutions were drawn on a

Figure 10.3 This simple and not very exciting cardboard model provided the necessary image of alternative futures for the potential occupants of the to-be-renovated basement space. The covered portions of the model represent areas that were not included in the project. (Model constructed by M. Hunt.)

map of the model. The graduate student* who coordinated the project then examined the various solutions to see if congruent plans were offered.

There were two outcomes of this modest project. First, when the coordinator presented the composite results to the architect assigned to the project, he commented that he had never before worked with a group that was so well prepared. Second, the teaching assistants' initial hostility to the move had given way to outright enthusiasm. They had become excited about the space they had helped structure and were eager to see the plan implemented.

The drain improvement project. When it rains the water that falls on the ground has to go somewhere. Often much of the water is absorbed into the ground, eventually reaching the water table. The remainder runs off into streams and rivers. Human habitation, however, has a tendency to reduce water absorption as the ground is covered by houses and buildings, by streets and parking lots. Thus what was once a natural process requiring no human intervention can become a problem. In some parts of the United States an elected official called a drain commissioner is responsible for dealing with these problems within a given geographical area. (A "drain" refers to the various means—streams, wetlands, underground pipes, etc.—by which the runoff water is contained and managed.)

Citizens living along a drain have the right to initiate action by making a complaint. It is then the responsibility of the drain commissioner to take appropriate action, which generally entails the expertise of engineers. In the present case however, landscape architects were also consulted, and they in turn sought the service of environmental psychologists. The latter were to determine how people perceive the drain and what their preferences were as far as alternative treatments were concerned.

The method used in this case was based on a picture questionnaire (R. Kaplan, 1979a). Photographs were taken of various portions of the drain. Because the drain under study did not represent all of the alternative solutions, additional photographs from other drains were included. The picture questionnaire included a total of 32 photographs printed on four pages (Figure 10.4). Participants were asked to rate each photographed scene both for how similar it was to where they lived and for how much they liked it. The questionnaire was distributed to the residences of people who live along the drain; a cover letter indicated the eagerness of the drain commissioner to obtain people's feelings about the various possible treatments.

---

*Linda Whitlock skillfully organized and guided the process.

Figure 10.4 A sample page of the photoquestionnaire used in the drain improvement project (cf. R. Kaplan, 1977a).

Responses were generally enthusiastic. A number of people specifically indicated how appreciative they were of the opportunity to offer input. Although there was widespread agreement among the participants as far as certain photographs were concerned, certain of the neighborhoods through which the drain passed had distinctive preferences. It was thus decided not to treat the entire length of the drain the same way, but to deal with different portions of it differently.

Among the scenes of ways the drain might look was one that was quite natural in appearance—there was no suggestion of human intervention. The photograph depicted a small stream running through an area of brush and small trees. The portion of the sample at the high end of the socioeconomic continuum liked this scene; it was otherwise not preferred. More widely liked were scenes characterized by controlled textures and a general impression of neatness. The possibility that order is an important component of preference, especially for people of limited economic resources, is clearly suggested by this study. It is a hypothesis that deserves further exploration.

The urban park project   A small parcel of downtown acreage was purchased by the city in order to create a park. The design was to be worked out by two landscape architects, with public input to be obtained with the help of a couple of environmental psychologists (R. Kaplan, 1978b). It was decided that obtaining reactions to photographs of various alternative arrangements would be an appropriate procedure. To make such photographs possible, simple models were constructed of three alternative park plans. (Actually the same model was successively rebuilt to provide the three different versions.) Numerous photographs were made of each version. From these, 24 photographs were selected to provide a variety of views and moods of the alternative plans (Figure 10.5). These were placed on display at two buildings near the site of the proposed park—the public library and a savings bank. People were invited to fill out a rating sheet indicating their reactions to the 24 views. An invitation to participate in this activity appeared in a newspaper article. In addition, the City Parks and Recreation Department sent letters to residents in the neighborhood of the park, inviting their participation.

Through this procedure many more people contributed their opinions than what would have been the case at a public hearing. The reactions were probably more informed and more focused than might be the case at a typical public hearing. The pictures effectively communicated what the alternatives would be like, and people's reactions were not restricted to a "yes" or "no" for the project or even to a vote among the alternatives. Rather, they responded separately to each of the photographs. The preferences were then subjected to a nonmetric factor analysis (see Chapter 9, Note 3). The resulting groupings of scenes showed

Figure 10.5 Here are four of the photographs used to represent alternative designs for the projected park. (C. Cares and T. Brown were the designers for this project.)

what sorts of patterns went together in the minds of the participants. By looking at the level of preference expressed for the scenes in each of these groupings, the designers could incorporate a variety of "people concerns" into their final proposal.

One of the outcomes of this study is particularly noteworthy. The city had originally indicated that the tiny park was to incorporate a modern sculpture (which had been awarded top prize in a competition). The designers felt the sculpture was out of place for the location, given the park's size and the proximity of an adjacent 1850s Greek Revival building. Nonetheless, one of the three designs was for the optimal inclusion of the sculpture, and thus eight of the photographs included a simulated version of it (e.g., upper right in Figure 10.4). One of the groupings resulting from the data analytic procedures comprised six of these scenes depicting the sculpture. These were by far the least liked scenes in the study. The question of the inclusion of the sculpture in the park was never again mentioned.

The park has since been constructed. It is a source of pride to the city administration and is well liked by the citizens (R. Kaplan, 1980, 1981). This conclusion is not based merely on observation of its use. The city requested a follow-up study, which not only showed widespread satisfaction but also found that many people who do not actually use the park indicated *how glad they were that it is there*. People were also asked what their feeling was about the fact that public input had played a role in the design. Their responses to that item were, not surprisingly, most enthusiastic.

Although the settings and even the purposes of these projects are quite different, there are several common themes that play a central role in effective participation:

☐   *The public was involved sufficiently early in the process so that their input would be incorporated readily into the ultimate decision.*

☐   *There were alternatives available to react to.* People were presented with examples that communicated a sense of the possibilities. What was called for on their part was an indication of preference—a straightforward response that is not dependent on verbal facility.

☐   *These possibilities were presented using a cognitively congenial medium.* The use of the visual/spatial material made it possible for people to visualize alternative futures. It allowed them to utilize some of that information-processing facility that is in principle such a powerful human asset.

Conditions that Facilitate Participation

A necessary and vital aspect of the participatory process is the exchange of information. Human understanding is prerequisite to human effectiveness. Conversely, failure to understand leads to the anger and frustration so evident in the participatory attempts that do not work.

The exchange of information—the transfer of knowledge—calls upon all the principles discussed in Chapter 8. Capacity limitations must be recognized. Connections must be made to prior cognitive structures, and effort must be expended to determine what the prior structure looks like. One cannot assume shared meaning of the key elements. These constructs must be understood by the information provider and recipient alike. If these various concerns are kept in mind, visual modes of presentation can be particularly effective. If they are not, the visual has little or no advantage over the verbal. The method is a guarantee of effectiveness not by itself but only in interaction with the cognitive requirements of the recipient.

Another important facet of the participatory process is *the nature of the reaction* requested of the participant. Time is one dimension that has considerable influence on the outcome. The more time required to acquire the necessary background, the smaller the number of people likely to participate. In some areas this may be unavoidable. Thus Wildavsky (1964) discussed the time requirements for participation in various governmental activities in a small town. He feels specialization is a necessity

for most people; they will have to choose some particular area of participation since the time required to acquire the necessary background for
multiple areas is likely to be prohibitive. On the other hand, in many
cases the time requirement can be greatly reduced if the type of reaction
sought is appropriately chosen.

One of the most common formats for obtaining public input is
probably one of the worst. People are asked, "What do you want?" Not
knowing what the possibilities are (since this is something experts know
a great deal more about than the public does), people find this a hard
question to answer. (Alternatively, people may be shown a finished design, beautifully displayed, and asked how they like it. This, of course,
is not participation; it barely has the appearance of participation.)

By contrast, people feel most comfortable and most willing to
plunge in without large prior time investment when the following conditions are met:

1.   There must be choices or alternatives they can react to.
2.   These choices must be in an easily understandable form.
3.   The reaction required of them must be something they do
readily and with facility. Preference ratings, for example, are something
people do quickly and easily. Explaining their preferences, by contrast, is
something people find very difficult to do (Canter, 1977; Zajonc, 1980).

Participation depends upon a system of relationships. Who decides
to participate is based on the nature of the information required, the
time required, and the type of reaction called for. Thus suiting one's
procedures to human cognitive requirements is not only likely to increase the quality of the feedback; it may increase the number of people
participating as well.

While people's decision whether or not to participate is crucial to
the effectiveness of the process, *how they feel afterward* matters, too. One
reason for this is what might be termed the "long-run perspective." Participation is presumably not a once-in-a-lifetime venture. Ideally it is a
relationship to the decision-making process that is available on many occasions. How people feel about one such experience has considerable
bearing on their future participation. How people feel afterward depends
in large part on whether they have the sense of having been listened to.
When the decision is already made and the people are invited to view a
beautiful model and appreciate it, the sense of having been listened to is
not likely to be present. Timing (that people have a role early enough)
and choice (the presence of alternatives that can be reacted to) are probably irreducible elements underlying this feeling.

The way people react to the experience also depends upon how the
information is presented and what is presented. If the procedures used

give a sense of grasp, of comprehension, then the participants will achieve not only a positive feeling about the participation process but also a better sense of relatedness to their environment. On the other hand, the exciting world of hypothetical futures can lead otherwise cautious people to lose their grasp on reality. Exploring far-out possibilities can be a stimulating exercise, but arousing false hopes is destructive in the context of that long-run perspective. People whose unrealistic expectations have been dashed by an uncooperative reality are not more likely to be effective participants in what goes on around them than those who hold no hopes from the start. People with unrealistic expectations can be made to feel helpless by the same course of events that might be seen as positive by people with more modest hopes (Chapter Note 2). In a creature whose action depends upon knowledge, misinformation can be as *dis*abling as correct information can be *en*abling.

BROADENING THE SCOPE OF PARTICIPATION

The advantages of using effective participatory procedures in the planning and design process can be substantial, but participation can also be viewed from a much broader perspective. The benefits of participatory relationships can be derived from many different facets of human/environment relationships. One domain where much can be done to foster a more participatory relationship involves the *results* of planning and design. Participation need not end when construction is completed. Environmental arrangements, in other words, can offer the opportunity for a continuing role.

It is also possible to go a step further; people can participate not only in the planning, but in the work involved as well. Sometimes referred to as "self-help," such procedures have become increasingly common where there are no viable economic alternatives. Although motivated by limitations in economic resources, such arrangements are also worth examining from the perspective of the psychological benefits they bring with them.

Perhaps the broadest perspective on participation involves looking at the environment as a whole—social, institutional, and cultural as well as physical—for an analysis of the extent to which one's efforts are sought, encouraged, or even required for the continued functioning of the system to which one belongs.

Building Participation into the Results of Design and Planning

While there is a great temptation to present the user with an elegantly finished package, gift-wrapped with a bow around it, some designers have emphasized the importance of not completely finishing a structure. Leaving room for individual taste, for personal expression, may make the result far more satisfying for the user.

While incompleteness can be an explicit strategy, settings that are in principle complete are still susceptible to personalization. Mautz and Kaplan (1974) found that personalization in a housing development may be undertaken explicitly for the purpose of increasing legibility; distinctiveness in this situation was used to help children pick out their own residences. F. D. Becker (1977) looked at the personalization of dormitory rooms. He found not only that personalization increased satisfaction, but that students were happy to inherit the personalization of the previous resident if it contributed to usable space or to uniqueness.

Canter (1975) cites work of the Building Performance Research Unit in Scotland that extends these findings to public buildings. Among the school buildings studied, a considerable decline in teacher satisfaction occurred during the first few years of a building's life. Thereafter, however, the satisfaction leveled off. Canter explains this by reference to the degree of "improvization" that had taken place. He computed a score that took into account the number of changes in the way the space was used and the number of spaces that had multiple usage. The greater the improvization, the *higher* the teacher satisfaction. Thus, Canter concludes that "the degree to which a person is able to act on and modify a building may well influence his preference for it" (p. 178).

There are opportunities for providing satisfying participation in the public sector on a far smaller and less dramatic scale. Watering trees in a nearby park can make a simple but vital contribution. People are happy to participate in this way if they are confident (a) that they know how to do it and (b) that they know that their doing it is appropriate. There are people who, in response to a park response survey, have explicitly requested to be allowed to weed the flower beds, and plant bulbs.

A dramatic example of this phenomenon involved an attempt to create a park in an area of New York City known as Hell's Kitchen (Reemer, 1971). A city-owned parcel of empty land in the area had been used for various purposes, but vandalism had been too severe. It was essentially a junkyard when an environmental group organized a community effort to clean up the area and establish a park. All of the equipment in the park was made of discarded material—even to the park benches, which had been auto seats in their former life. Neighbors kept the plantings watered and the litter picked up. Community effort produced what would otherwise have been impossible.

Langer (1981) cites a series of studies that she and Rodin carried out in the context of institutionalized elderly adults. The experimental group in the study was instructed that they "should be making all the decisions that they used to make for themselves" and were each given a plant to care for. A second group was also given plants, but they were told of the nursing home staff's "eagerness to take care of them and help them"—even to the extent of watering the plants for them. Both in the short-run and 18 months later, the experimental group was significantly superior on various measures of physical and psychological health. Although the interpretation the author makes is in the context of control, the manipulation could as well be considered as enhanced participation.

Lewis's (1972, 1979) documentation of the effects of the New York City Housing Authority's Tenant Gardening Competition, as well as others like it, further supports the role of personal involvement in increased psychological well-being. The involvement in these competitions invariably leads to participation in seemingly unrelated domains, which in turn gives rise to a greater sense of community, increased self-esteem, and a reduced sense of the stigma associated with living in public housing.

Another possible way of enhancing participation through planning and design involves creating environments that people can comprehend, environments where people can find the resources they require for the activities they wish to pursue. Wurman (1971) has persuasively argued that so much of what is important in a modern city is invisible to people. He has even produced a "yellow pages" to make some of these resources more understandable (Wurman, 1972). Comparably, Carr and Lynch (1968) argue that access to information about a city and, by implication, the opportunities for participation would be greatly enhanced by appropriate planning decisions. In particular they mention a cheap and easy-to-use transportation system and enhanced visibility of the important elements of a region. They also propose that, with appropriate labeling and the creation of visual access, urban industry could teach a great deal about what processes are going on.

Self Help

Less-developed countries have long been plagued with squatter settlements. People who could not afford to purchase housing, especially near urban areas, would construct shacks on unoccupied land. The typical response on the part of officialdom was to destroy these illegal settlements and initiate programs to construct appropriate housing for such people. In recent years it has become increasingly evident that governments are totally incapable of coming up with the resources necessary for such massive housing programs. It now appears that "self-help" efforts such as those that resulted in the squatter settlements offer the only economically viable alternative for creating housing on the scale required (Opat, 1976) (Figure 10.6).

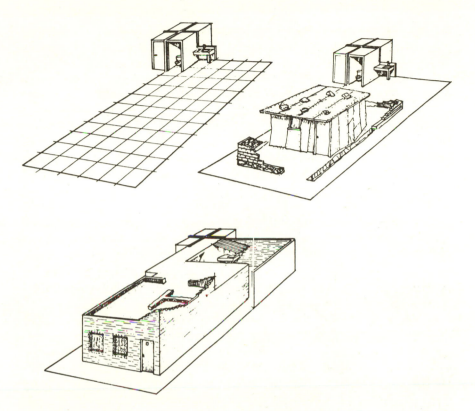

Figure 10.6 Top left sketch shows minimal facilities provided by the Panamanian government as a starting point for self-help housing. Top right and bottom sketches indicate late
steps in construction (Opat, 1976).
Reprinted from Design and Environment, *Spring 1976, vol. 7, no. 3.*

The controlling factor here was economics. This has generally been
the case in those instances where the self-help route has been taken.
The benefits, however, extend well beyond the economic. Terner and
Herz (1968) speak of "freedom" and "independence" and the "spirit of
the frontier" in describing the psychological impact on the low-income
individuals participating in creating their own housing.

Although the most major commitments to self-help housing have
been in Africa and South America, it should not be concluded that such
an approach must be restricted to less-developed countries. A system
designed for squatter settlements in Venezuela has, for example, been
applied in modified form in a Detroit inner-city neighborhood (Terner
and Herz, 1968). Perhaps one of the most interesting examples of self-
help principles applied to housing in the United States is described by
Goetze (1972). In this instance the individuals involved did not build a

dwelling from scratch, but helped renovate an older house in need of repair. This contribution of work as partial payment is commonly referred to as "sweat equity."

The program Goetze describes involved lower-income families in Rochester, New York. People had to qualify for the program by completing a course in money management. They then made commitments as to what aspects of the renovating they would do as down payments for the house they were to live in. Goetze characterizes this approach as bringing out "homeowner attitudes which accept normal maintenance in stride. . . . Some families which had been indifferent to their rented homes became fastidious and resourceful as homeowners" (p. 59). He contrasts this program with a more traditional HUD-FHA sponsored low-income housing program in the same city. The latter program also involved refurbishing older dwellings, but in this case they were repaired by contractors and then rented to low-income individuals. In this program maintenance has been a serious problem, and the houses involved have been subject to rapid deterioration. Money management courses offered by the program have not been taken seriously.

Goetze points out numerous advantages of the sweat equity/home ownership program. They range from lowered cost and better maintenance to more sensitive preservation of special features of the dwelling in the refurbishing process. He concludes his discussion of psychological benefits by noting that the *sense of having a choice* that the program fosters was central to the living patterns once the resident moved in.

While such programs lend themselves to individual housing units, programs with different form and at different scales have also been built around a self-help approach. The Local Initiatives Program, a Canadian program designed to reduce joblessness, attempted to meet community needs without going through an intervening bureaucracy. Described as "getting oats to the sparrows without going through the horse," the program looks to the unemployed to think up projects and apply for money. It has funded a great diversity of projects, is well received in the community, and, once again, taps powerful psychological benefits:

> First, regardless of the nature of the job—it can be a lousy, rotten job—if the community sees it as beneficial, that's a strong motivation to the worker.
>   That other important thing is that the individual must have some say in the decisions that affect him. People want to work, but not just at anything, or under any conditions. (Ann Arbor News, 1975, p. 43)

Recently, modest self-help programs have even been charged with rather major projects. An area in the South Bronx of New York City, so desolate as to have received a presidential visit and national attention, was to be the target of a $1.5 billion renovation effort, but this massive project was ultimately turned down. Hopes for rehabilitation of the area now rest on a variety of small-scale, self-help projects. Pierce (1979) provides a colorful description of some of these projects:

> On a banana-like curved section of Kelly Street, undeterred by the blocks of abandonment that surround them, one finds an intrepid band of remaining residents—The Banana Kelly Community Improvement Association. They are gutting and rehabilitating a block of five-story apartment buildings with a combination of their own sweat equity and small grants from foundations and government housing job projects. Their motto: "Don't Move, Improve."
>
> Off the Bronx's southernmost tip, facing Ryker's Island and Manhattan, I watched members of the Bronx Frontier Corporation, led by Jack Flanagan, a towering ex-policeman with a great flowing beard, erect a tall, heavy-duty windmill. It will provide energy to turn waste from nearby Hunt's Point vegetable markets into compost to be distributed free to South Bronx community groups trying to develop gardens and parks on empty lots.
>
> On Courtland Avenue, a seedy but busy retail street with a strong Latino flavor, the South Bronx Redevelopment Office—jointly funded by federal, state and city governments—has opened. And across the Harlem River in Manhattan, Edward Logue, the master-builder who changed the face of New Haven and Boston in the 1950s and '60s, has completed the first draft of a South Bronx redevelopment plan. It breaks sharply with the massive urban renewal projects of the past by emphasizing moderate housing rehabilitation, job creation and community participation.*

Participation has great potential for enhancing environmental design, but it is much more than that, too. It is a way of relating to the environment, a bringing together of the various coping strategies into a way of functioning that is satisfying, rewarding, and, one might even say, healthful for the human psyche. One would expect humans functioning in this way to be more effective and at the same time less frustrated, less destructive than humans so often are.

If participation is so desirable, encouraging, and enhancing, it must be of highest priority. We have looked in some detail at participation in the particular process of environmental design, but what of participation more broadly conceived? How are we to foster this way of relating people and the environments they inhabit?

Encouraging Participation

An appropriate place to begin the search for an answer to this question is with the ecological psychologists. They have addressed this issue quite directly with their "undermanning/overmanning" concept (see Wicker, 1979). In their classic *Big school, small school*, Barker and Gump

Reprinted by permission of The Washington Post Company, © 1979, pp. 322–23.

Wicker, 1979). In their classic *Big school, small school,* Barker and Gump (1964) have examined the level of participation in high schools of varying sizes. They found that, although the number of behavior settings was larger for large high schools, *the number of behavior settings per individual* was substantially larger in small high schools. Students in small high schools, in other words, experience not only more opportunity to participate, but also far more pressure to play a role in the various available settings. Individuals are more likely both to feel needed and to participate in settings that Barker and Gump characterize as "undermanned."

In this way the ecological psychology perspective demonstrates the vital role of scale in participation and hence in such psychological benefits as satisfaction. Not only small schools, but small towns (Denman, 1970; Williams, 1977) and small-scale technologies (Schumacher, 1973) fit this same pattern.

At the same time there are many circumstances where an analysis in terms of scale seems less well suited to a particular situation. There are many circumstances where the likelihood of participation seems more closely related to cognitive factors. The degree to which an individual comprehends a situation and understands what can be done is often crucial. The very perception an individual has of a situation may create or destroy the opportunity for participation. Let us examine some of these cognitive factors.

A striking example of the role of perception and comprehension can be found well distributed throughout the United States. There are innumerable situations requiring talent, skill, and help. There are children with learning difficulties requiring individual attention, elderly needing help with transportation or home maintenance or someone to talk to. There are valuable materials lost because effective recycling of such complex structures as derelict cars and refrigerators requires too much disassembly and sorting to be affordable within the current scheme of things. There are crops that rot in the fields because they ripened late and it is too expensive to run the harvester through again. Numerous volunteer organizations face overwhelming challenges with limited participation and minimal resources. At the same time there are innumerable people sitting in their homes feeling useless, dissatisfied, and unneeded. The settings are there in profusion, but people do not perceive them as being there. The problem is not one of lacking niches, but of having failed to communicate about them, of having failed to identify and package them so that people can understand and relate to them.

Another powerful cognitive factor in one's likelihood of participation is having a view of the world within which action is appropriate and meaningful. Certain patterns of participation are supported by the group with whom one shares a small-scale setting. Other patterns are the outcome of what one believes about the universe and one's relation to it. Frequently, of course, one affiliates with people who share one's world view and these two forces combine. On the other hand, many modern individuals (apparently unlike nonliterate cultures; see Stein, 1960) have no larger, well-organized belief system and thus lack that basis for participation.

Support both for the importance of participation and for its strong ties to cognition comes from several unexpected sources. Various investigators have commented on the use of participation in reducing vandalism (e.g., Clark, 1976; Magill, 1976; Ward, 1973). A quite different source of support comes from the work of Antonovsky (1979) in the area of medical sociology. He was interested in determining the psychological and life-history factors that predict physical health. This is an area where multiple causation is to be expected; it was thus with considerable surprise that Antonovsky discovered that one factor stood out above all others in importance and actually seemed to play a summarizing or integrating role as far as the other factors were concerned. He calls this factor the "sense of coherence," which he defines as "a global orientation that expresses the extent to which one has a pervasive . . . feeling of confidence that one's . . . environments are predictable and that there is a high probability that things will work out as well as can be reasonably expected" (p. 10).

This sense of coherence is, in Antonovsky's thinking, directly related to meaningful participation in activities that are pertinent to one's life. Thus he not only links cognitive variables to participation but also points to a tangible benefit of this configuration—namely, a higher level of human health.

Another unexpected source of support for the cognition/participation/satisfaction complex of factors comes from a NASA program relating to undersea habitats. Wortz and Nowlis (1975) were concerned with what they refer to as the "habitability" of confined spaces over extended periods of time. Their "laboratory" was the *Tektite II,* an undersea habitat which served as a base for scientific missions. Although their primary concern was with the adequacy of the design of this environment, they ultimately came to see habitability as more closely related to the psychology of the inhabitants than to design.

One of the observations that led them to this conclusion involved the food provided to the scientific missions using *Tektite II.* Seven of the missions received high-quality, preprogrammed foods which Wortz and Nowlis themselves considered to be excellent. The other three missions had self-selected foods which depended upon what was locally available. At times, due to tropical storms, these three missions were left with no food at all. Yet out of 40 complaints made about food during debriefing, 39 came from the groups that had received preprogrammed food.

Ultimately Wortz and Nowlis identify three factors they consider central to habitability. They are individuality, a sense of purpose, and a sense of choice. Participation necessarily assumes the existence of *choices or alternatives*. When one's actions are coerced, they do not constitute participation, and when there are no alternative possible outcomes, then participation is futile. Participation also implies *purpose*, since it necessarily occurs in the context of some goal or larger picture. Action in the context of a coherent view of the world is clearly purposive, as is action directed toward improving one's neighborhood or fixing one's roof. *Individuality* is a characteristic, if not a necessary, consequence of participation. What one does for oneself will be different from what others do for themselves. What the factory or the bureaucracy does for one is less likely to be individualized.

It is also interesting to note that Wortz and Nowlis refer to a *sense* of purpose and a *sense* of choice. These are cognitive factors, ways of experiencing the world. The mere existence of needs or opportunities does not encourage purpose unless they are perceived. Likewise, possible alternatives for action, potential choices, cannot influence people's lives if people do not know about them. The functional niche is the perceived niche.

SOME PAYOFFS OF EFFECTIVE PARTICIPATION

When it works effectively, participation can benefit both the people directly involved in the process—citizens and professionals—and the solution itself. Let us examine some of these payoffs in the context of environmental decision making.

For the Professional

One set of payoffs of participation for the professional involves some hard, cold realities that are increasingly difficult to ignore. To begin with, there is the ever-present possibility of error. While there is never a guarantee that error can be avoided, one of the most frequent factors in the failure of design and planning projects is people. Participation, properly structured, can be a powerful corrective for potential errors of this kind. It is probably less embarrassing to discover errors in this way than by having one's design creations (even one's award-winning creations) dynamited by public officials.

Another reality is legal in nature. Increasingly, public participation of some sort is required by law. To the extent that such events are mandated anyway, one may as well put them to good use. While the professional's inclination to remain in control might lead to minimizing the opportunities for participation, as we have seen, this stance invites confrontation, usually followed by mutual frustration. A more attractive alternative is to develop the skills to make participation effective. This not only has the advantage of enhancing one's sense of competence but also calls on talents with which the professional is often well endowed.

The two abilities that are perhaps the most central to making participation effective are the capacity to envision alternative solutions and the capacity to present them effectively so that others can comprehend them. While professionals tend not to use these capacities in quite this way, they come equipped with many of the essential tools. Granted, the professionals may have to resist deciding among the alternatives before people have a chance to see them. Environmental designers in particular may have to learn new ways of generating models and graphics that are simpler and cheaper than what is traditionally used. Professionals are in general effective problem-solvers and talented individuals; it seems likely that they could make the necessary adjustments.

Perhaps the biggest payoff for the professional involves not merely taking advantage of their capacities, but doing the very thing that gives them the greatest satisfaction. Professionals take enormous pride in meeting challenges in a creative way. One could hardly ask for a greater challenge than finding a solution that incorporates physical realities and public concerns. Professionals like challenges; as we saw in Chapter 7, constraints are central to structuring the problem space. It is hardly surprising, therefore, that professionals have been known to create their own constraints when the situation failed to provide them. Including human concerns, that is, taking seriously the input gained through public participation, should provide problems as challenging as anyone could ask for. Achieving an aesthetic solution requires doing something not just anyone could have done; it requires meeting difficult constraints. Perhaps responding effectively to "people input" could be the basis for a new aesthetic.

For People

People are inherently conservative animals. They have a considerable investment in the nearby environment in its present form. They have learned how to relate to it, to function in it, to make some sort of sense out of it. That is not to say that it could not be improved, but the impending change is rarely assumed to be for the better. Perhaps it was not always so, but in the modern world changes so often lead to an environment that is less natural, less responsive, and less legible. In this context one benefit of participation is quite obvious. People feel better about the process of change when they are part of it, when they have a chance to provide input about such often-ignored realities as their attachment to the land and the elements of the environment that they value, as well as about factors that affect their functioning.

Feeling better about the process when it includes participation goes hand in hand with feeling better about the environment. This is not only because of the input itself. It also stems from the greater knowledge about what is going on. Having thought about and contributed to decisions about the future of their environment, people are likely also to have a greater sense of involvement, of active concern for and pride in the physical world that surrounds them. They may also feel more secure about the stability of essential landmarks and other major features if they have had an opportunity to make their feelings known.

Finally, people who have participated in the decisions about their nearby environment are likely to have better feelings about themselves. They are more likely to feel competent and less likely to feel helpless. The more people feel attached to their neighborhood, the more vital it is for their self-esteem, and even for their sense of clarity, to understand what is happening and to feel that in some way they have been a part of it.

For the Project (or the Environment)

It is important to recognize that participation is not merely a procedure that has benefits for the participants. The quality of the solution is likely to be improved as well. One dimension of an effective solution must be the fit to the particular environment in question. Local people are far more likely to be able to bring to bear information concerning local resources, historical considerations, and the like.

Clarkson (1970) describes a prototypic confrontation between an agricultural expert and a native of a less-developed country. Based on maps and theory the expert suggests that a certain crop be grown in a certain field. The native refuses, referring to ghosts traditionally associated with that field. While this may seem to be a straightforward conflict between reason and superstition, Clarkson (a geographer) points out that the local is likely to be in possession of long-term, detailed information about the productivity of that particular field—despite the information on the generalized map and despite the local's failure to describe this information in a way understandable to the expert.

Perhaps a parallel situation arises from the lack of local input in the shaping of the urban environment. The sameness of residential communities, shopping malls, and industrial "parks" across the land is a consequence of insensitivity to what had been special places. Planners and managers tend not to be natives of the cities they work in, and they tend to be highly mobile. This makes appreciation of the local residents' perceptions and preferences difficult. Participation can contribute a great deal in terms of quality of fit.

A related problem of fit arises from the differences in preference patterns between environmental professionals and other people. Such differences have been documented repeatedly (e.g., E. Anderson, 1978; Buhyoff et al., 1978; Gifford, 1980; R. Kaplan, 1973b). They are so consistent that it is safe to say that the professional cannot count on personal preferences to be universal—except, perhaps, as far as other professionals are concerned. Here the issue is the fit not to the environment per se, but to the people who are likely to use the environment.

Another way in which participation enhances the quality of a solution is through the encouragement of diversity. Every community, every neighborhood is different. Even if the need is apparently similar, the solution will be different if it is responsive to the inputs of each particular community. Such diversity enhances the distinctiveness of different environments, aids legibility, and allows many different "experiments" to occur simultaneously across the whole country (see W. Johnson, 1978).

Thus information obtained through participation aids the professional in coming forth with a superior solution. Comparably, the quality of the project is enhanced through the impact this process has on the users. There is likely to be far more community support for changes that are the outcome of a participatory process. People will be more involved, and they will take better care of the project. The impact of the process can be even greater than this, however. Ward (1973) has put together a rather depressing book concerned with the problem of vandalism. In chapter after chapter one learns how few approaches do any good. The one exception is a chapter concerning participation and community involvement. This appears to be the only procedure known that is highly effective in warding off such destructive behavior.

The benefits of participation extend well beyond any specific project. People who participate in such activities become educated about what is going on in their community. They are likely to be both knowledgeable and willing to act on their knowledge, since the two-way information flow of the participatory process is far less likely to lead to cynicism than are such relatively one-way processes as reading the newspaper and voting. In this way the cumulative effect of a participatory mode of relating professionals to the environment and to the people who function in it is a citizenry whose actions are likely to be more responsive, more responsible, and better informed.

SOME CONCLUDING COMMENTS

Participation is a process that is strongly matched to the cognitive capacity and requirements of our species. We have saved the discussion of participation until late in the volume because it depends upon so much that has gone before. Throughout the book we have attempted to develop a description of effective human/environment functioning. Humans did not evolve as passive beings, eager to accept solutions from kindly experts. Rather, human evolution suggests that effective functioning is active and knowledge-based.

This also describes participation. It depends upon knowledge, upon understanding. This knowledge may be obtained through a sharing process, or it may be the outcome of an active search involving the collection and interpretation of data. Without such knowledge, problem solving is made difficult and coping impossible. Without such knowledge, clarity fails and the likely reaction is to avoid the issue if humanly possible.

Another important relationship between participation and previously discussed material involves the concept of control. As we have seen, a tendency to use this concept uncritically has led to an obscuring of some important distinctions. The inability to distinguish between participation in its broadest sense and control is one of these misuses. It thus may be helpful to look at some of the critical differences between these two concepts.

Kamps (1981) tells a story that helps make this contrast clearer. A trip to the hobby store found a grandfather unwilling to pay the price of impressive, super-fancy kites. Instead, he took his deeply disappointed grandsons back home, where they ended up creating their own kites. Using pieces from the woodpile, bright comics from the newspaper, and strips from old shirts, each of them fashioned his own creation. Flying the kites expressed more than the fun of the activity itself. The pride of accomplishment could hardly have been matched had their soaring objects been dragons from the Orient.

Underlying the distinctions between control and participation is a basic and critical difference: *control is defined in terms of outcome, but participation is defined in terms of process.* The outcome of control is necessarily positive since that is what control is all about. While a positive outcome is no less a desired consequence of participation, it is not a necessary consequence. Participation cannot guarantee any particular outcome.

As we have seen, control is also characterized by directness, by clear and relatively prompt links between effort and result. This is often not the case with participation. Participation may involve many factors and interacting forces. Frequently there is a resulting influence, but it may be difficult to identify or trace.

Making one's own kite lacks the guarantee assumed with a ready-made product, that the object will in fact fly. In this example, however, at least the directness between effort and result is relatively prompt and traceable. Many environmental decisions, by contrast, can provide no such directness of impact, but there can still be choices as far as process is concerned. We may not be able to determine how things will work, but we can help determine the way they will be approached. And the way things are approached can have substantial implications for the expert, for the citizen, and for the environment that is their common concern.

NOTES

1. Public Participation

There is a substantial literature on public participation, most of it concerned with issues quite different from those addressed here. For example, political scientists have been interested in the historical and theoretical aspects of democracy and participation. At a more practical level, numerous public agencies have had to come to terms with regulations about public input. The signing of the National Environmental Policy Act and the subsequent flurry of activity on participation in the context of environmental impacts are a good case in point.

Among planners there has been considerable emphasis on who participates and on how much real power the participators have. Burke (1968) confronted what he saw as a dilemma between participation and professional expertise. Arnstein (1969) responded with a proposed "ladder" indicating a unidimensional scale of goodness of participation (where goodness was equated with citizen power). Van Til and Van Til (1970) joined the fray, followed by Kasperson and Breitbart (1974) responding to all three papers. Throughout the discussion, "who" and "how much" remained the dominant themes.

A number of papers have considered participation in the context of policy making related to natural resources (e.g., Burch, 1976; Heberlein, 1976; Hendee, 1977; Sewell and Coppock, 1977). The general feeling is that current methods of participation are not entirely satisfactory and that there is considerable resistance to public input on the part of experts and decision makers.

The community-development context provides another arena for public participation. There are papers concerning goals (Yin, 1977), procedures (Connor, 1977), and benefits (Yates, 1972). Perhaps the most informative and certainly the most inspirational source is *The grass roots primer* (Robertson and Lewallen, 1975), which includes some colorful and ingenious examples drawn from the challenging New York City environment. What is actually happening appears to be far more diverse and harder to classify in terms of a power struggle than many of the articles on the topic would suggest.

2. Expectations and Adaptation Level

A compelling analysis of the damage that can be caused by inappropriate expectations can be found in the "utopia syndrome" described by Watzlawick, Weakland, and Fisch (1974). These authors would certainly subscribe to the satisficing maxim "the best is the enemy of the good." Another way to conceptualize the same issue is in terms of adaptation level. Brickman and Campbell (1971) provide an ingenious analysis of how adaptation levels (or expectations) would escalate if unchecked and how cultures are structured to keep them under control.

part six

PROSPECT

The complex of environmental problems that currently threaten our well-being and, ultimately, our continued existence can be characterized in simplest terms as problems of fragility and limits. The environmental resources we depend on are finite; the systems we depend on are fragile. These two facets of our world are closely linked. Careless agricultural practices in the past have created desert; continued productivity of the land, following current practices, depends on huge expenditures of resources that are in limited supply. We must care for these resources and systems as if they were all we shall ever have.

Such a relationship to the environment is not a new idea. It is well expressed by the term "stewardship." In the context of the framework we have presented, stewardship can be viewed as a participatory relationship with the environment, a relationship that is realistic with respect to time, to space, and to uncertainty.

There were patterns of life and work in the past, even in the relatively recent past, that were far less energy-expensive and yet at least as satisfying as present patterns. A return to the past is neither possible nor necessarily desirable; at the same time, a selective revival of certain patterns that were gentler and more respectful of the environment is in the best tradition of stewardship.

While some of the patterns may come from the past, the concern must be for the future and for the people who will follow us. The tragedy of the commons is a paradigm of the failure of stewardship. A concern for the future requires that one take the best care possible of the network of relationships on which life depends.

The role of space in stewardship involves a realization of the distribution of resources upon the face of the earth. To understand this distribution is to understand that the earth is finite, that the resources we depend upon have their limits. Given our wondrous technologies, it is difficult to have an appreciation for where things come from. Just as there is a rapid decline in an "away" where one can throw things, there are limited locations where food can be grown, where pure water can be found, where minerals can be mined. The reservoir of wild places, and especially of diverse habitats, is declining at a rapid rate. Knowing "what is where" and that the "wheres" are limited is a central aspect of stewardship.

A third element involves the realistic assessment of uncertainty. Steward-ship implies care; it implies use rather than ownership. Even more, it implies use of our resources in such a way that others can use them in the future. This sounds unconvincing to those who hold that technology will find a way out. Perhaps ways will be found to generate indefinite supplies of energy with mini-mal cost. Perhaps we can relocate on another, as yet unspoiled planet. Perhaps we can live in space colonies.

These are all possibilities. Although they seem highly improbable, they still cannot be ruled out. However, to reject stewardship on the grounds that such solutions might yet save us is not merely to entrust the future to a gamble; it is to gamble recklessly. If a stewardship approach is not adopted and these techno-logical salvations do not materialize, irreparable harm will have been done. On the other hand, little will have been lost if a stewardship approach to caring for the environment is adopted and the promised technological breakthroughs ulti-mately do materialize. The space program has already taught us that the earth is finite. Perhaps another lesson to be learned is that it is foolish to mess with one's life support system until an alternative is available and working.

Stewardship, then, is an appropriate and possibly an essential way of relat-ing to a world in trouble. But will this path be chosen? Will this creature who has done so much damage to the earth's ecosystem in so short a time reverse its pattern soon enough? The answer to this urgent question is not known. It is possible, however, to look at a number of factors that can contribute to the an-swer. One can look at the human abilities and concerns that could contribute to functioning in this way. One can also consider the requirements that would have to be met for human capabilities to be used in this direction. There are some en-couraging signs to point to. Despite all this, however, these remain unanswered questions.

Humans are supplied with abilities and concerns appropriate to the stewardship role:

☐   They can comprehend patterns of information; they are quick to grasp stories, especially stories that are pertinent to their lives. They can even compre-hend stories fraught with risk and uncertainty if such comprehension contributes to their overall sense of clarity.

☐   They have the capacity to appreciate the past, especially if it is a past well known to them. There is a conservative bias in human information process-ing, a tendency to place great weight on the lessons of the past.

☐   They can, when the circumstances are favorable, anticipate the future. While they are readily diverted from such calculations, they have the capacity for lookahead, for using future projection as a basis for decisions in the present.

☐   They can function despite considerable adversity, despite uncertainty and risk, if they have available a model to guide their behavior and a conception of a future goal. In such circumstances people often need both a future goal worth working for and a reasonable path to get there.

☐   They can solve problems with flexibility and ingenuity; further, they are capable of storing the solutions so as to be able to cope with similar difficul-ties in the future. Not only are they able to utilize their own solutions in this way, but they can absorb the accumulation of insights and stories provided by their culture and thus cope effectively with a far wider range of difficulties than a single individual could otherwise handle. They are, in other words, knowledge-generating and knowledge-utilizing creatures.

☐   They are concerned to comprehend, to make sense of what they experience. They are also inclined to extend their experience, to venture into the uncertain and the unknown, thus uncovering new material that must be organized and understood. Thus their motivation to achieve clarity is not contradictory with their inclination to welcome new challenges.

This description of human cognitive ability and inclination seems, on the whole, rather promising. It may, in fact, seem too promising. If the picture is so positive, why does the record look so bad? Why has such a potentially reasonable animal proved to be so destructive?

There is no simple answer to this question. In part the problem may be a rate of change so rapid that neither culture nor genes have had a chance to adapt. In part, it may be the very recent growth in numbers that makes humans such a menace to themselves and to other life forms on earth. Undoubtedly, the recent growth in the capacity to exploit physical energy, to multiply the impact of human decisions so widely and quickly, has been a factor.

Another way to look at the discrepancy between what humans are apparently capable of doing and what they in fact have done is in terms of the *requirements* of their cognitive capabilities. While the evidence is overwhelming that humans *can* comprehend, anticipate, solve problems, cope with uncertainty, and all the rest, it is not the case that this impressive facility applies to just any kind or form or amount of information. The human information-processing capacity evolved in a particular environment. This capacity is powerful, but it is by no means universal; it is by far more effective under some circumstances than others. It thus may be wise to pay some attention to what these circumstances are.

The first requirement that must be met if human cognition is to be used effectively and constructively is, not surprisingly, comprehension. As we have seen, comprehension is closely tied to the nature of the information people have available to them. It is hardly necessary at this point to review the many factors that operate here. At the same time it is worth pointing out that, for whatever reason (and there are probably many), most members of Western culture have little understanding or appreciation of the many systems upon which their continued existence depends.

The second requirement is for a framework within which the appropriate pattern of behavior—in this case, stewardship—makes sense. Behavior above and beyond the call of duty is behavior not likely to be repeated often. Behavior that is an expression and affirmation of the scheme by which people relate to the world is far more securely grounded. In fact, in a thriving culture such behavior is so securely grounded that one trusts others to do it, too. One thus runs little risk of being the only one who behaves that way, while others take advantage. This trust, which is a key factor in avoiding repetitions of the tragedy of the commons, can arise out of a cultural framework.

The third requirement is that there be opportunities to make a difference, that there be choices and that the choices matter. People are disinclined to exert themselves, to play an active role, in the interest of futile exercises. As cynicism becomes increasingly widespread, this becomes an increasing problem.

Experts play a central role in each of these requirements. They are often responsible for the limited comprehension on the part of the public, and they are frequently intolerant of the sort of belief system that could provide a coherent, meaningful framework. Most of all, they are often inclined to minimize the difference that ordinary people might make. Ours has become an expert-dominated culture, and this emphasis is unlikely to be favorable to the active and constructive exercise of the human cognitive capacity.

Stewardship is not an activity that can be entrusted to someone else. Nor is it a quick fix, a short-term modification in patterns of behavior. It is an enduring, continuing pattern of relationship. It requires effort and commitment, as participation generally does. At the same time, it promises some of the satisfactions inherent in participation. While it requires a coherent, meaningful framework, it can also contribute to one. Stewardship can become a pattern of human/environment relationship that itself gives meaning and significance to human actions.

REFERENCES

Abelson, R. P., 1963. Computer simulation of "hot" cognition, in S. S. Tomkins and S. Messick (eds.), *Computer simulation of personality*. New York: Wiley.

Acredolo, L. P., 1977. Developmental changes in the ability to coordinate perspectives of a large-scale space. *Developmental Psychology* 13:1.

Acredolo, L. P., 1981. Small- and large-scale spatial concepts in infancy and childhood, in L. S. Liben, A. H. Patterson, and N. Newcombe (eds.), *Spatial representation and behavior across the life span*. New York: Academic.

Acredolo, L. P., Pick, H. L., and Olsen, M. G., 1975. Environmental differentiation and familiarity as determinants of children's memory for spatial location. *Developmental Psychology* 11:495.

Alexander, C., 1965. A city is not a tree. *Architectural Forum* 122:58.

Alexander, C., Ishikawa, S., and Silverstein, M., 1977. *A pattern language*. New York: Oxford University Press.

Alexander, R. D., 1979. *Darwinism and human affairs*. Seattle: University of Washington Press.

Altman, I., and Chemers, M., 1980. *Culture and environment*. Monterey, Calif.: Brooks/Cole.

Anderson, B. F., 1975. *Cognitive psychology*. New York: Academic.

Anderson, E., 1978. Visual resource assessment: local perceptions of familiar natural environments. Doctoral dissertation, University of Michigan.

Ann Arbor News, 1975. Canadian project helps jobless create their own jobs. July 7.

Antonovsky, A., 1979. *Health, stress and coping*. San Francisco: Jossey-Bass.

Appleton, J., 1975. *The experience of landscape*. London: Wiley.

Appleyard, D., 1969. Why buildings are known. *Environment and Behavior* 1:131.

Appleyard, D., 1973. Professional priorities for environmental psychology, in R. Küller (ed.), *Architectural psychology*. Stroudsburg, Pa.: Dowden, Hutchinson and Ross.

Appleyard, D., 1977. Understanding professional media: issues, theory, and a research agenda, in I. Altman and J. F. Wohlwill (eds.), *Human behavior and environment,* vol. 2. New York: Plenum.

Appleyard, D., and Craik, K. H., 1974. The Berkeley environmental simulation project, in T. G. Dickert and K. R. Domeny (eds.), *Environmental impact assessment*. Berkeley: University of California Press.

Appleyard, D., and Lintell, M., 1972. The environmental quality of city streets. *Journal of the American Institute of Planners* 38:84.

Argyris, C., 1968. Some unintended consequences of rigorous research. *Psychological Bulletin* 70:185.

Arnstein, S., 1969. A ladder of citizen participation. *Journal of the American Institute of Planners* 35:216.

Attneave, F., 1957. Transfer of experience with a class-schema to identification-learning of patterns and shapes. *Journal of Experimental Psychology* 54:81.

Attneave, F., 1972. Representation of physical space, in A. W. Melton and E. Martin (eds.), *Coding processes and human memory*. Hillsdale, N.J.: Erlbaum.

Averill, J. R., 1973. Personal control over aversive stimuli and its relationship to stress. *Psychological Bulletin* 80:286.

Barash, D. P.,.1979. *The whisperings within*. New York: Harper and Row.

Barker, R. C., and Gump. P. V., 1964. *Big school, small school*. Stanford, Calif.: Stanford University Press.

Baron, R. M., 1981. Social knowing from an ecological-event perspective, in J. H. Harvey (ed.), *Cognition, social behavior and the environment*. Hillsdale, N.J.: Erlbaum.

Bartlett, F. C., 1932. *Remembering*. Cambridge: Cambridge University Press.

Bateson, G., 1972. *Steps to an ecology of mind*. New York: Chandler.

Baum, A., Singer, J. E., and Baum, C. S., 1981. Stress and the environment. *Journal of Social Issues* 37:4.

Bechtel, R. B., 1977. *Enclosing behavior*. Stroudsburg, Pa.: Dowden, Hutchinson and Ross.

Becker, E., 1973. *The denial of death*. New York: Free Press.

Becker, F. D., 1977. *Housing messages*. Stroudsburg, Pa.: Dowden, Hutchinson and Ross.

Berlyne, D. E., 1954. An experimental study of human curiosity. *British Journal of Psychology* 45:256.

Berlyne, D. E., 1960. *Conflict, arousal, and curiosity*. New York: McGraw-Hill.

Berlyne, D. E., 1966. Conditions of pre-questioning and retention of meaningful material. *Journal of Educational Psychology* 57:128.

Birnbaum, F., Coplon, J., and Scharff, I., 1973. Crisis intervention after a natural disaster. *Social Casework* 54:545.

Blaut, J. M., and Stea, D., 1974. Mapping at the age of three. *Journal of Geography* 73:5.

Blythe, R., 1969. *Akenfield.* New York: Pantheon.

Bransford, J. D., 1979. *Human cognition: learning, understanding and remembering.* Belmont, Calif.: Wadsworth.

Bransford, J. D., and Franks, J. J., 1971. The abstraction of linguistic ideas. *Cognitive Psychology* 2:31.

Bransford, J. D., and Franks, J. J., 1972. The abstraction of linguistic ideas: a review. *Cognition: International Journal of Cognitive Psychology* 1:211.

Bransford, J. D., and Johnson, M. K., 1973. Considerations of some problems of comprehension, in W. G. Chase (ed.), *Visual information processing.* New York: Academic.

Brickman, P., and Campbell, D. T., 1971. Hedonic relativism and planning the good society, in M. H. Appley (ed.), *Adaptation-level theory.* New York: Academic.

Briggs, R., 1976. Methodologies for the measurement of cognitive distance, in G. T. Moore and R. G. Golledge (eds.), *Environmental knowing.* Stroudsburg, Pa.: Dowden, Hutchinson and Ross.

Bronson, G., 1974. The postnatal growth of visual capacity. *Child Development* 45:873.

Brown, R., 1980. Natural categories and basic objects in the domain of persons. Colloquium at University of Michigan, April 25.

Bruner, J. S., 1957. On going beyond the information given, in *Contemporary approaches to cognition.* Cambridge, Mass.: Harvard University Press.

Brunswik, E., 1956. *Perception and the representative design of psychological experiments.* Berkeley: University of California Press.

Bufford, S., 1973. Beyond the eye of the beholder: aesthetics and objectivity. *Michigan Law Review* 71:1438.

Bufford, S., 1980. Beyond the eye of the beholder: a new majority of jurisdictions authorize aesthetic regulation. *UMKC Law Review* 48:125.

Buhyoff, G. J., Wellman, J. D., Harvey, H., and Fraser, R. A., 1978. Landscape architects' interpretations of people's landscape preferences. *Journal of Environmental Management* 6:255.

Burch, W. R., 1976. Who participates: a sociological interpretation of natural resource decisions. *Natural Resources Journal* 16:41.

Burden, E., 1970. *Architectural delineation*. New York: McGraw Hill.

Burke, E. M., 1968. Citizen participation strategies. *Journal of the American Institute of Planners* 34:287.

Burton, I., Kates, R. W., and White, G. F., 1968. The human ecology of extreme geophysical events, Natural Hazard Working Paper No. 1. Toronto: University of Toronto Press.

Cadwallader, M. T., 1976. Cognitive distance in intraurban space, in G. T. Moore and R. G. Golledge (eds.), *Environmental knowing*. Stroudsburg, Pa.: Dowden, Hutchinson and Ross.

Campbell, B. G., 1974. *Human evolution*. Chicago: Aldine.

Campbell, D. T., 1975. On the conflicts between biological and social evolution and between psychology and moral tradition. *American Psychologist* 30:1103.

Campbell, D. T., and Fiske, D. W., 1959. Convergent and discriminant validation by the multitrait-multimethod matrix. *Psychological Bulletin* 56:81.

Canter, D., 1975. Buildings in use, in D. Canter and P. Stringer (eds.), *Environmental interaction*. London: Surrey University Press.

Canter, D., 1977. *The psychology of place*. New York: St. Martin's Press.

Cantril, H., 1966. *The pattern of human concerns*. New Brunswick, N.J.: Rutgers University Press.

Caplan, N., 1976. Social research and national policy: what gets used, by whom, for what purposes, and with what effects? *International Social Science Journal* 28:187.

Carpenter, E., 1955. Space concepts of the Aivilik Eskimos. *Explorations* 5:131.

Carr, S., and Lynch, K., 1968. Where learning happens. *Daedalus* 17:1281.

Catton, W. R. Jr., 1975. Environmental optimism: cargo cults in modern society. *Sociological Focus* 8:27.

Chermayeff, S., and Alexander, C., 1963. *Community and privacy*. New York: Doubleday.

Clark, R. N., 1976. Control of vandalism in recreation areas: fact, fiction or folk-lore? in *Vandalism and outdoor recreation: symposium proceedings*, USDA Forest Service General Technical Report PSW-17.

Clarkson, J. D., 1970. Ecology and spatial analysis. *Annals of the Association of American Geographers* 60(4):700.

Clay, G., 1973. *Close-up*. New York: Praeger.

Cohen, S., 1978. Environmental load and the allocation of attention, in A. Baum, J. E. Singer, and S. Valins (eds.), *The urban environment*. Hillsdale, N.J.: Erlbaum.

Cohen, S., 1980. The aftereffects of stress on human performance and social behavior. *Psychological Bulletin* 88:82.

Cohen, S., and Weinstein, N., 1981. Nonauditory effects of noise on behavior and health. *Journal of Social Issues* 37:36.

Collier, J. Jr., 1967. *Visual anthropology: photography as a research method*. New York: Holt, Rinehart and Winston.

Collins, A. M., and Loftus, E. F., 1975. A spreading-activation theory of semantic processing. *Psychological Review* 82:407.

Connor, D. M., 1977. Starting the citizen participation process, in P. Marshall (ed.), *Citizen participation certification for community development*. Washington, D.C.: National Association of Housing and Redevelopment Officials.

Craik, K. H., 1975. Individual variations in landscape description, in E. H. Zube, R. O. Brush, and J. G. Fabos (eds.), *Landscape assessment*. Stroudsburg, Pa.: Dowden, Hutchinson and Ross.

Craik, K.J.W., 1943. *The nature of explanation*. London: Cambridge University Press.

Crandall, J. E., 1967. Familiarity, preference, and expectancy arousal. *Journal of Experimental Psychology* 73:374.

Cronbach, L. J., and Meehl, P. E., 1955. Construct validity in psychological tests. *Psychological Bulletin* 52:281.

Cross, J. G., and Guyer, M. J., 1980. *Social traps*. Ann Arbor: University of Michigan Press.

Danford, S., and Willems, E. P., 1975. Subjective response to architectural displays: a question of validity. *Environment and Behavior* 7:488.

Dawes, R. M., 1980. Social dilemmas. *Annual Review of Psychology* 31:169.

Day, M. C., 1975. Developmental trends in visual scanning, in H. W. Reese (ed.), *Advances in child development and behavior*, vol. 10. New York: Academic.

DeGroot, A. D., 1965. *Thought and choice in chess*. The Hague: Mouton.

DeJonge, D., 1962. Images of urban areas: their structure and psychological foundations. *Journal of the American Institute of Planners* 28:266.

Denman, C. C., 1970. Small towns are the future of America. *Congressional Record*, Extension of Remarks, March 16; E2025, E2026.

Devlin, A. S., 1976. The "small town" cognitive map: adjusting to a new environment, in G. T. Moore and R. G. Golledge (eds.), *Environmental knowing*. Stroudsburg, Pa.: Dowden, Hutchinson and Ross.

Downs, R. M., 1970. Geographic space perception, in C. Board, R. J. Chorley, P. Haggett, and D. R. Stoddart (eds.), *Progress in geography: international review of current research*, vol. 2. London: Edward Arnold.

Downs, R. M., and Stea, D. (eds.), 1973. *Image and environment*. Chicago: Aldine.

Downs, R. M., and Stea, D., 1977. *Maps in minds*. New York: Harper and Row.

Dreyfus, H. L., 1972. *What computers can't do*. New York: Harper and Row.

Duke, R. D., and Greenblat, C. S., 1979. *Game-generating games*. Beverly Hills, Calif.: Sage.

Edney, J. J., 1976. The psychological role of property rights in human behavior. *Environment and Planning A* 8:811.

Edney, J. J., 1980. The commons problem: alternative perspectives. *American Psychologist* 35(2):131.

Ehrlich, P. R., 1968. *The population bomb*. New York: Ballantine Books.

Evans, G. W., 1980. Environmental cognition. *Psychological Bulletin* 88:259.

Fischer, J. L., 1971. Art styles as cultural cognitive maps, in C. F. Jopling (ed.), *Art and aesthetics in primitive societies*. New York: Dutton.

Flannery, K. V., 1955. The ecology of early food production in Mesopotamia. *Science* 147:1247.

Foa, U. G., and Foa, E. B., 1974. *Societal structures of the mind*. Springfield, Ill.: Charles C Thomas.

Forrester, J. W., 1971. Counterintuitive behavior of social systems. *Technology Review* 73:52.

Fortune, 1976. The stock market is "efficient." June, p. 147.

Frankl, V., 1963. *Man's search for meaning*. New York: Washington Square Press.

Franzwa, D., 1973. Influence of meaningfulness, picture detail and presentation mode on visual rentention. *Audiovisual Communication Review* 20:209.

Freides, D., 1974. Human information processing and sensory modality. *Psychological Bulletin* 81:284.

Frey, J. E., 1981. Preferences, satisfactions, and the physical environments of urban neighborhoods. Doctoral dissertation, University of Michigan.

Fried, M., 1963. Grieving for a lost home, in L. J. Duhl (ed.), *The urban condition.* New York: Basic Books.

Fromkin, H. L., and Steufert, S., 1975. Laboratory experimentation, in M. D. Dunnette (ed.), *Handbook of industrial and organizational psychology.* Chicago: Rand McNally.

Gallagher, T. J., 1977. Visual preference for alternative natural landscapes. Doctoral dissertation, University of Michigan.

Gans, H. J., 1963. Effect of the move from city to suburb, in L. J. Duhl (ed.), *The urban condition.* New York: Basic Books.

Gibson, J. J., 1946. Perception of distance and space in the open air. In *Motion picture testing and research.* AAF Program, Report no. 7. (Reprinted in D. C. Beardslee and M. Wertheimer (eds.), *Readings in perception.* Princeton, N.J.: Van Nostrand, 1958.)

Gibson, J. J., 1966. *The senses considered as perceptual systems.* Boston: Houghton Mifflin.

Gibson, J. J., 1979. *The ecological approach to visual perception.* Boston: Houghton Mifflin.

Gifford, R. J., 1980. Judgments of the built environment as a function of individual differences and context. *Journal of Man-Environment Relations* 1:22.

Gladwin, T., 1970. *East is a big bird.* Cambridge, Mass.: Harvard University Press.

Glass, D. C., and Singer, J. E., 1972. *Urban stress.* New York: Academic.

Goetze, R., 1972. Urban housing rehabilitation: two approaches contrasted to illustrate productive and meaningful dweller participation, in J.F.C. Turner and R. Fichter (eds.), *Freedom to build.* New York: Macmillan.

Goldberg, M. E., and Wurtz, R. H., 1972. The activity of superior colliculus in behaving monkey: effect of attention on neuronal responses. *Journal of Neurophysiology* 35:560.

Goodchild, M. F., 1976. Perception, preferences and geometry: a commentary, in R. G. Golledge and G. Rushton (eds.), *Spatial choice and spatial behavior.* Columbus: Ohio State Press.

Gorman, D. A., 1973. Effects of varying pictorial detail and presentation strategy on concept formation. *Audiovisual Communication Review* 21:337.

Grabiner, J. V., and Miller, P. D., 1974. Effects of the Scopes trial. *Science* 185:832.

Green, I., Sedewa, B. E., Johnston, C. A., Jackson, W. N., and Deardorff, H. L., 1975. *Housing for the elderly.* New York: Van Nostrand Reinhold.

Greenbie, B. B., 1974. Social territory, community health and urban planning. *Journal of the American Institute of Planners* 40:74.

Greenbie, B. B., 1975. Problems of scale and context in assessing a generalized landscape for particular persons, in E. H. Zube, R. O. Brush, and J. G. Fabos (eds.), *Landscape assessment.* Stroudsburg, Pa.: Dowden, Hutchinson and Ross.

Haber, R. N., 1978. Visual perception. *Annual Review of Psychology* 29:31.

Halle, L. J., 1977. *Out of chaos.* Boston: Houghton Mifflin.

Hallowell, A. I., 1955. *Culture and experience.* Philadelphia: University of Pennsylvania Press.

Hammitt, W. E., 1979. Measuring familiarity for natural environments through visual images, in *Proceedings of Our National Landscape Conference*, USDA Forest Service, General Technical Report PSW-35.

Hammitt, W. E., 1981. A theoretical foundation for Tilden's interpretive principles. *Journal of Environmental Education* 12(3):13.

Hammond, K. R. (ed.), 1966. *The psychology of Egon Brunswik.* New York: Wiley.

Hardin, G., 1968. The tragedy of the commons. *Science* 162:1243.

Harris, M., 1974. *Cows, pigs, wars and witches.* New York: Random House.

Hebb, D. O., 1949. *The organization of behavior.* New York: Wiley.

Hebb, D. O., 1972. *Textbook of psychology*, 3rd edn. Philadelphia: Saunders.

Hebb, D. O., 1974. What psychology is all about. *American Psychologist* 29:71.

Hebb, D. O., 1980. *Essay on mind.* Hillsdale, N.J.: Erlbaum.

Heberlein, T. A., 1976. Some observations on alternative mechanisms for public involvement. *Natural Resources Journal* 16:197.

Held, R., 1970. Two modes of processing spatially distributed visual stimulation, in F. O. Schmitt (ed.), *The neurosciences: second study program.* New York: Rockefeller University Press.

Hendee, J. C., 1977. Public involvement in the U.S. Forest Service roadless-area review, in W.R.D. Sewell and J. T. Coppock (eds.), *Public participation in planning.* London: Wiley.

Herman, J. F., and Siegel, A. W., 1978. The development of cognitive mapping of the large-scale environment. *Journal of Experimental Child Psychology* 26:89.

Herzog, T. R., Kaplan, S., and Kaplan, R., 1976. The prediction of preference for familiar urban places. *Environment and Behavior* 8:627.

Herzog, T. R., Kaplan, S., and Kaplan, R., 1982. The prediction of preference for unfamiliar urban places. *Population and Environment* 5:43.

Hilden, O., 1965. Habitat selection in birds. *Annale Zoologici Fennici* 2:53.

Hoch, I., 1976. City size effects, trends and policies. *Science* 193:856.

Hohauser, S., 1970. *Architectural and interior models: design and construction.* New York: Van Nostrand Reinhold.

Holland, J. H., 1974. *Adaptation in natural and artificial systems.* Ann Arbor: University of Michigan Press.

Horn, R. E. (ed.), 1977. *Guide to simulations/games for educational and training,* 3rd edn. Cranford, N.J.: Didactic Systems.

Hubel, D. H., 1963. The visual cortex of the brain. *Scientific American* 209(5):54.

Hubel, D. H., and Wiesel, T. N., 1968. Receptive fields and functional architecture of monkey striate cortex. *Journal of Physiology (London)* 195:215.

Huttenlocher, J., 1976. Language and intelligence, in L. B. Resnick (ed.), *The nature of intelligence.* Hillsdale, N.J.: Erlbaum.

Ingram, H. M., 1973. Information channels and environmental decision making. *Natural Resources Journal* 13(1):150.

Ingram, H. M., and Ullery, S. J., 1977. Public participation in environmental decision making, in R. Sewell and J. J. Coppock (eds.), *Public participation in planning.* London: Wiley.

Jackson, J. B., 1970. The stranger's path, in E. H. Zube (ed.), *Landscapes: selected writings of J. B. Jackson.* Amherst: University of Massachusetts Press.

James, W., 1892. *Psychology: the briefer course.* [New York: Collier Books 1962].

Janis, I. L., and Mann, L., 1977. *Decision making.* New York: Macmillan.

Janke, R., 1968. *Architectural models.* New York: Praeger.

Janoff-Bulman, R., and Brickman, P., 1980. Expectations and what people learn from failure, in N. T. Feather (ed.), *Expectancy, incentive, and action.* Hillsdale, N.J.: Erlbaum.

Jay, A., 1971. *Corporation man.* New York: Random House.

Jensen, R., 1974. *Cities of vision.* New York: Halsted.

Jervis, R., 1973. Minimizing misperception, in G. M. Bonham and M. J. Shapiro (eds.), *Thought and action in foreign policy* (Proceedings of the London Conference on Cognitive Process Models of Foreign Policy), Interdisciplinary Systems Research no. 33.

Johnson, S., and Burdge, R. J., 1974. An analysis of community and individual reactions to forced migration due to reservoir construction, in D. R. Field, J. C. Barron, and B. F. Long (eds.), *Water and community development*. Ann Arbor, Mich.: Ann Arbor Science.

Johnson, W., 1978. *Muddling toward frugality*. Boulder, Colo.: Shambhala.

Jonides, J., 1980. Towards a model of the mind's eye movement. *Canadian Journal of Psychology* 34:103.

Jonides, J., 1982. Voluntary versus automatic control over the mind's eye movement, in J. B. Long and A. D. Baddeley (eds.), *Attention and Performance* vol. 9. Hillsdale, N.J.: Erlbaum.

Kahneman, D., and Tversky, A., 1973. On the psychology of prediction. *Psychological Review* 80:237.

Kamps, B., 1981. Soaring in the wind. *Organic Gardening* 28(5):75.

Kaplan, R., 1972. The dimensions of the visual environment: methodological considerations, in W. J. Mitchell (ed.), *Environmental design: research and practice*. Los Angeles: University of California.

Kaplan, R., 1973a. Some psychological benefits of gardening. *Environment and Behavior* 5:145.

Kaplan, R., 1973b. Predictors of environmental preference: designers and "clients," in W.F.E. Preiser (ed.), *Environmental design research*. Stroudsburg, Pa.: Dowden, Hutchinson and Ross.

Kaplan, R., 1974. A strategy for dimensional analysis, in D. H. Carson (ed.), *Man-environment interactions*. Stroudsburg, Pa.: Dowden, Hutchinson and Ross.

Kaplan, R., 1975. Some methods and strategies in the prediction of preference, in E. H. Zube, R. O. Brush, and J. G. Fabos (eds.), *Landscape assessment*. Stroudsburg, Pa.: Dowden, Hutchinson and Ross.

Kaplan, R., 1976. Way-finding in the natural environment, in G. T. Moore and R. G. Golledge (eds.), *Environmental knowing*. Stroudsburg, Pa.: Dowden, Hutchinson and Ross.

Kaplan, R., 1977a. Preference and everyday nature: method and application, in D. Stokols (ed.), *Perspectives on environment and behavior*. New York: Plenum.

Kaplan, R., 1977b. Patterns of environmental preference. *Environment and Behavior* 9:195.

Kaplan, R., 1978a. The green experience, in S. Kaplan and R. Kaplan (eds.), *Humanscape: environments for people*. Belmont, Calif.: Duxbury.

Kaplan, R., 1978b. Participation in environmental design, in *Humanscape*.

Kaplan, R., 1979a. A methodology for simultaneously obtaining and sharing information, in *Assessing amenity resource values*, USDA Forest Service General Technical Report RM-68.

Kaplan, R., 1979b. Visual resources and the public: an empirical approach, in *Proceedings of Our National Landscape Conference*, USDA Forest Service General Technical Report PSW-35.

Kaplan, R., 1980. Citizen participation in the design and evaluation of a park. *Environment and Behavior* 12:494.

Kaplan, R., 1981. *Evaluation of an urban vest-pocket park*. USDA Forest Service General Technical Report NC-195.

Kaplan, R., 1983. The role of nature in the urban context, in I. Altman and J. F. Wohlwill (eds.), *Behavior and the natural environment*. New York: Plenum.

Kaplan, R., Kaplan, S., and Deardorff, H. L., 1974. The perception and evaluation of a simulated environment. *Man-environment Systems* 4:191.

Kaplan, S., 1970. The role of location processing in the perception of the environment, in J. Archea and C. Eastman (eds.), *edra two* (Proceedings of the Second Annual Environmental Design Research Association Conference, Pittsburgh).

Kaplan, S., 1972. The challenge of environmental psychology: a proposal for a new functionalism. *American Psychologist* 27:140.

Kaplan, S., 1973a. Cognitive maps in perception and thought, in R. M. Downs and D. Stea (eds.), *Image and environment*. Chicago: Aldine.

Kaplan, S., 1973b. Cognitive maps, human needs, and the designed environment, in W.F.E. Preiser (ed.), *Environmental design research*. Stroudsburg, Pa.: Dowden, Hutchinson and Ross.

Kaplan, S., 1975. An informal model for the prediction of preference, in E. H. Zube, R. O. Brush, and J. G. Fabos (eds.), *Landscape assessment*. Stroudsburg, Pa.: Dowden, Hutchinson and Ross.

Kaplan, S., 1976. Adaptation, structure and knowledge, in G. T. Moore and R. G. Golledge (eds.), *Environmental knowing*. Stroudsburg, Pa.: Dowden, Hutchinson and Ross.

Kaplan, S., 1977a. Participation in the design process: a cognitive approach, in D. Stokols (ed.), *Perspective on environment and behavior*. New York: Plenum.

Kaplan, S., 1977b. Tranquility and challenge in the natural environment, in *Children, nature and the urban environment*, USDA Forest Service General Technical Report NE-30.

Kaplan, S., 1978a. Perception of an uncertain environment, in S. Kaplan and R. Kaplan (eds.), *Humanscape: environments for people*. Belmont, Calif.: Duxbury.

Kaplan, S., 1978b. On knowing the environment, in *Humanscape*.

Kaplan, S., 1978c. Attention and fascination: the search for cognitive clarity, in *Humanscape*.

Kaplan, S., 1979a. Concerning the power of content-identifying methodologies, in *Assessing amenity resource values*, USDA Forest Service General Technical Report RM-68.

Kaplan, S., 1979b. Perception and landscape: conceptions and misconceptions, in *Proceedings of Our National Landscape Conference*, USDA Forest Service General Technical Report PSW-35.

Kaplan, S., 1982. A process-oriented approach to human concerns in environmental decision making, in S. L. Hart, G. Enk and W. Hornick (eds.), *From checklist to social choice*. Boulder, Colo.: Westview.

Kaplan, S., and Kaplan, R. (eds.), 1978. *Humanscape: environments for people*. Belmont, Calif.: Duxbury.

Kaplan, S., Kaplan R., and Wendt, J. S., 1972. Rated preference and complexity for natural and urban visual material. *Perception and Psychophysics* 12:254.

Kaplan, S., and Talbot, J. F., 1983. Psychological benefits of a wilderness experience, in I. Altman and J. F. Wohlwill (eds.), *Behavior and the natural environment*. New York: Plenum.

Kasperson, R. E., and Breitbart, M., 1974. *Participation, decentralization, and advocacy planning*, Resource Paper No. 25. Washington, D.C.: Association of American Geographers.

Kates, R. W., 1962. *Hazard and choice perception in flood plain management*, Research Paper No. 78. Chicago: University of Chicago Press.

Kennedy, J. M., 1974. *A psychology of picture perception*. San Francisco: Josey-Bass.

Klein, D. C., 1978. Reflections on the psychology of new towns, in D. C. Klein (ed.), *Psychology and the planned community*. New York: Human Sciences Press.

Kosslyn, S. M., Ball, T. M., and Reiser, B. J., 1978. Visual images preserve metric spatial information: evidence from studies of image scanning. *Journal of Experimental Psychology* 4:47.

Kosslyn, S. M., Pick, H. L., and Fariello, G. R., 1974. Cognitive maps in children and men. *Child Development* 45:707.

Kuhn, T. S., 1962. *The structure of scientific revolutions.* Chicago: University of Chicago Press.

Lachman, J. L., and Lachman, R., 1979. Theories of memory organization and human evolution, in D. R. Puff (ed.), *Memory organization and structure.* New York: Academic.

Lachman, R., and Lachman, J. L., 1979. Comprehension and cognition, in F.I.M. Craik and L. S. Cermak (eds.), *Levels of processing in human memory.* Hillsdale, N.J.: Erlbaum.

Lang, J., and Burnette, C., 1974. A model of the designing process, in J. Lang, C. Burnette, W. Moleski, and D. Vachon (eds.), *Designing for human behavior.* Stroudsburg, Pa.: Dowden, Hutchinson and Ross.

Langer, E. J., 1981. Old age: an artifact? in *Biology, behavior and aging.* Washington, D.C.: National Research Council.

Langer, E. J., and Imber, L. G., 1979. When practice makes imperfect: debilitating effects of overlearning. *Journal of Personality and Social Psychology* 37:2014.

Laski, H. J., 1930. The limitations of the expert. *Harper's Magazine* 162:101.

Laszlo, E., 1977. *Goals for mankind.* New York: Dutton.

Laughlin, W. S., 1968. Hunting: an integrating biobehavior system and its evolutionary importance, in R. B. Lee and I. DeVore (eds.), *Man the hunter.* Chicago: Aldine.

Lazarus, R. S., 1980. The stress and coping paradigm, in C. Eisdorfer, D. Cohen, A. Kleinman, and P. Maxim (eds.), *Theoretical bases for psychopathology.* New York: Spectrum.

Lee, R. B., and DeVore, I., 1968. *Man the hunter.* Chicago: Aldine.

Lévy-Bruhl, L., 1923. *Primitive mentality* (translated by L. A. Clare). New York: Macmillan.

Lewin, R., 1982. Molecules come to Darwin's aid. *Science* 216:1091.

Lewis, C. A., 1972. Public housing gardens: landscapes for the soul, in *Landscape for living,* USDA Yearbook of Agriculture, pp. 277–282.

Lewis, C. A., 1979. Healing in the urban environment: a person/plant viewpoint. *Journal of the American Planning Association* 45:330.

Lindblom, C. E., 1964. The science of muddling through, in W. J. Gore and J. W. Dyson (eds.), *The making of decisions.* New York: Free Press.

Lindenthal, J. J., and Myers, J. K., 1979. The New Haven longitudinal survey, in I. Sarason and C. Spielberger (eds.), *Stress and anxiety,* vol. 6. Washington, D.C.: Hemisphere.

Lindsay, P. H., and Norman, D. A., 1977. *Human information processing*, 2nd edn. New York: Academic.

Lynch, K., 1960. *The image of the city*. Cambridge, Mass.: MIT Press.

MacCrimmon, K. R., and Taylor, R. N., 1975. Decision making and problem solving, in M. D. Dunnette (ed.), *Handbook of industrial and organizational psychology*. Chicago: Rand McNally.

Magill, A. W., 1976. The message of vandalism, in *Vandalism and outdoor recreation: symposium proceedings*, USDA Forest Service General Technical Report PSW-17.

Mandler, G., 1975a. *Mind and emotion*. New York: Wiley.

Mandler, G., 1975b. Memory storage and retrieval: some limits on the research of attention and consciousness, in P. M. Rabbitt and S. Dornic (eds.), *Attention and Performance*, vol. V. London: Academic.

Mandler, G., 1975c. Consciousness: respectable, useful, and probably necessary, in R. L. Solso (ed.), *Information processing and cognitive psychology*. Hillsdale, N.J.: Erlbaum.

Mandler, J. M., and Parker, R. E., 1976. Memory for descriptive and spatial information in complex pictures. *Journal of Experimental Psychology* 2:38.

Maslow, A. H., and Díaz-Guerrero, R., 1971. Adolescence and juvenile delinquency in two different cultures, in A. H. Maslow (ed.), *The farther reaches of human nature*. New York: Viking.

Mautz, R. K., and Kaplan, R., 1974. Residential modification as a mode of self-expression, in D. H. Carson (ed.), *Man-environment interactions*. Stroudsburg, Pa.: Dowden, Hutchinson and Ross.

Mayer, R. E., 1977. *Thinking and problem solving*. Glenview, Ill.: Scott, Foresman.

McCollough, C., 1965. Color adaptation of edge detectors in the human visual system. *Science* 149:1115.

McGrath, J. E., 1970. *Social and psychological factors in stress*. New York: Holt, Reinhart and Winston.

McGrath, J. E., 1977. Settings, measures and themes: an integrative review of some research on social-psychological factors in stress, in A. Monat and R. Lazarus (eds.), *Stress and coping*. New York: Columbia University Press.

McHarg, I. L., 1969. *Design with nature*. New York: Natural History Press.

McKechnie, G. E., 1977. Simulation techniques in environmental psychology, in D. Stokols (ed.), *Perspectives on environment and behavior*. New York: Plenum.

McNett, I., 1981. Federal research lab pursues work-personality connection. *APA Monitor* 4:1.

Menzel, E. W., 1969. Chimpanzee utilization of space and responsiveness to objects. *Proceedings of Second International Congress on Primatology,* vol. 1, pp. 72–80. Basel: Karger.

Menzel, E. W., 1973. Chimpanzee spatial memory organization. *Science* 182:943.

Midgley, M., 1978. *Beast and man: the roots of human nature.* Ithaca, N.Y.: Cornell University Press.

Miller, G. A., 1956. The magical number seven, plus or minus two: some limits in our capacity for processing information. *Psychological Review* 63:81.

Moates, D. R., and Schumacher, G. M., 1980. *An introduction to cognitive psychology.* Belmont, Calif.: Wadsworth.

Moore, E. O., 1981. A prison environment's effect on health care service demands. *Journal of Environmental Systems* 11(1):17.

Moore, G. T., and Golledge, R. G. (eds.), 1976. *Environmental knowing.* Stroudsburg, Pa.: Dowden, Hutchinson and Ross.

Morgan, C. T., 1951. Some structural factors in perception, in R. R. Blake and G. V. Ramsey (eds.), *Perception: an approach to personality.* New York: Ronald.

Moynihan, D. P., 1969. *Maximum feasible misunderstanding.* New York: Free Press.

Neisser, U., 1967. *Cognitive psychology.* New York: Appleton-Century-Crofts.

Neisser, U., 1976. *Cognition and reality.* San Francisco: Freeman.

Newman, O., 1972. *Defensible space.* New York: Macmillan.

Nisbett, R. E., Borgida, E., Crandall, R., and Reed, H., 1976. Popular induction: information is not necessarily informative, in J. S. Carroll and J. W. Payne (eds.), *Cognition and social behavior.* Hillsdale, N.J.: Erlbaum.

Nisbett, R. E., and Ross, L., 1980. *Human inference.* Englewood Cliffs, N.J.: Prentice-Hall.

Norman, D. A., 1976. *Memory and attention.* New York: Wiley.

O'Keefe, J., and Nadel, L., 1978. *The hippocampus as a cognitive map.* London: Oxford University Press.

Opat, E. J., 1976. Better housing through self-help. *Design and Environment* 7:36.

Ostrander, E. R., 1975. Behavioral research for design application: on making the myth a reality, in B. Honikman (ed.), *Responding to social change.* Stroudsburg, Pa.: Dowden, Hutchinson and Ross.

Partridge, L., 1978. Habitat selection, in J. R. Krebs and N. B. Davies (eds.), *Behavioral ecology: an evolutionary approach.* Sunderland, Mass.: Sinauer.

Pauling, L., 1970. *Vitamin C and the common cold*. San Francisco: Freeman.

Perlmuter, L. C., and Monty, R. A., 1979. *Choice and perceived control*. Hillsdale, N.J.: Erlbaum.

Peters, R., and Mech, L. D., 1975. Behavioral and intellectual adaptations of selected mammalian predators to the problem of hunting large animals, in R. Tuttle (ed.), *Socioecology and psychology of primates*. The Hague: Mouton.

Petrinovich, L., 1979. Probabilistic functionalism: a conception of research method. *American Psychologist* 34:373.

Pfeiffer, J. E., 1978. *The emergence of man*. New York: Harper and Row.

Piaget, J., and Inhelder, B., 1967. *The child's conception of space*. New York: Norton.

Pick, A. D., 1980. Cognition: psychological perspective, in H. C. Triandis and W. Lonner (eds.), *Handbook of cross-cultural psychology: basic processes*, vol. 3. Boston: Allyn and Bacon.

Pierce, N. R., 1979. Our premier urban wasteland may provide a turning point. *Ann Arbor News*, October 11.

Porteous, J. D., 1971. Design with people: the quality of the urban environment. *Environment and Behavior* 3:155.

Posner, M. I., 1973. *Cognition: an introduction*. Glenview, Ill.: Scott, Foresman.

Posner, M. I., 1978. *Chronometric explorations of mind*. Hillsdale, N.J.: Erlbaum.

Posner, M. I., and Keele, S. W., 1968. On the genesis of abstract ideas. *Journal of Experimental Psychology* 77:353.

Posner, M. I., and Keele, S. W., 1970. Retention of abstract ideas. *Journal of Experimental Psychology* 83:304.

Posner, M. I., and Rothbart, M. K., 1980. The development of attentional mechanisms, in J. H. Flowers (ed.), *Nebraska symposium on motivation*. Lincoln: University of Nebraska Press.

Proceedings of Our National Landscape Conference, 1979. USDA Forest Service General Technical Report PSW-35.

Proshansky, H., Nelson-Shulman, Y., and Kaminoff, R., 1979. The role of physical settings in life-crisis experiences, in I. Sarason and C. Spielberger (eds.), *Stress and anxiety*. Washington, D.C.: Hemisphere.

Pylyshyn, Z. W., 1973. What the mind's eye tells the mind's brain: a critique of mental imagery. *Psychological Bulletin* 80:1.

Rapoport, A., 1976. Environmental cognition in cross-cultural perspective, in G. T. Moore and R. G. Golledge (eds.), *Environmental knowing*. Stroudsburg, Pa.: Dowden, Hutchinson and Ross.

Rappaport, R. A., 1967. *Pigs for the ancestors*. New Haven: Yale University Press.

Reemer, R., 1971. Hell's Kitchen and the new Earth Park. *Fitness for Living*, May/June, p. 34.

Reif, F., 1974. Educational challenges for the university. *Science* 184:537.

Robertson, J., and Lewallen, J. (eds.), 1975. *The grass roots primer*. San Francisco: Sierra Club Books.

Robinson, A. H., and Petchenik, B. B., 1976. *The nature of maps*. Chicago: University of Chicago Press.

Rock, I., and Harris, C. S., 1967. Vision and touch. *Scientific American* 216:96.

Rodin, J., Rennert, K., and Solomon, S. K., 1980. Intrinsic motivation for control: fact or fiction, in A. Baum and J. E. Singer (eds.), *Advances in environmental psychology*, vol. 2. Hillsdale, N.J.: Erlbaum.

Rosch, E., 1978. Principles of categorization, in E. Rosch and B. B. Lloyd (eds.), *Cognition and categorization*. Hillsdale, N.J.: Erlbaum.

Saarinen, T. F., 1976. *Environmental planning*. Boston: Houghton Mifflin.

Saarinen, T. F., and Sell, J. L., 1980. Environmental perception. *Progress in Human Geography* 4:525.

Sadalla, E. K., and Staplin, L. J., 1980. An information storage model for distance cognition. *Environment and Behavior* 12:183.

Sanoff, H., 1979. *Design games*. Los Altos, Calif.: Kaufman.

Sarason, S. B., 1973. Jewishness, blackishness, and the nature-nurture controversy. *American Psychologist* 28:962.

Schneider, G. E., 1969. Two visual systems. *Science* 163:895.

Schumacher, E. F., 1973. *Small is beautiful: economics as if people mattered*. London: Blond and Briggs.

Scott, W. A., and Wertheimer, M., 1962. *Introduction to psychological research*. New York: Wiley.

Scudder, T., 1973. The human ecology of big projects. *Annual Review of Antropology* 2:45.

Seligman, M.E.P., 1975. *Helplessness*. San Francisco: Freeman.

Sewell, W.R.D., and Coppock, J. T., 1977. A perspective on public participation in planning, in W.R.D. Sewell and J. T. Coppock (eds.), *Public participation in planning*. London: Wiley.

Shepard, R. N., 1975. Form, formation and transformation of representations, in R. L. Solso (ed.), *Information processing and cognition*. Hillsdale, N.J.: Erlbaum.

Sherrod, D. R., and Cohen, S., 1978. Density, personal control, and design, in S. Kaplan and R. Kaplan (eds.), *Humanscape: environments for people*. Belmont, Calif.: Duxbury.

Sherrod, D. R., and Downs, R., 1974. Environmental determinants of altruism: the effects of stimulus overload and perceived control on helping. *Journal of Experimental Social Psychology* 10:468.

Shippee, G., Roitman, D., and Gregory, W. L., 1980. Social traps: five years later. *Journal of Man-Environment Relations* 1(1):32.

Shuttleworth, J., 1979. A report to Mother's readers. *The Mother Earth News*, no. 60, p. 42.

Shuttleworth, S., 1980. The evaluation of landscape quality. *Landscape Research* 5(1):14.

Siegel, A. W., and White, S. H., 1975. The development of spatial representations of large-scale environments, in H. W. Reese (ed.), *Advances in child development and behavior*, vol. 10. New York: Academic.

Silver, R. L., and Wortman, C. B., 1980. Coping with undesirable life events, in J. Garber and M.E.P. Seligman (eds.), *Human helplessness*. New York: Academic.

Simon, H. A., 1957. *Models of man: social and rational*. New York: Wiley.

Simon, H. A., 1978. Rationality as process and as product of thought. *American Economic Review* 68(2):1.

Slovic, P., Fischhoff, B., and Lichtenstein, S., 1976. Cognitive processes and societal risk taking, in J. S. Carroll and J. W. Payne (eds.), *Cognition and social behavior*. Hillsdale, N.J.: Erlbaum.

Slovic, P., Kunreuther, H., and White, G. F., 1974. Decision processes, rationality, and adjustment to natural hazards, in G. F. White (ed.), *Natural hazards, local, national, and global*. New York: Oxford University Press.

Smith, C. J., 1977. *Geography and mental health*, Resource Paper No. 76-4. Washington, D.C.: Association of American Geographers.

Smith, E. E., Shoben, E. J., and Rips, L. J., 1974. Structure and process in semantic memory: a feature model for semantic decisions. *Psychological Review* 81:214.

Sperling, W., 1965. Kind und landschaft: das geographische Raumbild des kindes. Stuttgart: (Der Erdkundeunterricht 5).

Stein, M. R., 1960. *The eclipse of community*. Princeton, N.J.: Princeton University Press.

Steinitz, C., 1981. Predicting the impacts of suburban development upon an historically valuable landscape, the Boston region South Shore. *Environmental Review* 4(3):2.

Steinitz, C., Parker, P., and Jordan, L., 1976. Hand-drawn overlays: their history and prospective uses. *Landscape Architecture* 66:444.

Sterling, P., and Wickelgren, B. G., 1969. Visual receptive fields in the superior colliculus of the cat. *Journal of Neurophysiology* 32:1.

Stokols, D., 1977. Origins and directions of environment-behavior research, in D. Stokols (ed.), *Perspectives on environment and behavior.* New York: Plenum.

Stokols, D., 1979. A congruence analysis of human stress, in I. Sarason and C. Spielberger (eds.), *Stress and anxiety,* vol. 6. Washington, D.C.: Hemisphere.

Strong, G. W., 1977. Religion, skill and responsibility. University of Michigan, unpublished.

Sullivan, J. L., and Feldman, S., 1979. *Multiple indicators.* Beverly Hills, Calif.: Sage.

Suttles, G. D., 1972. *The social construction of communities.* Chicago: University of Chicago Press.

Terner, D., and Herz, R., 1968. Squatter-inspired. *Architectural Design*, August, p. 367.

Tester, D. K. (ed.), 1974. *Designing the method.* Raleigh, N.C.: Student Publications of the School of Design, North Carolina State University.

Thomas, J. C., 1977. Cognitive psychology from the perspective of wilderness survival. IBM Research Report RC 6647 (#28603), July 19.

Toffler, A., 1970. *Future shock.* New York: Random House.

Tolman, E. C., 1948. Cognitive maps in rats and man. *Psychological Review* 55:189.

Trevarthen, C. B., 1968. Two mechanisms of vision in primates. *Psychologische Forschung* 31:299.

Tuan, Y.-F., 1974. *Topophilia: a study of environmental perception, attitude and values.* Englewood Cliffs, N.J.: Prentice-Hall.

Tuan, Y.-F., 1977. *Space and place.* Minneapolis: University of Minnesota Press.

Tversky, A., and Kahneman, D., 1973. Availability: a heuristic for judging frequency and probability. *Cognitive Psychology* 5:207.

Tversky, A., and Kahneman, D., 1981. The framing of decisions and the psychology of choice. *Science* 211:453.

Ulrich, R. S., 1974. *Scenery and the shopping trip.* Michigan Geographical Publication No. 12, University of Michigan.

Ulrich, R. S., 1979. Visual landscapes and psychological well-being. *Landscape Research* 4(1):17.

Van Kreveld, D., and Zajonc, R., 1966. The learning of influence structures. *Journal of Personality* 34:205.

Van Til, J., and Van Til, S. B., 1970. Citizen participation in social policy. *Social Problems* 17:313.

Voss, J. F., 1969. Associative learning and thought, in J. F. Voss (ed.), *Approaches to thought*. Columbus, Ohio: Charles E. Merrill.

Wagar, J. A., 1974. Interpretation to increase benefits for recreationists, in *Outdoor recreation research: applying the results*. General Technical Report NC-9, USDA Forest Service.

Ward, C. (ed.), 1973. *Vandalism*. New York: Van Nostrand Reinhold.

Washburne, R. F., and Wagar, J. A., 1972. Evaluating visitor response to exhibit content. *Curator* 15(3):248.

Watt, K.E.F., 1974. *The Titanic effect*. Stamford, Conn.: Sinauer.

Watzlawick, P., Weakland, J. H., and Fisch, R., 1974. *Change*. New York: Norton.

Weber, R., Brown, L., and Weldon, J., 1978. Cognitive maps of environmental knowledge and preference in nursing home patients. *Experimental Aging Research* 4:157.

Weisberg, R. W., 1980. *Memory, thought and behavior*. New York: Oxford University Press.

Weisman, G. D., 1981. Way-finding and the built environment: an evaluation of architectural legibility. *Environment and Behavior* 13:189.

White, G. F. (ed.), 1974. *Natural hazards, local, national and global*. New York: Oxford University Press.

White, R. W., 1974. Strategies of adaptation, in G. V. Coelho, D. A. Hamburg, and J. E. Adams (eds.), *Coping and adaptation*. New York: Basic Books.

Whyte, W. H., 1980. *The social life of small urban spaces*. Washington, D.C.: Conservation Foundation.

Wickelgren, W. A., 1979. *Cognitive psychology*. Englewood Cliffs, N.J.: Prentice-Hall.

Wicker, A. W., 1979. *An introduction to ecological psychology*. Monterey, Calif.: Brooks/Cole.

Wildavsky, A., 1964. *Leadership in a small town*. Totowa, N.J.: Bedminster.

Williams, H. S., 1977. Smallness and the small town. *Small Town* 8:7.

Wilson, E. O., 1978. *On human nature.* Cambridge, Mass.: Harvard University Press.

Wilson, F., 1975. *City planning: the games of human settlement.* New York: Van Nostrand Reinhold.

Witherspoon, G., 1977. *Language and art in the Navajo universe.* Ann Arbor: University of Michigan Press.

Wohlwill, J. F., 1973. The environment is not in the head! In W.F.E. Preiser (ed.), *Environmental design research,* vol. 2. Stroudsburg, Pa.: Dowden, Hutchinson and Ross.

Wohlwill, J. F., 1976. Environmental aesthetics: The environment as a source of affect, in I. Altman and J. F. Wohlwill (eds.), *Human Behavior and Environment,* vol. 1. New York: Plenum.

Wohlwill, J. F., 1980. The place of order and uncertainty in art and environmental aesthetics. *Motivation and Emotion* 4:133.

Wohlwill, J. F., and Harris, G., 1980. Response to congruity or contrast for manmade factors in natural-recreation settings. *Leisure Sciences* 3:349.

Wong, K. Y., 1979. Maps in minds: an empirical study. *Environment and Planning A* 11:1289.

Woodcock, D. M., 1982. A functional approach to environmental preference. Doctoral dissertation, University of Michigan.

Wortz, E. C., and Nowlis, D. P., 1975. The design of habitable environments. *Man-Environment Systems* 5:280.

Wurman, R. S., 1971. *Making the city observable.* Cambridge, Mass.: MIT Press.

Wurman, R. S., 1972. *Yellow pages of learning resources.* Cambridge, Mass.: MIT Press.

Wurtz, R. H., and Albano, J. E., 1980. Visual-motor function of the primate superior colliculus. *Annual Review of Neuroscience* 3:189.

Wurtz, R. H., and Mohler, C. W., 1976. Organizations of monkey superior colliculus: enhancing visual response of superficial layer cells. *Journal of Neurophysiology* 39:745.

Yancey, W. L., 1971. Architecture, interaction, and social control. *Environment and Behavior* 3:3.

Yates, D., 1972. Neighborhood government. *Policy Sciences* 3:209.

Yin, R. K., 1977. Goals for citizen involvement: some possibilities and some evidence, in P. Marshall (ed.), *Citizen participation certification for community develop-*

ment. Washington, D.C.: National Association of Housing and Redevelopment Officials.

Zajonc, R. B., 1980. Feeling and thinking: preferences need no inferences. *American Psychologist* 35:151.

Zube, E. H., 1976. Perception of landscape and land use, in I. Altman and J. F. Wohlwill (eds.), *Human behavior and environment*, vol. 1. New York: Plenum.

Zube, E. H., 1980. *Environmental evaluation.* Monterey, Calif.: Brooks/Cole.

NAME INDEX

279

SUBJECT INDEX